The Rough Guide

Beijing

written and researched by

Simon Lewis

ROUGH GUIDES

NEW YORK • LONDON • DELHI
www.roughguides.com

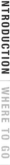

Introduction to
Beijing

Beijing is China at its most dynamic, a vivid metropolis spiked with high-rises, proud owner of over a hundred flyovers (some even commemorated on stamps), a city changing and growing at a furious, unfettered pace. However this forward-looking city is also where, for a thousand years, the drama of China's imperial history was played out, with the emperor sitting enthroned at the centre of the Chinese universe. Though Beijing is a very different city today, it remains spiritually and politically the heart of the nation. Shanghai and Hong Kong may be where the money is, but it's Beijing that pulls the strings,

and its lure is irresistible to many Chinese, who come here to fulfil dreams of success in business, politics or the arts.

The cranes that skewer the skyline, and the Chinese character *chai* (demolish), painted in white on old buildings, attest to the speed of change, affecting not just the city's architecture: as China embraces capitalism, **social structures** are also being revolutionized. The government is as determined as ever to repress dissent, but outside the political arena pretty much anything goes these days. Students in the latest street fashions while away their time in Internet cafés and *McDonald's*; dropouts dye their hair and mosh in punk clubs. Even red-light districts and gay bars have appeared. The new prosperity is evident everywhere

The 2008 Olympics

The only developing country with the resources to host the Olympic Games, and the narrow loser of the 2000 Olympic bid, China was a natural choice for the 2008 Games, although its dubious human rights record caused plenty of protest at the nomination. In preparation, billions of dollars are being spent on city improvements, including new subway lines, underground cables to ensure there are no embarrassing power cuts, and the relocation of polluting factories to the suburbs. Beijing is to become a showcase, demonstrating China's new modernity and internationalism. From a visitor's point of view, it's already improved immeasurably; there's grass in the parks, a brace of new museums have opened, previously neglected ancient structures have been renovated, and cabbies are studying English.

The focus of the games will be the Olympic Forest Park, a vast arcadia with a boulevard sweeping down the middle; it's located on the outskirts of Beijing, due north of the Forbidden City. Its centrepiece, surrounded by a dragon-shaped canal, is the 80,000-seater National Stadium, built by Swiss firm Herzog de Meuron and designed to resemble a nest. Not all events will take place here; the beach volleyball is actually slated for Tian'anmen Square. For more information, check out the official website ⑩beijing-2008.org.

– witness the Mercedes-driving businessmen and the many schoolkids with mobile phones – but not everyone has benefited: migrant day-labourers wait for work on the pavements, and homeless beggars, a rare sight ten years ago, are now as common as in Western cities.

First impressions of Beijing, for both foreigners and visiting Chinese, are often of a bewildering **vastness**, conveyed by the sprawl of uniform apartment buildings in which most of the city's population of twelve million are housed, and the eight-lane freeways that slice it up. It's an impression reinforced on closer acquaintance by the concrete desert of Tian'anmen Square, and the gargantuan buildings of the modern executive around it. The main tourist sights – the Forbidden City, the Summer Palace and the Great Wall – also impress with their scale, while more manageable grandeur is on offer at the

city's attractive temples, including the Tibetan-style Yonghe Gong, the Taoist Baiyun Guan, and the astonishing Temple of Heaven, once a centre for imperial rites.

With its sights, history and, by no means least, delicious **food** (all of China's diverse cuisines can be enjoyed relatively cheaply at the city's numerous restaurants and street stalls), Beijing is a place almost everyone enjoys. But it's essentially a private city, one whose surface, though attractive, is difficult to penetrate. The city's history and unique character are in the details. To find and experience these, check out the little **antique**

Dust storms

Every spring, Beijing suffers from dust storms, when fine dust and sand swirl through the city, turning the sky orange and drastically reducing visibility. The storms are caused by desertification in the lands west and north of the city, in Inner Mongolia, Gansu and Shanxi, where grassland and semi-forest have been turned into cultivated land, mostly during the Mao years. This has loosened the topsoil, which is then picked up by spring winds whipping off the Mongolian plains and dumped on the city. Massive efforts are under way to bring the problem under control. Vast tracts of land just north and west of the city have been planted with trees to form a natural windbreak – nicknamed the Great Green Wall – with the result that there were only a handful of storms in 2002 and 2003, compared to 32 in 2001.

markets; the local **shopping districts**; the smaller, quirkier sights; the **hutongs**, the city's twisted grey stone alleyways that are – as one Chinese guidebook puts it – "fine and numerous as the hairs of a cow"; and the **parks**, where you'll see Beijingers performing *tai ji* and old men sitting with their caged songbirds. Take advantage, too, of the city's burgeoning **nightlife** and see just how far the Chinese have gone down the road of what used to be called spiritual pollution. Keep your eyes open, and you'll soon notice that Westernization and the rise of a brash consumer society is not the only trend here. Just as marked is the revival of older Chinese culture, much of it outlawed during the more austere years of communist rule. Witness, for example, the sudden re-emergence of the **tea house** as a genteel meeting place, and the renewed interest in **imperial cuisine** – dishes once enjoyed by the emperors.

What to see

I n the absolute centre of Beijing, **Tian'anmen Square** is the physical and spiritual heart of the city. Some of the most significant sights are very close by, including the **Forbidden City**, two colossal museums, and the formidable buildings of the modern executive, as well as the corpse of Chairman Mao, lying pickled in his sombre mausoleum.

The road leading south from here, **Qianmen Dajie**, once the pivot of the ancient city, is now a busy market area that leads to the magnificent **Temple of Heaven**. These days the main axis of the city has shifted to the east–west road, a showcase of grandiose architecture, that divides Tian'anmen Square and the Forbidden City. Changing its name every few kilometres along its length, the thoroughfare is generally referred to as **Chang'an Jie**. Westward, this street takes you past the shopping district of **Xidan** to the **Military Museum**, monument to a fast-disappearing overtly communist ethos. Eastward, the road zooms past more giant buildings and glamorous shopping districts – notably **Wangfujing**, **Jianguomen** and the **Silk Market** – to the little oasis of calm that is the **Ancient Observatory**, where Jesuit priests once taught the charting of the heavens.

In between the grid lines formed by the major streets are the dark, twisting little alleys or **hutongs**, at their most numerous in the area north of Tian'anmen Square.

Chinese script

Chinese characters are simplified images of what they represent, and their origins as pictograms can often still be seen, even though they have become highly abstract today. The earliest known examples of Chinese writing are predictions which were cut into "oracle bones" over three thousand years ago during the Shang dynasty, though the characters must have been in use long before as these inscriptions already amount to a highly complex writing system. As the characters represent concepts, not sounds, written Chinese cuts through the problem of communication in a country with many different dialects. However, learning the writing system is ponderous, taking children an estimated two years longer than with an alphabet. Foreigners learning Mandarin use the modern *pinyin* transliteration system of accented Roman letters – used in this book – to help memorize the sounds. For more, see p.187.

Lurking here is a scattered collection of sights, many of them remnants of the imperial past, when this area was the home of princes, dukes and

A week is long enough to explore the city and its main sights, and get out to the Great Wall.

eunuchs. Easier to track down is **Beihai Park**, the imperial pleasure park, just north of the Forbidden City, and the fine **Yonghe Gong**, a Lamaist temple in the northern outskirts.

Beijing's sprawling outskirts are a messy jumble of farmland, housing and industry, but it's here you'll find the most pleasant places to retreat from the city's hectic pace, including the two **Summer Palaces**, the giant parks of **Badachu** and **Xiangshan**, and the **Tanzhe** and **Jietai temples**. Well outside the city – but within the scope of a day-trip – is the **Great Wall**, which winds over lonely ridges only a few hours' drive north of the capital.

A week is long enough to explore the city and its main sights, and get out to the Great Wall. With more time, try to venture further afield: the city of **Tianjin**, with its unexpected European architecture; the imperial pleasure complex of **Chengde**; and the old-fashioned town of **Shanhaiguan**, where the Great Wall meets the sea, are all directly accessible from the capital by train and bus.

When to go

T he best time to visit Beijing is in the **autumn**, in September and October, when it's dry and clement. Next best is the short **spring**, in April and May, when it's dry and comfortably warm, though a little windy. The spring dust storms that once plagued the city have lessened of late. In **winter** it gets very cold, down to -20°C (-4°F), and the mean winds that whip off the Mongolian plains feel like they're freezing your ears off. **Summer** (June to August) is muggy and hot, with temperatures up to 30°C (86°F) and sometimes beyond.

The run-up to **Chinese New Year** (falling in late January or early to mid-February) is a great time to be in the country – when everyone is in festive mood and the city is bedecked with decorations. This isn't a good time to move around, however, as much of the population is on the move and transport systems become hopelessly overstretched. It's best to avoid Beijing during the first three days of the festival itself, as everyone is at home with family, and a lot of businesses and sights are closed.

Climate

	°C (°F) Average daily		Rainfall Average daily
	max	min	mm (in)
Jan	1 (34)	-10 (14)	4 (0.2)
Feb	4 (39)	-8 (18)	5 (0.2)
March	11 (52)	-1 (30)	8 (0.3)
April	21 (70)	7 (45)	17 (0.7)
May	27 (81)	13 (55)	35 (1.4)
June	31 (88)	18 (64)	78 (3.1)
July	31 (88)	21 (70)	243 (9.6)
Aug	30 (86)	20 (68)	141 (5.6)
Sept	26 (79)	14 (57)	58 (2.3)
Oct	20 (68)	6 (43)	16 (0.6)
Nov	9 (48)	-2 (28)	11 (0.4)
Dec	3 (37)	-8 (18)	3 (0.1)

19

things not to miss

It's not possible to see everything Beijing has to offer on a short trip – and we don't suggest you try. What follows is a selective taste of the city's highlights: beautiful temples, fascinating markets, mouthwatering cuisine and great excursions beyond the city – all arranged in colour-coded categories to help you find the very best things to see and experience. All entries have a page reference to take you straight into the guide, where you can find out more.

01 **Great Wall at Simatai** Page **150** • A dramatic stretch of crumbly, vertiginous fortifications three hours from Beijing.

03 Beijing duck Page **112** • Though heavy on calories and very rich, Beijing's culinary speciality is supremely tasty.

02 Acrobatics Page **129** • The style may be vaudeville, but the cunning stunts, performed by some of the world's greatest acrobats, are breathtaking.

05 Baiyun Guan Page **66** • See China at prayer in this attractive and popular Taoist temple, where devotees play games such as throwing coins at the temple bell.

04 Yonghe Gong Page **87** A lively Tibetan temple, busy with devotees and monks.

06 **Dazhalan** Page **57** • An earthy, hectic shopping street with some grand facades and plenty of opportunities for bargain-hunting.

07 **The botanical gardens** Page **152** • Especially on sunny days in spring, Beijing's botanical gardens offer welcome respite from the city's sombre palette.

08
Nightlife Page **122** • Experience Beijing's cultural explosion by catching one of the new bands in a smoky bar, or just bop with the beautiful people.

09 Forbidden City Page **48** • For five centuries centre of the Chinese universe and private pleasure ground of the emperor, this sumptuous palace complex ranks as the city's main attraction.

11 Markets Page **135** • The city's jumbled cornucopias of bric-a-brac, souvenirs, curios and fake antiques are great for a browse and a haggle.

10 Hutongs Page **57** • The old tangle of alleys behind Qianmen reveals the city's real, private face.

12 Yiheyuan Page **97** • Once the exclusive retreat of the emperors, this beautiful landscaped park, dotted with imperial buildings, is now open to all.

13 Tea houses Page **114** • Experience the ancient and relaxing tea ceremony in one of Beijing's elegant new tea houses.

14 Boating at Houhai Lake Page **86** • Get out on the water in a duck-shaped pedalo, then idle over a cappuccino with the smart set at a lakeside bar.

15 Tian'anmen Square Page **42** • The grandiose heart of communist China, a concrete plain laden with historical resonances.

17 Beijing opera Page **127** • Largely incomprehensible to foreigners, and many Chinese, but still a great spectacle.

16 Temple of Heaven Page **60** • A gorgeous temple in an elegant park.

18 Mao's mausoleum Page **44** • Join the queue of awed peasants shuffling past the pickled corpse of the founder of modern China in his giant tomb.

19 Hotpot Page **112** • Eaten from a common pot, this tasty northern Chinese staple turns a meal into a real social occasion.

Contents

Using this Rough Guide

We've tried to make this Rough Guide a good read and easy to use. The book is divided into nine main sections, and you should be able to find whatever you want in one of them.

Front section

The front **colour section** offers a quick tour of Beijing and its surroundings. The **introduction** aims to give you a feel for the place, with tips on where to head for and when to go. Next, our author rounds up his favourite aspects of Beijing in the **things not to miss** section – whether it's an amazing temple, great food or a cultural performance. After this comes a full **Contents** list.

Basics

The **Basics** section covers all the **pre-departure** nitty-gritty to help you plan your trip and the practicalities you'll want to know once there. This is where to find out about how to get there, about money and costs, Internet access, transport and the local media, and other items of **general practical information**.

The City

This is the heart of the Rough Guide, divided into user-friendly chapters, each of which covers a city district. Every chapter starts with an introduction to help you decide where to go, followed by an extensive tour of the sights.

Listings

This section contains all the consumer information to make the most of your stay, with chapters on **accommodation**, places to **eat** and **drink**, **nightlife**, **entertainment** and **art galleries**, and **shopping**. There's also a directory of useful addresses.

Around the city

Here attractions elsewhere in Beijing Municipality and the surrounding provinces are covered, including the Great Wall and three cities – Tianjin, Chengde and Shanhaiguan.

Contexts

Read **Contexts** to get a deeper understanding of what makes Beijing tick. We include a brief **history** and a further reading section reviewing the best **books** relating to the city.

Language

The **language section** offers useful guidance for pronouncing **Mandarin Chinese** and includes a comprehensive **menu reader**. Here you'll also find a **glossary** of terms relating to Beijing's and China's history and culture.

Index and small print

Apart from a **full index**, which includes maps as well as places, this section covers publishing information, credits and acknowledgements, and also has our contact details in case you want to send us updates, corrections or suggestions for improving the book.

Colour maps

The back colour section contains additional maps and plans to help you explore the city.

Map and chapter list

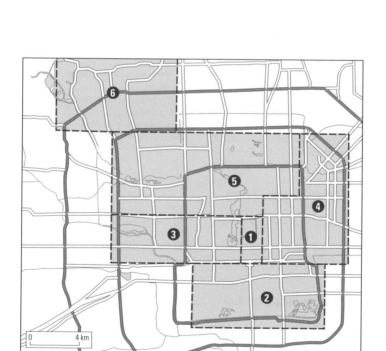

Contents

Around the city
145–171

Contexts
173–184

Language
185–201

Index and small print
203–211

Colour maps

Beijing and around
Beijing

Beijing transport

Map symbols

maps are listed in the full index using coloured text

– – – –	Chapter division boundary
▬ ▪ ▪ ▪	Province boundary
═══	Road
・・・・・	Path
▬▪═	Railway
───	River
▪▪▪▪	Wall
⊠	Gate
⊐⊏	Bridge
✈	Airport
Ⓜ	Bus stop/station
Ⓜ	Metro station
◉	Accommodation
▣	Restaurant

♦	Point of interest
▲	Hill
E	Embassy/consulate
♣	Museum
ⓘ	Tourist office
⊠	Post office
☏	Telephone office
⊞	Hospital
♠	Temple
⚲	Dagoba
♜	Mosque
⊞→	Church
▮	Building
▦	Park

Basics

Basics

Getting there

BASICS | Getting there

Beijing is China's main international transport hub, with plenty of direct flights from European capitals and from American, Australian and Asian cities. Though most travellers arrive by plane, there's also the possibility of arriving by rail from Hong Kong or, romantically, from Moscow (on the so-called Trans-Siberian train; see p.14).

Air fares vary with **season**, with the highest fares charged from Easter to October and around Christmas, New Year, and just before the Chinese New Year (which falls between mid-Jan and mid-Feb). Note also that flying at weekends is slightly more expensive; price ranges quoted below assume midweek travel.

You can often cut costs by going through a **specialist flight agent** – either a consolidator, who buys up blocks of tickets from the airlines and sells them at a discount, or a **discount agent**, who may also offer special student and youth fares plus travel insurance, rail passes, car rentals, tours and the like.

A further possibility is to see if you can arrange a **courier flight**, on which you shepherd a parcel through customs in return for a deeply discounted ticket. To take advantage, however, your schedule will have to be very flexible (especially as courier flights to Beijing aren't common – Hong Kong is a better bet). Furthermore, you may have to be satisfied with quite a short stay; courier flights are often best suited to lone travellers with very little luggage.

If your time is limited, or you can't face the hassles of travelling on your own, or if you have a specialist interest such as cycling or Chinese opera, then an **organized tour**, with transport and accommodation (and sometimes flights) included, might be worth considering. Though convenient, a tour is likely to work out more expensive than if you were travelling independently.

Booking flights online

Many airlines and discount travel websites offer you the opportunity to book your tickets **online**, cutting out the costs of agents and middlemen. Good deals can often be found through discount or auction sites, as well as through the airlines' own websites.

It's worth considering arriving in Beijing **via Hong Kong**. Entry regulations to Hong Kong are relaxed, with most nationalities not requiring a visa, and an onward visa for the rest of China is easy to obtain and valid for a longer period than one obtained abroad (see p.15 for more).

The cheapest way to reach Beijing from Hong Kong is the daily **train**, which leaves Hung Hom station in Kowloon at 3pm and arrives the next day at Beijing west station at 7pm. A hard-sleeper ticket – for a berth in a six-bed open compartment – costs around HK$600 ($75).

Online booking agents

ⓦ**www.cheapflights.com** Bookings from the UK and Ireland only. Flight deals, travel agents, plus links to other travel sites.

ⓦ**www.cheaptickets.com** Discount flight specialists.

ⓦ**www.expedia.com** Discount air fares, all-airline search engine and daily deals.

ⓦ**www.flyaow.com** Online air travel info and reservations site.

ⓦ**www.lastminute.com** UK bookings only. Offers good last-minute holiday package and flight-only deals.

ⓦ**www.flychina.com** Online broker specializing in flights between the US and China, as well as Chinese domestic flights. Use their fare finder to submit a request, then wait for their emailed confirmation or suggestion. Staff are helpful and special offers are posted frequently.

ⓦ**www.hotwire.com** Bookings from the US only. Last-minute savings of up to forty percent on regular fares. Travellers must be at least 18; no refunds, transfers or changes are allowed.

ⓦ **www.priceline.com** Name-your-own-price website that has deals at around forty percent off standard fares. Tickets are non-refundable, non-transferable and non-changeable.

ⓦ **www.travelocity.com** Provides access to the travel agent system SABRE, the most comprehensive central reservations system in the US.

ⓦ **www.travelshop.com.au** Australian website offering discounted flights, packages, insurance, online bookings.

From the UK and Ireland

The only **nonstop flights** to Beijing from the UK go from **London Heathrow** (10hr). It's not a problem to fly from other UK airports or from the Republic of Ireland, though you'll end up either catching a connecting flight to London or flying via your airline's hub city.

From the UK, the lowest available fares to Beijing from London start from around £400 in low season, rising to £600 in high season. If you're flying from the Republic of Ireland, reckon on €1000 in low season, €1500 in high season. Unfancied airlines such as Air China and Aeroflot offer competitive fares. Even the more upmarket airlines such as British Airways can be worth approaching to see if they are running any special offers or promotions – if you catch them at the right time you can enjoy the luxury of a nonstop flight at a budget price.

Airlines

Aeroflot UK ☎020/7355 2233,
ⓦ www.aeroflot.co.uk. London–Moscow flights, with daily connections to Beijing. Rather cheerless, but cheap.

Air China UK ☎020/7630 0919 or 7630 7678,
ⓦ www.air-china.co.uk. Five weekly nonstop flights from London Heathrow to Beijing, with keen fares.

Air France UK ☎0845/084 5111,
ⓦ www.airfrance.co.uk; Republic of Ireland ☎01/605 0383, ⓦ www.airfrance.com/ie. Daily flights to Beijing via Paris.

Austrian Airlines UK☎020/7766 0300,
ⓦ www.aua.com. Daily flights to Beijing via Vienna at competitive prices.

British Airways UK ☎0845/773 3377, Republic of Ireland ☎1800/626 747, ⓦ www.ba.com. Nonstop from London Heathrow to Beijing four times a week. Connections available from many UK airports.

Finnair UK ☎020/7408 1222, Republic of Ireland ☎01/844 6565, ⓦ www.finnair.com. From London Heathrow, Manchester and Glasgow to Helsinki, with three weekly flights from there to Beijing.

KLM UK ☎0870/507 4074, ⓦ www.klmuk.com. Flies from many UK regional airports to Amsterdam, with four flights weekly on to Beijing.

Lufthansa UK ☎0845/773 7747,
ⓦwww.lufthansa.co.uk. Daily flights to Beijing via Frankfurt, with connections from UK and Irish airports.

Pakistan International Airlines UK ☎020/7499 5500, ⓦ www.fly-pia.com. London–Islamabad, with two weekly connections to Beijing; requires an overnight stop. Usually an inexpensive option.

Singapore Airlines UK ☎0870/608 8886, Republic of Ireland ☎01/671 0722,
ⓦwww.singaporeair.com. A classy airline but a circuitous route, via Singapore from London Heathrow and Manchester, with a daily connection to Beijing.

Swiss International Airlines UK ☎0845/601 0956, ⓦ www.swiss.com. Daily flights to Beijing, with connections to their Zürich hub from London, Birmingham, Manchester and Dublin.

Thai Airways UK ☎0870/606 0911,
ⓦ www.thaiairways.com. Daily flights to Beijing from London Heathrow via Bangkok.

Flight agents and courier flight brokers

UK

Destination Group ☎020/7400 7045,
ⓦ www.destination-group.com. Good discount air fares.

Flightbookers ☎0870/010 7000,
ⓦ www.ebookers.com. Low fares on scheduled flights.

Flynow ☎0870/444 0045, ⓦ www.flynow.com. Large range of discounted tickets.

International Association of Air Travel Couriers ☎0800/0746 481 or 01305/216 920, ⓦ www.aircourier.co.uk. Courier flights to Beijing and Hong Kong from London Gatwick or Heathrow.

North South Travel ☎ & ☎01245/608 291,
ⓦ www.northsouthtravel.co.uk. Discounted fares worldwide; profits are used to support projects in the developing world, especially the promotion of sustainable tourism.

STA Travel ☎0870/1600 599,
ⓦ www.statravel.co.uk. Worldwide specialists in low-cost flights and tours for students and under-26s, though other customers welcome.

Top Deck ☎020/7244 8000,
ⓦ www.topdecktravel.co.uk. Long-established agent dealing in discount flights.

Trailfinders ☎020/7628 7628,
ⓦ www.trailfinders.com. One of the best-informed and most efficient agents for independent travellers.

Travel Bag ☎0870/890 1456,
🖳 www.travelbag.co.uk. Discount flights.
Travel Cuts ☎020/7255 2082 or 7255 1944,
🖳 www.travelcuts.co.uk. Canadian-owned company specializing in budget, student and youth travel.

Republic of Ireland

Apex Travel ☎01/241 8000,
🖳 www.apextravel.ie. Discount flight specialists.
Aran Travel International ☎091/562 595,
🖳 homepages.iol.ie/~arantvl/aranmain.htm. Good-value flights.
CIE Tours International ☎01/703 1888,
🖳 www.cietours.ie. General flight and tour agent.
Joe Walsh Tours ☎01/676 0991,
🖳www.joewalshtours.ie. General budget-fares agent.
Lee Travel ☎021/277 111. Flights and holidays.
McCarthy's Travel ☎021/427 0127,
🖳 www.mccarthystravel.ie. General flight agent.
Trailfinders ☎01/677 7888,
🖳 www.trailfinders.ie. Knowledgeable firm geared up for independent travellers.
USIT ☎01/602 1600, 🖳 www.usitnow.ie. Student and youth flight specialists.

Organized tours

UK-based tour operators generally include Beijing as one of a number of destinations in a whistlestop tour of China. A particularly good deal are the very cheap off-season **flight-and-hotel** packages to Beijing which, at prices that often go below £500, provide six or seven nights in a four-star hotel effectively for free, considering the cost of the flight alone. Don't forget, though, that quoted prices in brochures usually refer to the low-season minimum, based on two people sharing – the cost for a single traveller in high season will always work out far more expensive.

Specialist tour operators

China Travel Service (CTS) UK ☎020/7836 9911, 🖳 www.ctshorizons.com. An extensive range of tours including very cheap off-season hotel-and-flight packages to Beijing.
Destinations Worldwide Holidays Republic of Ireland ☎01/855 6641, 🖳 www.destinations.ie. Undemanding two-week tours that include Hong Kong and Beijing.
Hayes and Jarvis UK ☎0870/898 9890,
🖳 www.hayesandjarvis.co.uk. Their Beijing flight-and-hotel-only packages can be among the most inexpensive around.

Kuoni Worldwide UK ☎01306/740500
🖳 www.kuoni.co.uk. A handful of China guided tours; a twelve-day package taking in Beijing, Shanghai and other cities starts at around £2400 including flights.
Regent Holidays UK ☎0117/921 1711,
🖳www.regent-holidays.co.uk. Offers interesting Trans-Siberian packages for individual travellers in either direction and with various stopover permutations. The basic Moscow–Beijing package, including a night in a Moscow hotel, costs around £400.
The Russia Experience UK ☎020 8566 8846,
🖳 www.trans-siberian.co.uk. Besides detailing their Trans-Siberian packages, their website is a veritable mine of information about the railway.
World Expeditions UK ☎020/8870 2600,
🖳 www.worldexpeditions.co.uk. Offers a 21-day Great Wall trek, starting in Beijing and getting well off the beaten track, for £1600 excluding flights.

From the US and Canada

There is no shortage of flights to Beijing from North America. It takes around thirteen hours' **flying time** to reach Beijing from the West Coast; add seven hours or more to this if you start from the East Coast (including a stopover on the West Coast en route).

In low season, expect to pay $600–800/C$950–1250 from the West Coast (Los Angeles, San Francisco, Vancouver), or $800–1100/C$1250–1750 from the East Coast (New York, Montreal, Toronto). To get a good fare during high season it's important to buy your ticket as early as possible, in which case you probably won't pay more than $200/C$320 above what you would have paid in low season.

Airlines

Aeroflot US ☎1-888/340-6400, Canada ☎416/642-1653, 🖳www.aeroflot.com. Inexpensive flights from several North American cities to Moscow; useful if you're considering the Trans-Siberian train to Beijing.
Air Canada ☎1-888/247-2262,
🖳 www.aircanada.ca. Daily direct flights to Beijing from Toronto, via Vancouver.
Air China US ☎1-800/982-8802 or 1-800/986-1985, Canada ☎416/581-8833,
🖳 www.airchina.com.cn. Daily nonstop flights to Beijing from New York, San Francisco, Los Angeles and Vancouver. Also flies daily to Beijing from Montreal and Toronto via Vancouver. US connecting

flights available with Northwest Airlines.
All Nippon Airways ☎1-800/235-9262,
🌐svc.ana.co.jp/eng/index.html. Japanese carrier
with daily direct flights from New York, Washington,
San Francisco, Los Angeles, Vancouver and Toronto
to Tokyo, for onward flights to Beijing.
American Airlines ☎1-800/433-7300,
🌐www.aa.com. Daily nonstop flights from New
York, Dallas, Chicago and Los Angeles to Tokyo and a
connection to Beijing.
Asiana Airlines ☎1-800/227-4262,
🌐us.flyasiana.com. Korean airline flying nonstop to
Seoul, with connections to Beijing, from Los Angeles
(daily), San Francisco and Seattle (4 weekly), as well
as direct from New York (4 weekly).
Cathay Pacific ☎1-800/233-2742,
🌐www.cathay-usa.com & 🌐www.cathay.ca. Daily
service to Hong Kong from Los Angeles, New York,
San Francisco, Toronto and Vancouver, with
connections to Beijing.
China Eastern Airlines ☎1-800/200-5118,
🌐www.ce-air.com. Daily flights from Los Angeles to
Beijing.
Japan Air Lines ☎1-800/525-3663,
🌐www.japanair.com. Daily nonstop service to Tokyo
from New York, Los Angeles, San Francisco, Chicago
and Vancouver, with connections to Beijing.
Korean Airlines ☎1-800/438-5000,
🌐www.koreanair.com. Daily flights to Beijing via
Seoul from New York, Los Angeles, Chicago, Dallas,
Washington, San Francisco and Atlanta.
Northwest/KLM Airlines ☎1-800/447-4747,
🌐www.nwa.com, 🌐www.klm.com. Daily flights to
Tokyo from Honolulu, Seattle, San Francisco, Los
Angeles, Minneapolis, Detroit and New York, with
connections to Beijing.
United Airlines ☎1-800/538-2929,
🌐www.ual.com. Daily nonstop from Chicago and
Seattle to Beijing.

Travel agents and courier flight brokers

Air Brokers International ☎1-800/883-3273,
🌐www.airbrokers.com. Consolidator.
Council Travel ☎1-800/2COUNCIL,
🌐www.counciltravel.com. Nationwide organization
that mostly specializes in student/budget travel.
Flights from the US only.
**International Association of Air Travel
Couriers** ☎308/632-3273, 🌐www.courier.org.
New York–Beijing courier flights. Annual membership
required ($45).
STA Travel ☎1-800/781-4040, 🌐www
.sta-travel.com. Worldwide specialists in
independent travel.

TFI Tours ☎1-800/745-8000 or 212/736-1140,
🌐www.lowestairprice.com. Consolidator.
Travac ☎1-800/TRAV-800,
🌐www.thetravelsite.com. Consolidator.
Travelers Advantage ☎1-877/259-2691,
🌐www.travelersadvantage.com. Discount travel
club; annual membership required.
Travel Avenue ☎1-800/333-3335,
🌐www.travelavenue.com. Full-service travel agent
that offers discounts in the form of rebates.
Travel Cuts Canada ☎1-800/667-2887, US ☎1-
866/246-9762, 🌐www.travelcuts.com. Canadian
student-travel organization.
Worldtek Travel ☎1-800/243-1723,
🌐www.worldtek.com. Discount travel agency for
worldwide travel.

Tour operators

Prices below exclude flights to China unless
otherwise stated.
Abercrombie & Kent ☎1-800/323-7308 or
630/954-2944, 🌐www.abercrombiekent.com.
Luxury tours; $4000 buys you a twelve-day
"Highlights of China" trip covering Shanghai, Guilin,
Xi'an and Beijing.
Absolute Asia ☎1-800/736-8187,
🌐www.absoluteasia.com. Numerous tours of China
of between 6 and 23 days' duration and offering
first-class accommodation; their 14-day "Art and
History of China" tour starts at $3700.
Adventure Center ☎1-800/228-8747 or 510/654-
1879, 🌐www.adventure-center.com. Their 21-day
"Essence of China" package ($1500) starts out in
southern China and ends up in Beijing, with walking,
hiking and biking opportunities along the way.
Adventures Abroad ☎1-800/665-3998 or
360/775-9926, 🌐www.adventures-abroad.com.
Small-group specialists offering a 13-day tour that
weaves its way from Beijing to Shanghai ($2100).
Asia Transpacific Journeys ☎1-800/642-2742,
🌐www.southeastasia.com. Their "China: Beyond
the Wall" deluxe 18-day hiking tour – commencing in
Beijing – starts at $4800.
Backroads ☎1-800/GO-ACTIVE or 510/527-
1555, 🌐www.backroads.com. Cycling and hiking
throughout Beijing; ten-day packages start at $4000.
IST Cultural Tours ☎1-800/833-2111,
🌐www.ist-tours.com. Their "China – New and Old"
tour takes in Beijing and Shanghai ($700).
Mir Corp ☎206-624-7289, 🌐www.mircorp.com.
Specialists in Trans-Siberian rail travel, for small
groups as well as individual travellers.
Pleasant Holidays ☎1-800/742-9244,
🌐www.pleasantholidays.com. Air/hotel packages to
Beijing; five nights start at a very reasonable $900.

Worldwide Quest Adventures ☎1-800/387-1483 or 416/633-5666, ⓦwww.worldwidequest.com. On their 21-day "Hike the Great Wall" you get 11 days of trekking along the wall, all for $2600.

From Australia and New Zealand

The closest entry point into China from Australia and New Zealand is Hong Kong, from where it's easy to pick up a connecting flight to Beijing, though from Australia it's also possible to fly to Beijing without changing planes. Once in Hong Kong, you have the option of continuing your journey on the Kowloon–Beijing train (see p.9).

From Australia, some of the cheapest fares are with Royal Brunei Airlines, though they only serve Brisbane and Darwin. Their return fares, via a stopover in Brunei, are around A$1100 to Hong Kong from Brisbane or Darwin. Other good deals include Air China from Melbourne or Sydney direct to Beijing (A$1500); and Cathay Pacific direct to Hong Kong (A$1500 in low season; their fares are steep at other times). Qantas or British Airways are the only two operators to fly direct from Perth to Hong Kong (A$1800).

Flights **from New Zealand** are limited and therefore expensive: about the best deal is on Air New Zealand or Singapore from Auckland to Hong Kong (NZ$1750). Air New Zealand, Malaysia and other carriers also fly via other Southeast Asian cities to Hong Kong and Beijing.

Airlines

Air China Australia ☎02/9232 7277, ⓦwww.airchina.com.cn/index_en.html. From Sydney or Melbourne, they fly five times a week to Beijing.
Air New Zealand New Zealand ☎0800/737 000, ⓦwww.airnz.com. Auckland to Hong Kong five times a week, with connections to Beijing; also flights from various New Zealand cities to Singapore, for a connection to Beijing with Singapore Airlines.
British Airways Australia ☎02/8904 8800, New Zealand ☎0800/274 847, ⓦwww.britishairways.com. Daily from Australian east-coast capitals to Hong Kong, with connections to Beijing.
Cathay Pacific Australia ☎13 17 47, New Zealand ☎09/379 0861 or 0508/800 454,

ⓦwww.cathaypacific.com. Daily from Australian east-coast capitals to Hong Kong, with connections to Beijing with their sister airline Dragonair.
Malaysia Airlines Australia ☎13 26 27, New Zealand ☎09/373 2741, ⓦwww.mas.com.my. Five flights a week from Australian east-coast capitals, plus Perth and Adelaide, to Beijing.
Qantas Australia ☎13 13 13, ⓦwww.qantas.com.au. Flights at least daily from Australian east-coast capitals to Hong Kong, with connections on Chinese airlines to Beijing.
Royal Brunei Airlines Australia ☎07/3017 5000, ⓦwww.royalbruneiairlines.com.au. From Brisbane and Darwin to Hong Kong weekly, via Brunei, with connections on Chinese airlines to Beijing.
Singapore Airlines Australia ☎13 10 11, New Zealand ☎09/303 2129, ⓦwww.singaporeair.com. Several flights weekly from Brisbane, Sydney, Melbourne and Auckland to Singapore, with connections to Beijing.
Thai Australia ☎1300/651 960, ⓦwww.thaiair.com. Several flights weekly from Brisbane, Sydney and Melbourne, via Bangkok, to Beijing.
Vietnam Australia ☎02/9283 1355, ⓦwww.vietnamairlines.com.vn. Twice weekly to Beijing from Sydney and Melbourne, via Hanoi.

Travel agents

All About Asia Australia ☎1800/066 526 or 07/3221 4417, ⓦwww.allaboutasia.com.au. Discount air fares plus hotel packages.
Budget Travel New Zealand ☎09/366 0061 or 0800/808 040, ⓦwww.budgettravel.co.nz.
Destinations Unlimited New Zealand ☎09/373 4033.
Flight Centres Australia ☎13 31 33 or 02/9235 3522, New Zealand ☎09/358 4310, ⓦwww.flightcentre.com.au.
Northern Gateway Australia ☎08/8941 1394, ⓦwww.northerngateway.com.au.
STA Travel Australia ☎1300/733 035, ⓦwww.statravel.com.au; New Zealand ☎0508/782 872, ⓦwww.statravel.co.nz.
Student Uni Travel Australia ☎02/9232 8444, ⓦwww.sut.com.au; New Zealand ☎0800/874 823, ⓦwww.sut.co.nz.
Trailfinders Australia ☎02/9247 7666, ⓦwww.trailfinders.com.au.

Specialist tour operators

The Adventure Travel Company New Zealand ☎09/379 9755, ⓦwww.adventuretravel.co.nz. China tours, including Trans-Siberian rail trips.

China Tours and Travel Australia ☎08/9321 3432, ℻03/9321 2190. Six-day to three-week packages to China – starting or ending in Beijing – by air, road, rail and river.

China Travel Service Australia ☎02/9211 2633, New Zealand ☎09/309 6458, ⊛www.chinatravel.com.au. Package tours and accommodation bookings for Beijing and elsewhere in China.

Gateway Travel Australia ☎02/9745 3333, ⊛www.russian-gateway.com.au. Trans-Siberian bookings.

Intrepid Adventure Travel Australia ☎1300 360 667 or 03/9473 2626, New Zealand ☎0800/174 043, ⊛www.intrepidtravel.com.au. Small-group tours, with the emphasis on cross-cultural contact and low-impact tourism. Covers the staples, including hikes along the Great Wall near Beijing.

Passport Travel Australia ☎03/9867 3888, ⊛www.travelcentre.com.au. A few city-based packages to Beijing, plus Trans-Siberian bookings.

Via Moscow: The Trans-Siberian Train

One of the classic overland routes to China is through Russia on the so-called **Trans-Siberian Express**. As a one-off trip, the journey is highly recommended, and is a memorable way to begin or end your stay in China. The awesome views of stately birch forests, velvety prairies, misty lakes and arid plateaus help time pass, and there are frequent stops during which you can wander the station platform, purchasing food and knick-knacks. The trains are comfortable and clean: second-class compartments contain four berths, while first-class have two and even boast a private shower.

There are actually two rail lines from Moscow to Beijing: the **Trans-Manchurian** line, which runs almost as far as the sea of Japan before turning south through Dongbei (Manchuria) to Beijing; and the **Trans-Mongolian** express, which cuts through Mongolia from Siberia. The Manchurian train takes about six days, the Mongolian train about five; the latter is more popular with foreigners, not just because it's a little quicker but also because of the allure of Mongolia. Trans-Mongolian Chinese Train #4 is the most popular service for foreign tourists, a scenic route that rumbles past Lake Baikal

and Siberia, the grasslands of Mongolia, and the desert of northwest China, skirting the Great Wall.

Meals are included while the train is in China. In Mongolia, the dining car accepts payment in both Chinese and Mongolian currency; while in Russia, US dollars or Russian roubles can be used. It's worth having small denominations of US dollars as you can change these on the train throughout the journey, or use them to buy food from station vendors along the way. Note that trains via Manchuria arrive in Beijing at 5.20am, so remember to change money at the border stop if you're using this route.

Tickets and packages

Booking tickets can be problematic, especially in summer, when you may need to book two or three months ahead to ensure a seat. Furthermore, sorting out your travel arrangements from abroad is a complex business – you'll need transit visas for Russia, and if you use the Trans-Mongolian train you may have to apply for visas for Mongolia as well (US citizens don't need these). It's therefore highly advisable to use an experienced **travel agent** who can organize all tickets, visas and stopovers if required, in advance. One firm offering these services as well as rail packages that you can book from abroad is Monkey Business (⊛www.monkeyshrine.com), who have offices in Hong Kong and Beijing; for details of companies **at home** which can sort out Trans-Siberian travel, see the lists of specialist travel agents for your country earlier in this section. If you want to book a ticket yourself, reckon on paying the equivalent of at least US$200 for second-class travel from Moscow to Beijing.

If you're planning to take the train home, you could attempt to buy your train ticket in Beijing, at the CITS office in the *International Hotel* (see p.106). This is an inexpensive option (tickets for Moscow start at about £120/$190; visas will cost another £50/$80 or so), but it involves a fair amount of hassle. Staff there will tell you the hoops to jump through to get the necessary visas.

Red tape and visas

To enter China, all foreign nationals require a visa, available worldwide from Chinese embassies and consulates and through specialist tour operators and visa agents.

Single-entry tourist visas must generally be used within three months of issue, and cost US$30–50 or the local equivalent. They're generally valid for a month, but the authorities might grant a request for a two- or three-month visa, at least outside peak season.

To apply for a tourist visa you have to submit an application form, one or two passport-size photographs, your passport (which must be valid for at least another six months from your planned date of entry into China, and have at least one blank page for visas) and the fee. If you apply in person, processing should take between three and five working days. You'll be asked your occupation – it's wise not to admit to being a journalist or writer as you might be called in for an interview. At times of political sensitivity you may be asked for a copy of any air tickets and hotel bookings in your name.

A **business visa** is valid for three months and can be valid for multiple journeys, though you'll need an official invitation from a government-recognized Chinese organization to apply for one. Twelve-month **work visas** again require an invitation, plus a health certificate from your doctor. Students intending to study in Beijing for less than six months need an invitation or letter of acceptance from a college there in order to apply for **student visas**. If you're intending to go on a longer course, you have to fill in an additional form, available from Chinese embassies, and will also need a health certificate.

Getting visas in Hong Kong

In Hong Kong, it's somewhat easier to obtain visas that are valid for longer than the usual thirty-day period. The standard one-month tourist visa for China can be obtained from any of the numerous travel agencies or direct from the visa office at the Ministry for Foreign Affairs, Floor 5, Low Block, China Resources Building, 26 Harbour Rd (☎2827 1881). For a sixty- or ninety-day multiple-entry visa, issued in two days, visit the China Travel Service (CTS) at 78–83 Connaught Road or 27–33 Nathan Road. Note that these visas are valid from the date of issue, not the date of entry. You can get a six-month multiple-entry business visa at Shoestring Travel, 27–33 Nathan Rd, for HK$600. No invitation letter is required, just a business card. For a next-day, no questions asked, one-year business visa costing HK$900, visit Forever Bright Trading Ltd, 707, New Mandarin Plaza, Tower B, 14 Science Museum Road.

British and Irish citizens, nationals of most other European countries, Canadians, Australians and New Zealanders can stay in Hong Kong without a visa for three months; Americans and South Africans for thirty days.

Chinese embassies and consulates

Australia 15 Coronation Drive, Yarralumla, ACT 2600 ☎02/6273 4780,
ⓦwww.chinaembassy.org.au. Also consulates at 77 Irving Rd, Toorak (visa & passport enquiries ☎03/9804 3683) and 539 Elizabeth St, Surry Hills (☎02/9698 7929).
Canada 515 St Patrick St, Ottawa, Ontario K1N 5H3 ☎613/234 2682,
ⓦwww.chinaembassycanada.org. Visas can also be obtained from the consulates in Calgary, Toronto and Vancouver.
India 50-D Shantipath, Chanakyapuri, New Delhi, 110021, ☎26781585.
Ireland 40 Ailesbury Road, Dublin 4 ☎01/2691707.
Laos Thanon Wat Nak Yai, Vientiane ☎315103.
New Zealand 2–6 Glenmore Street, Wellington ☎04/474 9631, ⓦwww.chinaembassy.org.nz; plus a consulate in Auckland ☎09/525 1589, ⓦwww.chinaconsulate.org.nz.

B

Russia ul. Druzhby 6, Moscow ☎095/145-1543 ✆www.chinaembassy.ru.

UK 31 Portland Place, London W1B 1QD ☎020/7631 1430; Denison House, Denison Rd, Victoria Park, Manchester M14 5RX ☎0161/224 7480; ✆www.chinese-embassy.org.uk.

USA 2300 Connecticut Ave NW, Washington, DC 20008 ☎202/3282517, ✆www.chinese-embassy .org. Also consulates in Chicago, Houston, Los Angeles, New York and San Francisco.

Vietnam Tran Phu, Hanoi (round the corner from the main embassy building at 46 Hoang Dieu) ☎04/823 5517.

Visa extensions

Once in China, a first extension to a tourist visa, valid for a month, is easy to obtain; most Europeans pay ¥160 for this, Americans a little less. To apply for an extension, go to the "Aliens Entry Exit Department" of the Public Security Bureau (**PSB**) at 2 Andingmen Dong Dajie, 300m east of Yonghe Gong subway stop (Mon–Fri 8am–noon & 1.30–4pm; ☎010/84015292). The officious staff will keep your passport for a week; note that you can't change money, or even book into a new hotel, while they've got it. Subsequent applications for extensions will be refused unless you have a good reason to stay. They'll reluctantly give you a couple of extra days if you have a flight out of the country booked, otherwise you'll be brusquely ordered to leave the country. Don't; simply go to Chengde (see p.162), which has a friendly PSB office where you can get month-long second extensions on the spot.

Don't overstay your visa even for a few hours – the fine is ¥500 per day, and if you're caught at the airport with an out-of-date visa the hassle that will follow may mean you miss your flight.

Customs allowances

You're allowed to **import** into China up to four hundred cigarettes, two litres of alcohol, twenty fluid ounces of perfume and up to fifty grams of gold or silver. You can't take in more than ¥6000, and foreign currency in excess of US$5000 or the equivalent must be declared. It's illegal to import printed matter, tapes or videos critical of the country, but don't worry too much about this, as confiscation is rare in practice.

Finally, note that **export restrictions** apply on any items over 100 years old that you might buy in China. Taking these items out of the country requires an export form, available from the Friendship Store (see p.135); ask at the information counter for a form, and take along the item and your receipt and approval is given on the spot. You needn't be unduly concerned about the process – the "antiques" you commonly see for sale are all fakes.

Insurance

You'd do well to take out an insurance policy before travelling to cover against theft, loss and illness or injury. Before paying for a new policy, however, it's worth checking whether you are already covered: some all-risks home insurance policies may cover your possessions when overseas, and many private medical schemes include cover when abroad.

In Canada, provincial health plans usually provide partial cover for medical mishaps overseas, while holders of official student/teacher/youth cards in Canada and the US are entitled to (meagre) accident coverage and hospital inpatient benefits. Students will often find that their student health coverage extends during the vacations and for one term beyond the date of last enrolment.

Rough Guides travel insurance

Rough Guides offers its own low-cost travel insurance, especially customized for our statistically low-risk readers by a leading British broker, provided by the American International Group (AIG) and registered with the British regulatory body, GISC (the General Insurance Standards Council). There are five main Rough Guides insurance plans: **No Frills** for the bare minimum for secure travel; **Essential**, which provides decent all-round cover; **Premier** for comprehensive cover with a wide range of benefits; **Extended Stay** for cover lasting four months to a year; and **Annual Multi-Trip**, a cost-effective way of getting Premier cover if you travel more than once a year. Premier, Annual Multi-Trip and Extended Stay policies can be supplemented by a "Hazardous Pursuits Extension" if you plan to indulge in sports considered dangerous, such as scuba-diving or trekking. For a policy quote, call the Rough Guides Insurance Line: toll-free in the UK ☏0800/015 09 06 or ☏+44 1392 314 665 from elsewhere. Alternatively, get an online quote at ⓦwww.roughguides.com/insurance.

After exhausting these possibilities, you might want to contact a specialist travel-insurance company. A typical travel insurance policy usually provides cover for the loss of baggage, tickets and – up to a certain limit – cash or cheques, as well as cancellation or curtailment of your journey. Most of them exclude so-called dangerous sports unless an extra premium is paid: this can mean skiing and trekking as well as bungee jumping. Many policies can be chopped and changed to exclude coverage you don't need – for example, sickness and accident benefits can often be excluded or included at will. If you do take medical coverage, ascertain whether benefits will be paid as treatment proceeds or only after return home, and whether there is a 24-hour medical emergency number. When securing baggage cover, make sure that the per-article limit – typically under £500/$750 – will cover your most valuable possession.

To make a claim, you should keep receipts for medicines and medical treatment, and in the event you have anything stolen, you must obtain an official statement from the police.

Health

The most common health hazard in Beijing is the host of flu infections that strike down a large proportion of the population, mostly in the winter months. The problem is compounded by the overcrowded conditions, chain-smoking, pollution and the widespread habit of spitting, which rapidly spreads infection. Initial symptoms are fever, sore throat, chills and a feeling of malaise, sometimes followed by a prolonged bout of bronchitis. If you do come down with something like this, drink lots of fluids and get plenty of rest, and seek medical advice if symptoms persist.

Diarrhoea is the another common illness to affect travellers, usually in a mild form while your stomach gets used to unfamiliar food. The sudden onset of diarrhoea with stomach cramps and vomiting indicates food poisoning. In both instances, get plenty of rest, drink lots of water, and in serious cases replace lost salts with oral rehydration solu-

SARS

A previously unknown, infectious form of atypical pneumonia, **SARS** – severe acute respiratory syndrome – caused a major health crisis in Beijing in 2003. The disease, caused by a virus similar to one type of common cold virus, results in death in around five percent of cases.

It is thought that the virus might have originated in civet cats, and crossed into humans in Guangzhou province in the south of the country, where these cats are a delicacy. In April 2003, after weeks of insisting that everything was under control, the Chinese government admitted that they had over seven hundred cases in Beijing, ten times as many as previously acknowledged. The admission caused mass panic and Beijing virtually shut down for weeks: citizens took to wearing masks and staying at home, tourist sights were deserted, many businesses were closed, and the Rolling Stones cancelled their Chinese tour. The smell of disinfectant was pervasive, and, for once, public spitting was socially unacceptable. Rumours about SARS abounded – smoking cigarettes and burning incense were said to prevent it, pets and dirty money to spread it. Anyone travelling around the country was regarded with suspicion and roadside temperature checks and rather arbitrary quarantine measures were introduced.

In the event, SARS had a low transmission rate, and the epidemic petered out after a few weeks. Scientists feel the world got off rather lightly; had the disease been as infectious as flu, the consequences would have been catastrophic. A small blessing to come out of the whole episode was a ban on the consumption of wild animals.

tion (ORS); this is especially important with young children. Take a few sachets with you, or make your own by adding half a teaspoon of salt and three of sugar to a litre of cool, previously boiled water. While down with diarrhoea, avoid milk, greasy or spicy foods, coffee and most fruit, in favour of bland foodstuffs such as rice, plain noodles and soup. If symptoms persist, or if you notice blood or mucus in your stools, consult a doctor.

Eat at places which look busy and clean, stick to fresh, thoroughly cooked food, and you'll have few problems. Beware of food that has been pre-cooked and kept warm for several hours. Shellfish are a potential hepatitis A risk in Asia, and best avoided. Fresh fruit you've peeled yourself is safe; other uncooked foods may have been washed in unclean water. The other thing to watch out for is **dirty chopsticks**, though many restaurants provide disposable sets; if you want to be really sure, bring your own pair.

Hospitals, clinics and pharmacies

Medical facilities in Beijing are adequate: there are some high-standard international clinics, most big hotels have a resident doctor, and

for minor complaints, there are plenty of pharmacies which can suggest remedies. Most doctors will treat you with Western techniques first, but will also know a little Traditional Chinese Medicine (TCM).

If you don't speak Chinese, you'll generally need to have a good phrasebook or to be accompanied by a Chinese-speaker. However, the following hospitals have **foreigners' clinics** where some English is spoken: Beijing Hospital at 1 Dahua Lu (☎010/65132266); Friendship Hospital, 95 Yongan Lu, west of Tiantan Park (☎010/63014411); and Sino Japanese Friendship Hospital, in the northeast of the city just beyond Beisanhuan Dong Lu (daily 8–11.30am & 1–4.30pm; ☎010/64221122). For a service run by and for foreigners, try the International Medical and Dental Centre at S111 in the Lufthansa Centre, 50 Liangmaqiao Lu (☎010/64651384); the Hong Kong International Clinic on the third floor of the Swissotel Hong Kong Macao Centre, Dongsi Shitiao Qiao (daily 9am–9pm; ☎010/65012288 ext 2346); or the United Family Hospital, the only completely foreign-operated clinic, at 2 Jingtai Lu (☎010/64333960). For real emergencies, the AEA International Clinic has English-speaking staff and offers a comprehensive (and expensive) service at 14 Liangmahe Lu, not far from the Lufthansa Centre (clinic ☏010/64629112, emergency calls ☏010/64629100).

Pharmacies are marked by a green cross. There are large ones at 136 Wangfujing and 42 Dongdan Bei Dajie, or you could try the famous Tongrentang Pharmacy on Dazhalan for traditional remedies (see p.57). For imported non-prescription medicines, try Watsons (daily 9am–9pm) at the *Holiday Inn Lido*, Shoudujichang Lu, in the northeast of the city, or at the Full Link Plaza on Chaoyangmenwai Dajie (daily 10am–9pm).

Information, websites and maps

China's tourist offices abroad are run by the China National Tourist Office (CNTO). They will offer a little information and a lot of glossy brochures, but don't expect them to be too helpful as their main role is to sell tours.

In Beijing, **BTS** (Beijing Travel Service) is a new tourist agency focusing on the capital, its main role, again, being to sell tours. However they will also book train and plane tickets for a small commission and hand out free maps. They have offices at the locations below (daily 9am–6pm). For more information on their tours check ⊛english.bjta .gov.cn. There's also a **tourism hotline** for enquiries or complaints (☏010/065130828).

Of the many other agencies, the government-run **CITS** (China International Tourist Service) and **CYTS** (China Youth Travel Service) are the largest. Again, they run tours and sell tickets but don't expect too much from them.

Chinese tourist offices abroad

For additional locations, see ⊛www.cnto.org /offices.htm.

Australia 19th floor, 44 Market St, Sydney, NSW 2000 ☏02/9299 4057.

Canada 480 University Ave, Suite 806, Toronto, Ontario M5G 1V2 ☏0416/5996636.

UK 4 Glentworth St, London NW1 5PG ☏020/7373 0888.

USA Suite 6413, 350 Fifth Ave, Empire State Building, New York, NY 10018 ☏212/760-8218; Suite 201, 333 W Broadway, Glendale, CA 91024 ☏818/545-7505.

BTS offices in Beijing

South Lobby, Modern Plaza, Dong Dai shopping Centre, 40 Zhongguancun Nan Dajie, Haidian District ☏010/62622895.

10 Dengshikou Xi Jie, Dongcheng District, opposite Lao She's Residence ☏010/65123043.

First floor, Xidan Science and Technology Plaza, 131 Xidan Bei Dajie, Xicheng District ☏010/66160108.

27 Gongrentiyuchang Bei Lu, Chaoyang District.

Beijing Zhan Jie, just south of the COFCO Plaza.

Useful publications

The English-language *Beijing This Month* has listings and light features aimed at tourists, and is available free in the lobbies of the upmarket hotels. You can also pick up glossy free leaflets, containing basic tourist information, at the upmarket hotels, from any tourist office or the counter inside the front door at the Friendship Store on Jianguomenwai Dajie.

Much more useful, though, are the free magazines aimed at the expat community, which contain up-to-date entertainment and restaurant listings and are available at expat bars and restaurants (the *Subway* chain of fast-food restaurants is a good place to look if you can't make it to the Chaoyang district, where most expat services are). *City Edition* and *Metro* are upmarket monthlies, but by far the most useful publication is the irreverent and informative monthly **That's Beijing** (ⓦ www.thatsbeijing.com), whose giant listings section includes club nights, art happenings and the more underground gigs, with addresses written in *pinyin* and Chinese.

Anyone intending to live in Beijing should get hold of the fat *Beijing Guidebook* published by Middle Kingdom Press, which includes information on finding housing and doing business. It's available in the Friendship Store.

Online resources

There's plenty of online information about China in general and Beijing specifically, though as a general rule, avoid websites run by official agencies such as CITS; they're dry as dust. Here's a selection of sites to start you off:

The Beijing Page ⓦ www.beijingpage.com A comprehensive and well-organized page of links, with sections on tourism, entertainment, reference and industry.

Beijing Opera Page
ⓦ www.geocities.com/Vienna/Opera/ 8692/index0.html More than most people would want to know about Beijing opera, including story rundowns and a frank essay about why hardly anyone bothers watching it any more.

Beijing Guo'an
ⓦ www.soccerage.com/en/02/01278.html All about Guo'an, Beijing's football team, including fixture lists.

CCTV 9 ⓦ www.cctv-9.com. The website of Chinese state television's English-language channel, featuring a live video stream plus other programmes available to watch on demand.

China Business World ⓦ www.cbw.com A corporate directory site with a useful travel section, detailing tours and allowing you to book flights and hotels.

China Vista ⓦ www.chinavista.com China-based website with snippets about Chinese culture, history, attractions, and food.

Friends of the Great Wall
ⓦ www.friendsofgreatwall.org/english Covers efforts to maintain and clean up the Great Wall, with useful links.

Niubi ⓦ www.niubi.com This website, named after a very rude phrase in Chinese, is dedicated to Beijing's more underground rock bands.

Sinomania ⓦwww.sinomania.com A California-based site with links to current Chinese news stories and a good popular music section, with MP3s available.

Yesasia ⓦ www.yesasia.com Online shopping for Chinese movies, CDs, books, collectables etc.

Zhongwen.com ⓦ www.zhongwen.com Especially interesting if you're a student of Chinese, this site includes background on the Chinese script, several classic texts (with links to some English translations) and even a bunch of suggested renderings into Chinese of common Christian names.

Maps

A large fold-out **map** of the city is vital. In general, the free tourist maps – available in large hotels and printed inside tourist magazines – don't show enough detail. A wide variety of city maps are available at all transport hubs and from street vendors, hotels and bookshops. The best such map is the **Beijing Tourist Map** (¥8), which is labelled in English and Chinese and has bus routes, sights and hotels marked. The most detailed maps of the city are to be found in book form in *Shenghuo Ditu*, available from all bookshops (see p.138), though it's labelled only in Chinese.

Maps of Beijing that are worth seeking out before you go are the Berndtson and Berndtson, which is laminated, and the Periplus Beijing map, which has all the street names, including those of many *hutongs* (alleyways), in English. Whatever map you get, you can gauge if it's really up to date by whether it includes the newer subway lines.

Map outlets

UK and Ireland

Blackwell's Map and Travel Shop 50 Broad St, Oxford OX1 3BQ ☎01865/793 550, ⓦ maps.blackwell.co.uk.
Heffers 20 Trinity St, Cambridge CB2 1TJ ☎01865/333 536, ⓦ www.heffers.co.uk.
Hodges Figgis Bookshop 56–58 Dawson St, Dublin 2 ☎01/677 4754.
The Map Shop 30a Belvoir St, Leicester LE1 6QH ☎0116/247 1400, ⓦ www.mapshopleicester.co.uk.
Newcastle Map Centre 55 Grey St, Newcastle-upon-Tyne, NE1 6EF ☎0191/261 5622.
Stanfords 12–14 Long Acre, London WC2E 9LP ☎020/7836 1321, ⓦ www.stanfords.co.uk.
The Travel Bookshop 13–15 Blenheim Crescent, W11 2EE ☎020/7229 5260, ⓦ www.thetravelbookshop.co.uk.

US and Canada

Adventurous Traveler.com US ☎1-800/282-3963, ⊛adventuroustraveler.com.
Distant Lands 56 S Raymond Ave, Pasadena, CA 91105 ☎1-800/310-3220, ⊛www.distantlands.com.
Elliot Bay Book Company 101 S Main St, Seattle, WA 98104 ☎1-800/962-5311, ⊛www.elliotbaybook.com.
Globe Corner Bookstore 28 Church St, Cambridge, MA 02138 ☎1-800/358-6013, ⊛www.globercorner.com.
Map Link 30 S La Patera Lane, Unit 5, Santa Barbara, CA 93117 ☎1-800/962-1394, ⊛www.maplink.com.
Rand McNally US ☎1-800/333-0136, ⊛www.randmcnally.com.
The Travel Bug Bookstore 2667 W Broadway,

Vancouver V6K 2G2 ☎604/737-1122, ⊛www.swifty.com/tbug.
World of Maps 1235 Wellington St, Ottawa, Ontario K1Y 3A3 ☎1-800/214-8524, ⊛www.worldofmaps.com.

Australia and New Zealand

The Map Shop 6–10 Peel St, Adelaide, SA 5000 ☎08/8231 2033, ⊛www.mapshop.net.au.
Mapland 372 Little Bourke St, Melbourne, Victoria 3000 ☎03/9670 4383, ⊛www.mapland.com.au.
MapWorld 173 Gloucester St, Christchurch ☎0800/627 967 or 03/374 5399, ⊛www.mapworld.co.nz.
Perth Map Centre 900 Hay St, Perth, WA 6000 ☎08/9322 5733.
Specialty Maps 46 Albert St, Auckland 1001 ☎09/307 2217.

Costs, money and banks

In terms of costs, Beijing is a city of extremes. You can, if you wish to live it up, spend as much here as you would visiting any Western capital; on the other hand, it's also quite feasible to live extremely cheaply – most locals survive on less than US$150 a month.

Generally, your biggest expense is likely to be **accommodation**, which is priced at Western levels. Food and transport, on the other hand, are relatively cheap. The minimum you can live on comfortably is about £10/US$16 a day, if you stay in a dormitory, get around by bus and eat in simple restaurants. On a budget of £32/$50 a day, you'll be able to stay in a modest hotel, travel in taxis and eat in good restaurants. To stay in an upmarket hotel, you'll need to have a budget of around £80/$130 a day.

It used to be government policy to **surcharge foreigners** on fares on public transport and for admission to sights. This is no longer the case but the practice lives on, and you might well find price discrimination being exercised by unscrupulous shopkeepers. Discounts on admission prices are avail-

able to **students** in China on production of the red Chinese student identity card. A youth-hostel card gets a small discount at hostels.

Tipping is never expected, and though you might sometimes feel it's warranted, resist the temptation – you'll set an unwelcome precedent.

Money

Chinese **currency** is formally called the **yuan** (¥), more colloquially known as **renminbi** (RMB) or **kuai**; a yuan breaks down into units of ten **mao** or **jiao**. One mao is equivalent to ten fen, though these are effectively worthless – you'll only ever be given them in official currency transactions, or see the tiny yellow and green notes folded up into little twists and used to build model dragons or boats. Paper money was invented in China and is still the main form of exchange, available in ¥100, ¥50, ¥20, ¥10, ¥5, and ¥1 notes, with a similar selection of mao. At the time of writing the exchange rate was approximately ¥13 to £1, ¥8 to $1.

China is suffering from a rash of **counterfeiting**. A few years ago you were only likely to see fake ¥100 notes, but these days there are even fake ¥5 notes in circulation. Check your change carefully, as the locals do – hold them up to the light and rub them; fakes have no watermarks and the paper feels different.

Banks and ATMs

Banks are usually open seven days a week (9am–noon & 2–5pm), though foreign exchange (there's generally a particular counter for this, marked in English) is sometimes only available Monday to Friday. All banks are closed on New Year's Day, National Day, and for the first three days of the Chinese New Year, with reduced hours for the following eleven days.

The **Commercial Bank** (Mon–Fri 9am noon & 1–4pm) in the CITIC Building, 19 Jianguomenwai Dajie, next to the Friendship Store, offers the most comprehensive exchange service: here, you can change money and traveller's cheques, or use most credit cards to obtain cash advances or buy American dollars (if you present exchange certificates).

All branches of the **Bank of China** will give cash advances on Visa cards, incurring a three percent commission. Their main branch is at 108 Fuxingmennei Dajie (Mon–Fri 9am–noon & 1.30–5pm), off Chaoyangmen Dajie, just north of the international post office; it looks impressive (the building was designed by the renowned architect I.M. Pei) but doesn't do anything the smaller branches can't. You'll find other branches in the SCITECH Plaza (Mon–Fri 9am–noon & 1–6.30pm), the World Trade Centre (Mon–Fri 9am–5pm, Sat 9am–noon), the Sun Dong'an Plaza (Mon–Fri 9.30am–noon & 1.30–5pm), and the Lufthansa Centre (Mon–Fri 9am–noon & 1–4pm), among others.

Cirrus and Plus cards can be used to make cash withdrawals from **ATMs** operated by the Bank of China, the Industrial and Commercial Bank of China, China Construction Bank and Agricultural Bank of China.

Traveller's cheques

Traveller's cheques are the best way to carry your funds around, as they can be replaced if lost or stolen – for which contingency, it's worth keeping a list of the serial numbers separate from the cheques. They also attract a slightly better rate of exchange than cash. Available through banks and travel agents, they can be cashed only at branches of the Bank of China and at tourist hotels.

It's still worth taking along a small quantity of foreign currency – such as US, Canadian or Australian dollars, or British pounds or euros – as cash is more widely exchangeable than traveller's cheques. Don't try to change money on the black market as you'll almost certainly get ripped off.

Credit cards and wiring money

Major **credit cards**, such as Visa, American Express, and MasterCard, are accepted at big tourist hotels and restaurants, and by some tourist-oriented shops. It's straightforward to obtain cash advances on a Visa card at many Chinese banks (however, the commission is a steep three percent). Visa card holders can also get cash advances using ATM machines bearing the "Plus" logo.

It's possible to wire money to Beijing through **Western Union** (®www.westernunion.com); funds can be collected from one of their agents in the city, in post offices and the Agricultural Bank of China.

Arrival and city transport

Beijing's ring roads, freeways arranged in nested rectangles centring on Tian'anmen Square, are rapid-access corridors around the city. The second and third ring roads, Erhuan and Sanhuan Lu, are the two most useful; cutting down on journey times but extending the distance travelled, they are much favoured by taxi drivers. Within the second ring road lie most of the historical sights, while many of the most modern buildings – including the fanciest hotels, restaurants, shopping centres and office blocks – are along or close to the third. You'll soon become familiar with the experience of barrelling along a freeway in a bus or taxi while identical blocks flicker past, not knowing which direction you're travelling in, let alone where you are.

To get a sense of the city's **layout**, make mental notes of the more obvious **landmarks**: the Great Hall of the People in Tian'anmen Square, the Telecom Office on Xichang'an Jie, and the *Beijing Hotel* on Dongchang'an Jie; note also the Friendship Store and World Trade Centre, further east on Dongchang'an Jie. At the western intersection of the second ring road and Chang'an Jie, the astronomical instruments atop the ancient observatory stand out for their oddness, as does the white dagoba in Beihai Park, just northwest of the Forbidden City.

Arriving by air

The first experience many visitors have of Beijing, and one that straight away confounds many expectations, is arrival at the gleaming, ultramodern **Beijing Capital Airport**, 29km northeast of the centre, and the traffic jams along a modern freeway into the city. Banks and an ATM are on the right as you exit Customs (and there are more ATMs upstairs). There's an accommodation-booking service opposite Customs, but you may get lower prices if you call the hotels yourself and bargain for a discount.

You'll be pestered in the arrivals hall itself by charlatan taxi drivers; ignore them. To avoid getting ripped off by unlicensed drivers, use the **taxi rank** to the left of the main exit from Arrivals (just outside gate 9). Tariffs vary; a red sticker in the window states the rate per kilometre. A trip to the city centre will cost around ¥80 in a ¥1.2 taxi (including a ¥15 toll for use of the expressway).

There are plans for a new light railway from the airport to Dongzhimen, but it won't open until at least 2007. In the meantime, the

Beijing transport terminals

Beijing	北京	*běijīng*
Beijing Capital Airport	北京首都机场	*běijīng shǒudū jīchǎng*
Bus stations		
Deshengmen bus station	德胜门公共汽车站	*déshèngmén gōnggòng qìchēzhàn*
Dongzhimen bus station	东直门公共汽车站	*dōngzhímén gōnggòng qìchēzhàn*
Haihutun bus station	海户屯公共汽车站	*hǎihùtún gōnggòng qìchēzhàn*
Zhaogongkou bus station	赵公口公共汽车站	*zhàogōngkǒu gōnggòng qìchēzhàn*
Train stations		
Beijing Zhan	北京站	*běijīng zhàn*
Xi Zhan	西站	*xī zhàn*
Xizhimen Zhan	西直门站	*xīzhímén zhàn*
Yongdingmen Zhan	永定门站	*yǒngdìngmén zhàn*

most convenient public transport to the centre is the comfortable if cramped **airport buses**, which can be found outside gate 11. Buy tickets (¥16) from the desk directly in front of the exit. They leave regularly on two routes, A and B. **Route A** buses stop at the *Hilton*, the Lufthansa Centre, Dongzhimen subway stop, *Swissotel*, and Chaoyangmen subway stop, before terminating outside the *International Hotel*, just north of Beijing Zhan, the central **train station**, also served by the subway. **Route B** buses make stops on the northern and western sections of the third ring road, including the *SAS Royal Hotel*, Asian Games Village, and *Friendship Hotel*, before terminating at the *Xinxing Hotel*, at the intersection of Chang'an Jie and Xisanhuan Bei Lu, close to the Gongzhufen subway stop. If the airport bus doesn't pass close to where you want to end up, It's a good idea to do the remainder of your journey by taxi rather than tussle with more buses, as the public transport system is confusing at first and the city layout alienating. But be wary of the taxi drivers waiting at the bus stop – hail a cab from the street instead. The vast majority of Beijing's cab drivers are trustworthy, but there are a few bad apples who look out for new arrivals.

Arriving by train

Beijing has two main train stations. **Beijing Zhan**, the central station, just south of Jianguomennei Dajie, is where trains from destinations north and east of Beijing arrive.

At the northeastern edge of the concourse is the subway stop, on the network's loop line. The taxi rank is over the road and 50m east of the station; another 50m on is a major bus terminal, from where buses serve most of the city.

Approaching from the south or west of the capital, you'll arrive at the west station, **Xi Zhan**, Asia's largest train terminal and the head of the Beijing–Kowloon line. There are plenty of buses from here – bus #122 heads to Beijing Zhan, bus #21 to Fuchengmen subway stop – as well as taxis, from the rank 50m in front of the main entrance.

You're unlikely to use Beijing's other train stations unless you're on a suburban train from, for example, the Great Wall at Badaling. Beijing North, also known as **Xizhimen Zhan**, is at the northwestern edge of the second ring road, near the subway; Beijing South, or **Yongdingmen Zhan**, is just inside the third ring road, with a bus terminus outside.

City transport

Beijing's **public transport system** is extensive but overstretched. Most of the burden is carried by the heaving buses; the subway is fast, comfortable and not too crowded, but serves few destinations. Many visitors tire of the hassle of buses pretty quickly and end up taking rather more taxis than they'd planned. The scale of the city militates against taking "bus #11" – Chinese slang for walking – almost anywhere, and most of the

---

Street names

Beijing street names look bewildering at first, as a road can have several names along its length, but once you know the system they are easy to figure out. Each name varies by the addition of the word for inside or outside – **nei** or **wai** respectively – which indicates the street's position relative to the former city walls, then a direction – **bei**, **nan**, **xi**, **dong** and **zhong** (north, south, west, east and middle respectively). Central streets often also contain the word **men** (gate), which indicates that they once passed through a walled gate along their route. **Jie** and **lu** mean respectively "street" and "road"; the word **da**, which sometimes precedes them, simply means "big". Thus Jianguomenwai Dajie literally refers to the outer section of Jianguomen Big Street. More confusingly, in the northwest section of the Third Ring Road you'll come across both Beisanhuan Xi Lu (for the bit east of the northwest corner) and Xisanhuan Bei Lu (the stretch running south of that corner). Some of these compound street names are just too much of a mouthful and are usually shortened; Gongrentiyuchang Bei Lu, for example, is usually referred to as Gongti Bei Lu.

main streets are so straight that getting around on foot soon gets tedious. Cycling, still the preferred mode of transport for the majority of the population, is an excellent alternative to both public transport and walking, with plenty of rental outlets in the city.

Incidentally, Beijing is divided into **districts** which, unfortunately, aren't marked on standard city maps; it's helpful to know these districts when trying to locate addresses. Broadly, **Dongcheng** is the eastern half of the centre, **Xicheng** the western half. **Xuanwu** is the southwest, **Chongwen** the southeast, **Haidian** the north and west outside the second ring road, and **Chaoyang** north and east outside the second ring road.

Buses

Even though every one of the city's 140 bus and trolleybus services runs about once a minute, you'll find getting on or off at busy times hard work (rush hours are Mon–Sat 7–9am & 4.30–6pm). Forget about trying to see anything of the city from the window, as views tend to be limited to the backs of other passengers' necks.

Beijing buses are notable for their distinctive aroma, something like garlic and boiled cabbage. Less fragrant and a little more comfortable, if slower, are the **minibuses**, which ply the same routes as the buses. **Double deckers**, operated on five services, are more comfortable – you're more likely to get a seat on these – and run along main roads. **Luxury buses**, which run around certain tourist sights, are modern, air-conditioned, and actually quite pleasant. **Tourist buses** – which look like ordinary buses but have route numbers written in green – make regular trips (mid-April to mid-Oct) between the city centre and certain out-of-town attractions, including sections of the Great Wall; we've listed useful routes in the text.

The **fare** depends how far you are going, though it's usually around ¥0.5 and never exceeds ¥2.5. Double-decker buses charge ¥2 a trip, as do the minibuses. On luxury buses, fares are between ¥3 and ¥10, on tourist buses between ¥10 and ¥20. In all cases a conductor will collect fares.

Bus routes are efficiently organized and easy to understand – a useful feature, since stops tend to be a good kilometre apart. The routes are indicated by red or blue lines on all good maps; a dot on the line indicates a stop. Next to the stop on the map you'll see tiny Chinese characters giving the stop's name; you need to know it for the conductor to work out your fare (the *Beijing Tourist Map* has stops marked in *pinyin*; see p.187). The conductor will alert you when it's time to get off.

A word of warning: be very wary of **pickpockets** on buses. Beijing is not a particularly crime-ridden city, but the pickpockets here target foreigners.

Useful bus routes

All buses display their **route numbers** prominently. Routes numbered 1–25 run around the city centre; numbers in the 100s are trolleybuses; buses numbered in the

Long-distance bus stations

There are many termini for long-distance buses, each terminus serving buses from only a few destinations. Stations are located on the city outskirts, matching the destination's direction.

Dongzhimen, on the northeast corner of the second ring road, is the largest bus station, connected by subway to the rest of the city; it handles services to and from Shenyang and the rest of the northeast. **Deshengmen** (Beijiao), the north station serving Chengde and Datong, is just north of the second ring road; it's on the route of bus #328, which terminates at Andingmen, from where you can catch the subway's loop line. **Zhaogongkou**, on the south side of the third ring road (Nansanhuan Lu), serves southern and eastern destinations including Tianjin; it's on the route of bus #17 from Qianmen. Close by to the west, **Haihutun**, at the intersection of the third ring road and Yongdingmenwai Dajie, is for buses for Tianjin and cities in southern Hebei; it's connected with the centre by bus #2 to Qianmen.

200s run only at night; numbers in the 300s navigate the periphery of the city centre; and numbers in the 800s are the luxury buses.

Bus #1 and Double-decker bus #1 From Xi Zhan east along the main thoroughfare, Chang'an Jie.

Double-decker bus #2 From the north end of Qianmen Dajie, north to Dongdan, the Yonghe Gong and the Asian Games Village.

Double-decker #4 From Beijing Zoo to Qianmen via Fuxingmen.

Bus #5 From Deshengmen, on the second ring road in the northwest of the city, south down the west side of the Forbidden City and Tian'anmen to Qianmen Dajie.

Bus #15 From the zoo down Xidan Dajie, past Liulichang, ending at the Tianqiao area just west of Yongdingmennei Dajie, close to Tiantan Park.

Bus #20 From Beijing Zhan to Yongdingmen Zhan, south of Taoranting Park.

Bus #52 From Xi Zhan east to Lianhuachi Qiao, Xidan Dajie, Tian'anmen Square, then east along Chang'an Jie.

Trolleybus #103 From Beijing Zhan, north up the east side of the Forbidden City, west along Fuchengmennei Dajie, then north up Sanlihe Lu to the zoo.

Trolleybus #104 From Beijing Zhan to Hepingli train station in the north of the city, via Wangfujing.

Trolleybus #105 From the northwest corner of Tiantan Park to Xidan Dajie, then west to the zoo.

Trolleybus #106 From Yongdingmen Zhan to Tiantan Park and Chongwenmen, then up to Dongzhimennei Dajie.

Night bus #210 From Wangfujing south down Qianmen to the third ring road, terminating within walking distance of the *Jinghua Hotel.*

Bus #300 Circles the third ring road.

Bus #332 From Beijing Zoo to Beijing University and Yiheyuan, the Summer Palace.

Luxury bus #808 From just northwest of Qianmen to the Yiheyuan.

Luxury bus #802 Xi Zhan to Panjiayuan Market in the southeast.

The subway

Clean, efficient and very fast, the subway, which operates daily from 5.30am to 11pm, is an appealing alternative to the bus – though again, be prepared for enforced intimacies during rush hour. Station entrances are marked by a **logo** of a rectangle inside a "G" shape. All stops are marked in *pinyin*, and announced in English and Chinese over the intercom when the train pulls in.

A **loop line** runs around the city, making useful stops at Beijing Zhan, Jianguomen (under the flyover, close to the Ancient Observatory and the Friendship Store), Yonghe Gong (50m north of the temple of the same name), Gulou (near the Drum Tower) and Qianmen, at the northern end of Qianmen Dajie. The **east–west line** runs across the city from the western suburbs, through Tian'anmen, Wangfujing and the World Trade Centre, and terminates out beyond the eastern section of the third ring road; buses leave from the westernmost stop, Pingguoyuan, for Xiang Shan and Badachu. There are **interchanges** between this and the loop line at Fuxingmen and Jianguomen stations.

The third line, **line 13**, newest at the time of writing, serves the far north of the city. Built to serve the forthcoming Olympic Village, it's in fact an overground light rail system, though the stations use the same logo as the subway. You can get onto it from the loop line at Xizhimen or Dongzhimen, though you have to leave the station, walk a short distance and buy new tickets to do so. The only useful stations for tourists are Dazhongsi – for the Great Bell Temple – and Wudaokou – for Beijing University and the summer palaces.

The subway lines discussed above are shown on the **transport map** at the back of this book. In addition, **line 5**, due for completion in 2007, will run north–south with interchanges at Yonghegong, Dongdan and Chongwenmen; its central stops are shown on our transport map. Various other new lines are due to open in time for the 2008 Olympics, though we've not shown these on the transport map as the details were still to be finalized at the time of writing. Among these, **line 6** will connect the airport to Dongzhimen and should be ready in 2005, while other projected lines will run north–south between Xi Zhan and Yiheyuan (the summer palace), between Haidian and Guomao (for the China World Trade Centre) and between the two main train stations.

Tickets, which take the form of undated slips of paper, cost ¥3 per journey and can be bought from the ticket offices at the top of the stairs leading down to the platforms. It's worth getting a few tickets at once to save queuing every time you use the system. You need to give your ticket to an attendant before you descend to the platform.

Taxis

All **licensed taxis** have a sticker in the back window which indicates the rate per kilometre. Rare, luxury sedans are the most expensive, at ¥2 per kilometre, with a minimum fare of ¥12; the common red "bulletheads", as they're dubbed in Chinese, cost ¥1.2 or ¥1.6 per kilometre, with a minimum charge of ¥10. The antenna of the vehicle tells you the rate: a ¥1.2 vehicle has its at the side, a ¥1.6 car in the middle. Using a taxi after 11pm will incur a surcharge of twenty percent. Drivers are good about using their meters; if they don't put them on, insist by saying "*dǎbiǎo*".

Don't let yourself get hustled into a taxi, as unscrupulous drivers look out for newly-arrived foreigners with luggage; walk a short distance and hail one, or find a rank (there's one outside each train station). It's best to avoid the cabs that park outside tourist hotels as the drivers may be out to rip off visitors; hail one from the street instead.

Having a map open on your lap deters some drivers from taking unnecessary detours. If you feel aggrieved at a driver's behaviour, take his number (displayed on the dashboard) and report it to the taxi complaint office (☎010/68351150). Indeed, just the action of writing his number down can produce a remarkable change in demeanour. If a cab has a red star on the roof, the driver has been voted as exemplary by members of the public.

In preparation for the Olympics, all cab drivers have been issued English study cassettes – they might even play them for you.

Rickshaws

Don't use the ordinary cycle-rickshaws you'll see in backstreets. The drivers almost inevitably attempt to overcharge foreigners and use unpleasant tactics such as demanding more money when you get out than originally agreed.

Around the northwestern *hutongs*, drivers in bright waistcoats are employed by tour companies to give tourists rides around the area. You can approach them directly to go on a scenic trip, but be sure to bargain hard.

Bike rental

As a positive alternative to public transport, it's worth renting a bike, giving yourself much more independence and flexibility. Almost all hotels – certainly all the hostels – rent out bikes for around ¥20 a day (you may be able to barter that down) plus a ¥200–400 deposit. Classier hotels charge ¥50 a day for the same bikes.

Always test the brakes on a rented bike before riding off, and get the tyres pumped up. Should you have a problem, you can turn to one of the bike repair stalls – there are plenty of these on the pavement next to main roads.

Though the traffic's bad, cycling around Beijing is actually less daunting than riding around many Western cities. There are **bike lanes** on all main roads and you'll be in the company of plenty of other cyclists. Despite massive increases in car ownership recently, cycling is still by far the most common mode of transport – there are more than eight million privately owned bicycles in Beijing. The Chinese cycling pace is sedate, as the roads can be unpredictable, with cars sometimes going the wrong way round roundabouts, impatient taxi drivers in the cycle lane, buses veering suddenly towards the pavement, and jaywalkers aplenty. If you feel nervous at busy junctions, just dismount and walk the bike across – plenty of Chinese do.

You're supposed to park your bike at one of the numerous **bike parks**, where you pay ¥0.3 to the attendant, though plenty of people risk a fine (rarely enforced) by leaving their cycle propped up against railings or on the pavement. The parks outside subway stations are open all night. If you have a new bike or a mountain bike, get a lock and chain as well, as theft is very common.

Car rental

Given the state of Beijing's traffic, you'd have to be pretty intrepid to want to **drive** yourself around the city, though this is quite feasible to arrange. The best place to rent a car is from one of the rental firms at the airport; reckon on ¥300 per day plus fuel. You'll need an international driving licence and a credit card to cover the deposit.

City tours

Organized tours of the city and its outskirts offer a painless, if expensive, way of seeing the main sights quickly. All big hotels offer them, and CITS has a variety of one- and two-day tour packages, on "Dragon Buses" which you can book from their offices (see Directory, p.144), from a BTS office (see p.19) or from the information desk in the Friendship Store. These tours aren't cheap, though the price includes lunch and pays for a tour guide: Beijing By Night – a trip to the opera and a meal at a duck restaurant – costs ¥330; a trip to the Summer Palace,

Yonghe Gong and zoo is ¥260. Similar tours are run by two other official agencies, CTS and CYTS.

One good, inexpensive tour that's more imaginative than most is the **hutong tour** (see p.56 and p.85), which offers the opportunity to see a more private side of the city. The one-day tours offered by the cheaper hotels offer better value than similar jaunts run by classier places, and you don't have to be a resident of theirs to go along. The budget tour operation run from the *Fenglong Hotel* (see p.108), with branches at all the youth hostels, offers good-value evening trips to the **acrobatics** shows and the **opera** a few times a week, and day- (and occasionally overnight) trips to Simatai and Jinshanling Great Wall (April–Oct daily, Nov–March weekly; ¥60–80; see p.150). You must book these at least a day in advance.

Communications

Beijing's communications system has much improved in recent years – indeed, too much for the government's liking; at the time of writing, they had recently closed down thousands of Internet cafes. International phone calls are reasonably priced, and it's easy to phone or fax abroad, while the international mail service is reliable. Domestic calls are nearly as dependable, and mail delivery within the country is very rapid.

Mail

The Chinese **postal service** is, on the whole, fast and reliable. Overseas postage rates are becoming expensive; a postcard costs ¥4.2, while a standard letter is ¥5.4 or more, depending on the weight. As well as at post offices, you can post letters in green **postboxes**, or at tourist hotels, which usually have a postbox at the front desk. Envelopes can be frustratingly scarce; try the stationery sections of department stores.

An Express Mail Service (**EMS**) operates to most countries and to most destinations within China. Besides cutting delivery times, the service ensures the letter or parcel is sent by registered delivery – though note that the

courier service of DHL (see p.141) is rather faster, and costs about the same. To use the EMS service, head to the **EMS office** at 7 Qianmen Dong Dajie (☎010/65129948), or to the **International Post Office** on Chaoyangmen Dajie, just north of the intersection with Jianguomen Dajie (Mon–Sat 8am–7pm). At the latter office it's also possible to rent a PO Box, use their packing service for parcels, and buy a wide variety of collectable stamps, but staff are not very helpful.

The International Post Office is also where **poste restante** letters end up, dumped in a box; you'll have to rifle through them all to find your mail and pay ¥2.3 for the privilege (you'll also need to bring your passport as identification). Have letters addressed to you c/o Poste Restante, GPO, Beijing. Letters are only kept for a month and are then quickly sent back. You can also leave a message for someone in the poste restante box, but you'll have to buy a stamp.

There are other post offices in the basement of the World Trade Centre; on Xi Chang'an Jie, just east of the Concert Hall; on Wangfujing Dajie, near *Dunkin' Donuts*; and at the north end of Xidan Dajie (all Mon–Sat 9am–5pm). Main post offices are open seven days a week between 9am and 5pm; smaller offices may close for lunch or at weekends.

Parcels

To send **parcels**, turn up at the International Post Office with the goods you want to send and the staff will help you pack them, a service which costs only a few yuan; don't try to wrap the parcel in advance, as the package will have to be unpacked to ensure it is packed correctly. You can buy boxes at the post office, or your goods will be sewn into a linen packet like a pillowcase. Once packed, but before the parcel is sealed, it must be checked at the customs window in the post office.

As an indication of costs, a one-kilogram parcel should cost upwards of ¥70 to send surface mail, ¥120 by airmail to Europe. You'll have to complete masses of paperwork, with forms in Chinese and French (the international language of postal services) only. If you are sending valuable goods bought in China, put the receipt or a photocopy of it in with the parcel, as it may be opened for customs inspection farther down the line.

Phones

Local calls are free from land lines, and long-distance China-wide calls are fairly cheap. Note that everywhere in China has an **area code** which must be used when phoning from outside that locality; area codes are given for Chinese phone numbers throughout the book. International calls cost at least ¥16 a minute (much cheaper if you use an IP internet phone card – see below).

You can make international calls from the **China Telecom Building** on Xidan Dajie. You pay a deposit of ¥200 and are told to go to a particular booth where you dial the number directly. When your call is finished, the charge is worked out automatically and you pay at the desk. You may find that a minimum charge for three minutes applies. Calls to Britain cost ¥15 per minute, to the US and Australia ¥18, and to Hong Kong ¥5. You can also make IDD calls from streetside telephone shops (generally displaying "IDD" on a sign). These usually charge by the minute, but always check in advance.

Card phones are the cheapest way to make domestic long-distance calls (¥0.2 for 3min), and can also be used for international calls (generally over ¥10 for 3min). They take **IC Cards** (*I-C kǎ* in Mandarin), which are sold at every little store and in hotels, in units of ¥20, ¥50 and ¥100. There's a fifty percent discount after 6pm and at weekends. You will be cut off when the credit left on the card drops below the amount needed for the next minute.

Yet another option is the **IP** (Internet Phone) **card**, which can be used from any phone, and comes in ¥50 and ¥100 denominations. You dial a local number, then a PIN, then the number you're calling. Rates are as low as ¥2.4 per minute to the USA and Canada, ¥3.2 to Europe. The cards are widely available and connections generally reliable.

Tourist hotels offer direct dialling abroad from your room, but will add a surcharge, and a minimum charge equivalent to between one and three minutes will be levied even if the call goes unanswered. The **business centres** in most big hotels offer fax, telephone, Internet and telex services (as well as photocopying and typing), and you don't have to be a guest to use them – though prices for all these are typically extortionate. Hotels also charge for receiving faxes, usually around ¥10 per page.

Mobile phones

Your home **cellular phone** may already be compatible with the Chinese network (visitors from North America should ensure their phones are GSM/Triband), though note that you will pay a premium to use it abroad, and that callers within China have to make an international call to reach your phone. For more information, check the manual that

Useful dialling codes

To call mainland China from abroad, dial your international access code (☎00 in the UK and the Republic of Ireland, ☎011 in the US and Canada, ☎0011 in Australia, and ☎00 in New Zealand), then 86 (China's country code), then the number (minus the initial zero).

To call Hong Kong from abroad, dial your international access code followed by ☎852, then the number.

Phoning abroad from China

To call abroad dial ☎00 from mainland China, or ☎001 from Hong Kong, then the country code (see below), then the area code (if any, omitting the initial zero), then the number.

UK ☎44   Ireland ☎353   US & Canada ☎1   Australia ☎61   New Zealand ☎64

came with your phone, or with the manufacturer and/or your telephone service provider. Alternatively, once in Beijing you can buy a GSM SIM card from any China Mobile shop, which allows you to use your phone as though it's a local mobile, with a new number. The card costs around ¥100, with some variation depending on the degree of luck in the number it gives you – favoured sixes and eights bump up the price, unlucky fours make it cheaper. Additionally, you'll need to buy prepaid cards to pay for the calls. In big cities you can even **rent mobile phones** – look for the ads in expat magazines. Making and receiving domestic calls this way costs ¥0.6 per minute.

Internet access

Smoky Internet cafés full of kids playing Counterstrike used to be legion, but in 2002 a deadly fire in one was used as an excuse to close down three thousand establishments – Beijing's vice mayor called them the new opium dens. Those still open are heavily regulated, and you'll be asked to show your passport before being allowed near a computer. They're almost all far from the centre in **university districts** – there's usually one close to the entrance to each college. Try IVNT at 45 Zhongguancun Dajie, Haidian (both daily 8am–midnight; ¥6/hr). Beijing Library also has terminals for ¥5/hr though you'll have to become a temporary member to use them (¥5; see p.143).

At the time of writing, the only central Internet cafés are the Qianyi, on the third floor of The Station, the shopping centre on the east side of Qianmen; and Hailetong at 84 Xisi Nan Dajie (the northern extension of Xidan Bei Dajie). Note that there are actually two cafés up at the former, one inexpensive at ¥7 per hour, the other charging ¥20 an

The new Great Wall of China

If the Chinese regime was discomfited by news faxes sent from abroad during the Tian'anmen massacre in 1989, imagine the headache the **Internet** is giving them. Tireless as ever in controlling what its citizens know, the government has built a sophisticated **firewall** – nicknamed the new Great Wall of China – that blocks access to undesirable websites. The way this is administered shifts regularly according to the mood of the powers that be – restrictions were loosened, for example, while Beijing was campaigning to be awarded the 2008 summer Olympics (the government was anxious to be seen not to be oppressing its subjects). In general, you can be pretty sure you won't be able to access the BBC, CNN, the White House, or anything about Tibetan freedom, though newspaper websites tend to be left unhindered. Access to the search engine **Google** has even been cut off from time to time; in 2002, for example, it was unavailable for a few days (because, officials claimed, if you typed "Jiang Zemin" – the Chinese premier at the time – into it, a satirical game appeared among the top ten results).

hour – unfortunately, the owners tend to turn foreigners away from the former.

All hotels have business centres where you can get online, but this can be ridiculously expensive, especially in the classier places.

Better value are the **backpacker hostels** (see the "Accommodation" chapter for details), where getting online costs around ¥10 an hour.

The media

Xinhua, the Chinese news agency, is a mouthpiece for the state, whose propaganda you can read in the English-language *China Daily*, available from the Friendship Store (see p.135, the Foreign Language Bookstore (see p.138), and the bigger hotels and most newsagents, including the ones on subway platforms. The only thing you can believe in the *China Daily* is the handy section listing cultural events, though more detailed listings can be found in the city's expat-oriented magazines (see p.19). *Beijing Today* (¥2) is a much better English-language newspaper, also on sale on subway platforms, but doesn't carry listings.

Heavy **censorship** continues to affect the Chinese-language press, though stories sometimes break that the Party would rather people didn't know about. In 2001, for example, the press exposed a scandal about blood-donation vans spreading AIDS through entire villages; and in 2002 the appalling conditions of mineworkers and overtaxed peasants became a national issue thanks to crusading journalists. It's a brave editor who prints such stuff, however. Locals reckon the Beijing paper most willing to fly close to the wind is the *Beijing Youth Daily*. Imported publications (sometimes censored) such as *Time, Newsweek* and the *Far Eastern Economic Review*, and Hong Kong's *South China Morning Post*, can be bought at the Friendship Store.

TV and radio

There is the occasional item of interest on Chinese **television**, though you'd have to be very bored to resort to it for entertainment. Domestic travel and wildlife programmes are common, as are song-and-dance extravaganzas, the most entertaining of which feature dancers in weird fetishistic costumes, watched by party officials with rigor-mortis faces. Soap operas and historical dramas are popular, and often feature a few foreigners; also screened are 20-year-old American thrillers and war films. Chinese war films, in which the Japanese are shown getting mightily beaten, at least have the advantage that you don't need to speak the language to understand what's going on. The same goes for the flirty dating gameshows, where male contestants proudly state their height and qualifications.

CCTV, the state broadcaster, has two English-language channels: CCTV9 has a news programme at 10pm nightly, while CCTV5 is a sports channel and often shows European football games. CCTV2 and CCTV4, and local channel BTV1, all have English-language news programmes at 11pm. **Satellite TV** in English is available in the more expensive hotels.

On the **radio** you're likely to hear the latest ballads by pop-robots from the Hong Kong and Taiwan idol factories, or versions of Western pop songs sung in Chinese. Easy FM (91.5FM) is an expat-geared English-language station carrying music programmes and local information.

Opening hours, public holidays and festivals

Offices and government agencies are open from Monday to Friday, usually from 8am to noon, then from 1pm to 5pm; some open on Saturday and Sunday mornings too. Shops are generally open from 9am to 7pm Monday to Saturday, with shorter hours on Sunday. Museums are either open all week or are shut on one day, usually Monday.

The best time to **sightsee** is during the week, as all attractions are swamped with local tourists at weekends. Some attractions have separate low- and high-season opening times and prices; in high season (end March to early November) places are usually half an hour earlier to open, half an hour later to close, while prices rise by ¥5 or ¥10.

Public holidays and festivals

Public holidays have little effect on business, with only government departments and certain banks closing. However, on New Year's Day, during the first three days of the Chinese New Year, and on National Day, most businesses, shops and sights will be shut, though some restaurants stay open.

The rhythm of **festivals** and religious observances that marked the Chinese year was interrupted by the Cultural Revolution, and only now, nearly forty years on, are old traditions beginning to re-emerge. The majority of festivals celebrate the turning of the seasons or propitious dates, such as the ninth day of the ninth lunar month, and are times for gift-giving, family reunions and feasting.

A festivals and holidays calendar

Traditional festivals take place according to dates in the Chinese **lunar calendar**, in which the first day of the month is when the moon is a new crescent, with the middle of the month marked by the full moon; by the Gregorian calendar, these festivals fall on a different date every year.

January/February

New Year's Day (Jan 1).
Spring Festival (commences between late Jan and mid-Feb) The Chinese New Year celebrations extend over the first two weeks of the new lunar year (see box, opposite).
Tiancang (Granary) Festival Chinese peasants celebrate this on the twentieth day of the first lunar month, in the hope of ensuring a good harvest later in the year.

March

Guanyin's Birthday Guanyin, the goddess of mercy and probably China's most popular Buddhist deity, is celebrated on the nineteenth day of the second lunar month, most colourfully in Taoist temples.
International Working Women's Day (March 8).

April

Qingming Festival (April 4 & 5). This festival, Tomb Sweeping Day, is the time to visit the graves of ancestors, leave offerings of food, and burn ghost money – fake paper currency – in honour of the departed.

May

Labour Day (May 1). A week-long holiday.
Youth Day (May 4). Commemorating the student demonstrators in Tian'anmen Square in 1919, which gave rise to the nationalist "May Fourth" movement. It's marked in Beijing with flower displays on a vast scale.

June

Children's Day (June 1). Most school pupils are taken on excursions at this time, so if you're visiting a popular tourist site, be prepared for mobs of kids in yellow baseball caps.

September/October

Moon Festival Also known as the Mid-Autumn Festival, this is marked on the fifteenth day of the eighth lunar month. It's a time of family reunion, celebrated with fireworks and lanterns. Moon cakes, containing a rich filling of sweet paste, are eaten, and plenty of *maotai* – a strong white spirit distilled from rice – is consumed.

Spring Festival

The **Spring Festival**, usually falling in late January or the first half of February, is two weeks of festivities marking the beginning of a new year in the lunar calendar (and thus also called Chinese New Year). In Chinese astrology, each year is associated with a particular **animal** from a cycle of twelve – 2004 is the Year of the Monkey, for example – and the passing into a new astrological phase is a momentous occasion. There's a tangible sense of excitement in the run-up to the festival, when China is perhaps at its most colourful, with shops and houses decorated with good-luck messages and stalls and shops selling paper money, drums and costumes. However the festival is not an ideal time to travel – everything shuts down, and most of the population is on the move, making travel impossible or extremely uncomfortable.

The first day of the festival is marked by a family feast at which *jiaozi* (dumplings) are eaten, sometimes with coins hidden inside. To bring luck, people dress in red clothes (red being regarded as a lucky colour) – a particularly important custom if the animal of their birth year is coming round again – and each family tries to eat a whole fish, since the word for fish sounds like the word for surplus. **Firecrackers** are let off in the countryside to scare ghosts away and, on the fifth day, to honour **Cai Shen**, god of wealth. In central Beijing, where fireworks are banned, enterprising stallholders sell cassette tapes of explosions as a substitute. Another ghost-scaring tradition you may notice is the pasting up of images of door gods at the threshold.

The most public expression of festivities – a must for visitors – is to be had at the **temple fairs**, held in the evening on the first few days of the festival. At these boisterous affairs the air is thick with incense, and locals queue to kowtow to altars and play games that bring good fortune, such as trying to hit the temple bell by lobbing coins at it; priests are on hand to perform rituals and write prayers. The biggest temple fairs in Beijing are at the Tibetan Yonghe Gong (see p.87) and the Taoist Baiyun Guan (see p.66): pick one or the other to visit, as it's regarded as inauspicious to get to both during the same festival. To help you decide, Taoist festivals concentrate on renewal, Tibetan Lamaist ones on enlightenment. Other new-year fairs are held in the daytime at Ditan and Longtan parks, and on Liulichang (see p.57). Here you'll find plenty of food and colourful tat for sale, as well as performing opera singers, acrobats, and martial artists.

Double Ninth Festival Nine is a number associated with *yang*, or male energy, and on the ninth day of the ninth lunar month qualities such as assertiveness and strength are celebrated. It's believed to be a good time for the distillation (and consumption) of spirits.

Confucius Festival (Sept 28). The birthday of Confucius (see p.89) is marked by celebrations at all Confucian temples.

National Day (Oct 1). On which everyone has a week off to celebrate the founding of the People's Republic, and state TV is even more dire than usual, packed with programmes celebrating the achievements of the Communist Party.

December

Christmas (Dec 25). Though Beijing's Christian community is relatively small, Christmas is widely celebrated, an excuse for a feast and a party.

Crime and personal safety

It's easy to forget, but beneath the careful showcasing of modernity, Beijing is the heart of a brutal police state that has terrorized its subjects for much of its short, inglorious history. Not that this should worry visitors too much; the state is as anxious to keep guests happy as it is to incarcerate independent-minded journalists and the like. Indeed, Chinese who commit crimes against foreigners are treated much more harshly than if their victims had been compatriots.

Crime is a growth industry in China. Much of it is put down to spiritual pollution by foreign influences, the result of increasing liberalization. But serious social problems such as mass unemployment and appalling disparities in income are really to blame, as is the get-rich-quick attitude that has become the prevailing ideology. Official corruption is so rampant that even the party perceives it as a threat, and the state now routinely shoots scapegoats in an effort to cut it down.

While there is no need for obsessive paranoia – Beijing is still safer than most Western cities – you do need to take care. Tourists are an obvious target for **petty thieves**. Passports and money should be kept in a concealed money belt; a bum bag offers much less protection and is easy for skilled pickpockets to get into. It's a good idea to keep around US$200 separately from the rest of your cash, together with your traveller's-cheque receipts, insurance policy details, and photocopies of your passport and visa. Be wary on **buses**, the favoured haunt of pickpockets, and **trains**, particularly in hard-seat class and on overnight journeys. Take a chain and padlock to secure your luggage in the rack.

Hotel rooms are on the whole secure, dormitories much less so – in the latter case it's often fellow-travellers who are the problem.

Most hotels should have a safe, but it's not unusual for things to go missing from these.

On the street, flashy jewellery and watches will attract the wrong kind of attention, and try to be discreet when taking out your cash. Not looking obviously wealthy also helps if you want to avoid being ripped off by street traders and taxi drivers, as does telling them you are a student – the Chinese have a great respect for education, and much more sympathy for foreign students than for tourists.

The police

If you do have anything stolen, you'll need to get the police, known as the Public Security Bureau or **PSB**, to write up a **loss report** in order to claim on your insurance. Their main office is at 2 Andingmen Dajie, 300m east of Yonghe Gong subway stop.

The police are recognizable by their dark blue uniforms and caps, though there are a lot more around than you might at first think, as plenty are undercover. They have much wider powers than most Western police forces, including establishing the guilt of criminals – trials are often used only for deciding the sentence of the accused, though China is beginning to have the makings of an independent judiciary. Laws are harsh, with execution – a bullet in the back of the head – the penalty for a wide range of serious crimes,

Bogus art students

Spend any time in tourist areas of the capital and you will inevitably be approached by youths claiming to be art students. They aren't, of course; mostly they are ex-students from teacher training schools putting their language skills to dubious use. Their aim is to get you to visit a bogus art gallery and pay ridiculous prices for prints purporting to be paintings; they'll go to huge lengths to befriend foreigners. They're not aggressive though, and they can be useful if you need directions.

Emergency numbers

Police ☏110
Fire ☏119
Ambulance ☏120

from corruption to rape, though if the culprit is deemed to show proper remorse, the result can be a more lenient sentence.

The PSB also have the job of looking after foreigners, and you'll most likely have to seek them out for **visa extensions** (see p.16). While individual police can be very helpful and go out of their way to help foreigners, the PSB itself has all the problems of any police force in a nation rife with corruption, and it's best to minimize contact with them.

Cultural hints

When Confucius arrives in a country, he invariably gets to know about its society. Does he seek this information, or is it given him? Confucius gets it through being cordial, good, respectful, temperate and deferential.

Confucius, The Analects, 1.10

Privacy is largely an unheard-of luxury in China – indeed Chinese doesn't have an exact translation of the word. Public toilets are built with low partitions, no one eats alone in restaurants, all leisure activities are performed in noisy groups, and a curiosity – such as a visiting Caucasian, or "big nose" as the Chinese like to say – can find himself or herself the subject of frank stares and attention. The best thing to do in such situations is smile and say nǐhǎo. A desire to be left alone can baffle the Chinese, and is occasionally interpreted as arrogance. Conversely, behaviour seen as antisocial in the West, notably spitting and smoking, is quite normal here. Government campaigns to cut down on both have had little effect.

Skimpy clothing is fine (indeed fashionable), but looking scruffy will only induce disrespect. All foreigners are – correctly – assumed to be comparatively rich, so why they would want to dress like peasants is quite beyond the Chinese.

Shaking hands is not a Chinese tradition, though it is now fairly common between men. Businessmen meeting for the first time exchange business cards, with the offered card held in two hands as a gesture of respect – you'll see polite shop assistants doing the same with your change.

In a restaurant, the Chinese don't share the bill, so don't offer to pay your share, as the notion may cause embarrassment to your hosts. Instead, diners contest for the honour of paying it, with the most respected usually winning. You should make some effort to stake your claim but, as a visiting guest, you can pretty much guarantee that you won't get to pay a jiao.

If you visit a Chinese house, you'll be expected to present your hosts with a **gift**, which won't be opened in front of you – that would be impolite. Imported whisky and ornamental trinkets are suitable as presents, though avoid giving anything too practical as it might be construed as charity.

Sex and gender issues

Women travellers in Beijing usually find the incidence of **sexual harassment** much less of a problem than in other Asian countries. Chinese men are, on the whole, deferential and respectful. Being ignored is a much more likely complaint, as the Chinese will generally assume that any man accompanying a woman will be doing all the talking.

Prostitution, though illegal, has made a big comeback – witness all the new "hairdressers", saunas and massage parlours, every one a brothel. Single foreign men are likely to be approached inside hotels; it's common practice for prostitutes to phone around hotel rooms at all hours of the night. Bear in mind that China is hardly Thailand – consequences may be dire if you are caught with a prostitute – and that **AIDS** is rife and the public largely ignorant of sexual health issues.

Homosexuality, though officially regarded as a foreign eccentricity, is increasingly tolerated, though discretion is advised. See gay Beijing, p.126, for more.

Travellers with disabilities

Beijing makes few provisions for disabled people. Undergoing an economic boom, the city resembles a building site, with uneven, obstacle-strewn paving, intense crowds and vehicle traffic, and few access ramps. Public transport is also generally inaccessible to wheelchair users, though a few of the upmarket hotels have experience in assisting disabled visitors; in particular, Beijing's several *Holiday Inns* and *Hiltons* often have rooms designed for wheelchair users.

Given the situation, it may be worth considering an **organized tour** – the contacts given below will be able to help you arrange this or assist you in researching your own trip. Make sure you take spares of any specialist clothing or equipment, extra supplies of drugs (carried with you if you fly), and a prescription including the generic name – in English and Chinese characters – in case of emergency. If there's an association representing people with your disability, contact them early on in the planning process.

Contacts for travellers with disabilities

UK and Ireland

Irish Wheelchair Association Blackheath Drive, Clontarf, Dublin 3 ☎01/818 6400, ⓕ833 3873, ⓦwww.iwa.ie. A source of useful information on travelling abroad with a wheelchair.
Tripscope Alexandra House, Albany Rd, Brentford, Middlesex TW8 0NE ☎0845/7585 641, ⓕ020/8580 7021, ⓦwww.tripscope.org.uk. Advice on transport for those with a mobility problem.

US and Canada

Access-Able ⓦwww.access-able.com. Online resource for travellers with disabilities, with limited coverage of Beijing.
Directions Unlimited 123 Green Lane, Bedford Hills, NY 10507 ☎1-800/533-5343 or 914/241-1700. Travel agency specializing in bookings for people with disabilities.
Disability Travel ⓦwww.disabilitytravel.com. Arranges all aspects of travel for the mobility-impaired, including tours to Beijing.
Society for the Advancement of Travelers with Handicaps (SATH) 347 5th Ave, New York, NY 10016 ☎212/447-7284, ⓦwww.sath.org. Non-profit educational organization that has actively represented travellers with disabilities since 1976.

Australia and New Zealand

ACROD (Australian Council for Rehabilitation of the Disabled) PO Box 60, Curtin ACT 2605; Suite 103, 1st floor, 1–5 Commercial Rd, Kings Grove 2208; ☎02/6282 4333, TTY ☎02/6282 4333, ⓕ6281 3488, ⓦwww.acrod.org.au. Provides lists of travel agencies and tour operators for people with disabilities.
Disabled Persons Assembly 4/173–175 Victoria St, Wellington, New Zealand ☎04/801 9100 (also TTY), ⓕ801 9565, ⓦwww.dpa.org.nz. Resource centre with lists of travel agencies and tour operators for people with disabilities.

Working or studying in Beijing

There are increasing opportunities to work or study in Beijing. Many foreign workers are employed as English-language teachers, and most universities and many private colleges now have a few foreign teachers.

Foreigners are now allowed to **reside** anywhere in the city, though most live in housing targeted at them, often in Chaoyang in the east of the city. Rent in these districts is expensive, usually at least US$2000 a month, which gets you a tolerable imitation of a Western apartment. Living in ordinary neighbourhoods is much cheaper: a central, furnished two-bedroom apartment can cost around US$500 a month. The easiest way to find an apartment is through a real-estate agent, who will usually take a month's rent as a fee. There are plenty of agents, and many advertise in the expat magazines. Another good place to look is ⓦwww.9992.net, where landlords advertise. Yet another possibility is to lodge with a Chinese family, in which case you will need to be registered with the local PSB office as a guest.

The education sector

There are schemes to place foreign teachers in Chinese educational institutions – contact your nearest Chinese embassy (see p.15 for addresses) for details, or check the list of organizations given on p.38. Some employers ask for a **TEFL** (Teaching English as a Foreign Language) qualification, though a degree, or simply the ability to speak the language as a native, is usually enough.

Teaching at a **university**, you'll earn about ¥1500 a month, more than your Chinese counterparts do, though your workload of between ten and twenty hours a week is correspondingly a lot heavier. The pay isn't enough to allow you to put any aside, but is bolstered by on-campus accommodation – a room in a foreigners' dormitory, usually without a phone. Contracts are generally for one year. Most teachers find their students keen, hard-working, curious and obedient, and report that it was the contact with them that made the experience worthwhile. That said, avoid talking about religion or politics in the classroom, as this could get you into trouble.

You'll earn more – up to ¥150 per hour – in a **private school**, though be aware of the risk of being ripped off (you might be given more classes to teach than you'd signed up for). Check out the institution thoroughly before commiting yourself.

Studying in Beijing

Universities welcome foreign students for the extra revenue they bring. Courses cost about US$3500 a year, or US$1000 a semester. Accommodation costs around US$10 a day. It's possible to study just about anything, but note that most courses are in Chinese (for details of courses in the Chinese language itself, see below), and that if you want to study acupuncture, martial arts or Chinese medicine, courses run in the West are often better.

Beijing Daxue (usually referred to as Beida; see p.95; ⓦwww.pku.edu.cn) and **Tsinghua Daxue** (ⓦwww.tsinghua.edu.cn), both in Haidian in the northwest of the city, are the most famous universities in China, and therefore the most expensive. Beida's courses on history and culture are popular with foreigners. **Beijing Yuyuan Daxue** (ⓦwww.blcu .edu.cn) has a good reputation for language teaching and a wide range of courses. Other institutions to consider are **Renmin Daxue** (ⓦwww.ruc.edu.cn) and **Beijing Normal University** (ⓦwww.bnu.edu.cn). Otherwise, you can write to your nearest Chinese embassy for a list of universities, then contact the colleges themselves. It's best not to sign up for a course until you've visited the campus, and be wary of paying up front, as you won't get a refund.

Studying Chinese

You can do short courses (from two weeks to two months) in Mandarin Chinese at

Beijing Foreign Studies University, 2 Xi Erhuan Lu (☎010/68468167, ⊛www .bfsu.edu.cn); at the Bridge School in Jianguomenwai Dajie (☎010/64940243), which offers evening classes; or the Cultural Mission at 7 Beixiao Jie in Sanlitun (☎010/65323005), where most students are diplomats. A cheap and easy way to study basic Mandarin, though, is to find a Chinese student of English and get them to teach you. You'll have to negotiate a fee, but they don't charge very much, perhaps ¥15 an hour. For courses in Chinese lasting six months to a year, apply to the Beijing International School at Anzhenxili, Chaoyang (☎010/64433151, ⊛www.isb.bj.edu.cn); Beida in Haidian (see above); or Beijing Normal University (see above). Expect to pay around ¥10,000 in tuition fees for a year.

Commercial opportunities

Besides teaching, there are plenty of other white-collar jobs available for foreigners in mainland China, mostly with foreign firms, though some facility with Chinese is usually required. It's best to turn up and trawl around the offices or through the expat magazines.

China's vast markets and recent WTO membership present a wealth of **business opportunities**, usually in joint-venture operations where the Chinese have a controlling interest. However, anyone wanting to do business in China should do thorough research beforehand. The difficulties are formidable – red tape and corrupt and shady business practices abound. Remember that the Chinese do business on the basis of mutual trust and pay much less attention to contractual terms or legislation. Copyright and trademark laws are often ignored. You'll need to develop your **guanxi** – connections – assiduously, and cultivate the virtues of patience, propriety, and bloody-mindedness.

Useful resources

Council on International Educational Exchange ⊛www.ciee.org. Exchange programmes for US students of Mandarin or Chinese studies, with placements in Beijing.

Chinatefl ⊛www.chinatefl.com. Gives a good overview of English-teaching opportunties in the Chinese public sector.

Zhaopin ⊛www.zhaopin.com. A huge jobs site, in Chinese and English.

The City

The City

Tian'anmen Square and the Forbidden City

The first stop for any visitor to Beijing is **Tian'anmen Square**, at over 400,000 square metres, the greatest public square on earth. Right in the city centre, the square is symbolically the heart of China, and the events it has witnessed have shaped the history of the People's Republic from its inception. The square is a modern creation in a city that traditionally had no places where crowds could gather. As one of the square's architects put it: "Beijing was a reflection of a feudal society . . . We had to transform it, we had to make Beijing into the capital of socialist China." So they created a vast concrete plain dotted with worthy statuary and bounded by stern, monumental buildings: the **Great Hall of the People** to the west and the **Museums of History** and the **Revolution** to the east. To the north you'll see **Tian'anmen**, a gateway of great significance to both imperial and communist China.

Beyond it, and in its luxury and ornament a complete contrast to the square's austerity, is the Gugong, or Imperial Palace, better known in the West by its unofficial title, the **Forbidden City** – a reference to its exclusivity. Indeed, for the five centuries of its operation, through the reigns of 24 emperors of the Ming and Qing dynasties, ordinary Chinese were forbidden from even approaching the walls. With its maze of eight hundred buildings and nine thousand chambers, it was the symbolic heart of the capital, the empire, and (so the Chinese believed) the universe. From within, the emperors, the **Sons of Heaven**, issued commands with absolute authority to their millions of subjects. It remains an extraordinary place today, unsurpassed in China for monumental scale, harmonious design and elegant grandeur.

The Chairman Mao Memorial Hall	毛主席纪念堂	*máozhǔxí jìniàntáng*
The Forbidden City	故宫	*gùgōng*
The Great Hall of the People	人民大会堂	*rénmín dàhuìtáng*
Museum of Chinese History	中国历史博物馆	*zhōngguó lìshǐ bówùguǎn*
Museum of the Revolution	中国革命博物馆	*zhōngguó géming bówùguǎn*
Tian'anmen	天安门	*tiān'ānmén*
Tian'anmen Square	天安门广场	*tiān'ānmén guǎngchǎng*

Tian'anmen Square

For many Chinese tourists, Tian'anmen Square is a place of pilgrimage. Crowds flock to see the corpse of Chairman Mao in his **mausoleum** and to see the most potent symbols of power in contemporary China: the Great Hall of the People and Tian'anmen Gate. Some quietly bow their heads before the **Monument to the People's Heroes**, a thirty-metre-high obelisk commemorating the victims of the revolutionary struggle. Its foundations were laid on October 1, 1949, the day that the establishment of the People's Republic was announced. Basreliefs around it illustrate key scenes from China's revolutionary history; one of these, on the east side, shows the Chinese burning British opium (see p.176) in the nineteenth century. The calligraphy on the front is in Mao Zedong's handwriting and reads "Eternal glory to the Heroes of the People". The platform on which the obelisk stands is now discreetly guarded, and a prominent sign here declares that commemorative gestures, such as the laying of wreaths, are banned. In 1976, riots broke out when wreaths commemorating the death of the popular politician Zhou Enlai were removed; the demonstrations of 1989 began here with the laying of wreaths to a recently deceased liberal politician.

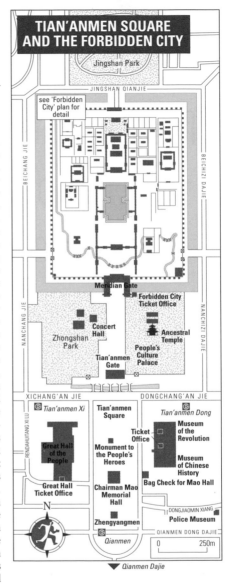

For an overview of the square, head to the south gate, **Zhengyangmen** (daily 9am–4.30pm; ¥5). Similar to Tian'anmen (the north gate), this squat, 40-metre-high structure with an arched gateway through the middle once marked the boundary between the imperial city and the commoners outside. Avoid the tacky souvenir stores on the first two floors and head to the top for the views; you'll get a good idea of how much more impressive the square looked before Mao's mausoleum was stuck in the middle of it. Inside, there's a model of what

Dissent in Tian'anmen Square

Though it was designed as a space for mass declarations of loyalty, Tian'anmen Square has as often been a venue for expressions of popular **dissent**. The first mass protests here occurred on May 4, 1919, when students gathered in the area to demonstrate against the disastrous terms of the Treaty of Versailles, under which the victorious Allies granted several former German concessions in China to the Japanese. The protests, and the movement they spawned, marked the beginning of the painful struggle for Chinese modernization. In 1925, the inhabitants of Beijing again occupied the square, to protest over the massacre in Shanghai of Chinese demonstrators by British troops. The following year, protesters angered at the weak government's capitulation to the Japanese marched on government offices and were fired on by soldiers.

The first time the square became the focus of protest in the communist era was in 1976, when thousands assembled here, without government approval, to voice their dissatisfaction with their leaders; in 1978 and 1979, large numbers came to discuss new ideas of democracy and artistic freedom, triggered by writings posted along "Democracy Wall" on the edge of the Forbidden City. People gathered again in 1986 and 1987, protesting at the Party's refusal to allow limited municipal elections to be held. But it was in **1989** that Tian'anmen Square became the venue for the largest expression of popular dissent in China in the twentieth century; from April to June of that year, nearly a million protesters demonstrated against the slowness of reform, lack of civil liberties and widespread corruption. A giant statue of a woman carrying a torch in both hands, the Goddess of Liberty, was created in the square by art students and set up facing Mao's portrait that hangs on Tian'anmen to the north. The government, infuriated at being humiliated by their own people, declared martial law on May 20, and on June 4 the military moved into the square. The ensuing **killing** was indiscriminate; tanks ran over tents and machine guns strafed the avenues. No one knows exactly how many demonstrators died in the massacre – probably thousands; hundreds were arrested afterwards and some remain in jail (though others have since joined the administration).

The problems the protesters complained of have still not been dealt with – some, such as corruption, are even viewed as having worsened – and the government remains sensitive about the events of June 1989: on the tenth anniversary of the uprising, the square was conveniently closed for repaving. These days the square is occasionally the venue for small protests by foreigners or members of the cultish sect Falun Gong – hence the many closed-circuit TV cameras and the large numbers of Public Security men, not all in uniform; look out, for example, for the plain-clothes bruisers who stand either side of Tian'anmen's Mao painting.

the area looked like in 1750, and photos taken before the communists' reconstruction.

At dawn, the flag at the northern end of the square is raised in a military ceremony. It's lowered again at dusk, which is when most people come to watch, though foreigners complain that the regimentation of the crowds at the ceremony is oppressive. After dark, the square is at its most appealing and, with its sternness softened by mellow lighting, it becomes the haunt of strolling families and lovers.

As a transport hub, the square is easy to get to: Qianmen **subway stop** is just south of the square, with Tian'anmen Xi and Tian'anmen Dong stops nearby to the west and east respectively; you can also get here on buses #1, #4, #10, #22, #52 or #57.

The Chairman Mao Memorial Hall

Mao's **mausoleum** (daily 8.30–11.30am, also 2–4pm on Mon, Wed & Fri in high season; free), constructed in 1977 by an estimated million volunteers, is an ugly building, looking like a drab municipal facility. It contravenes the principles of *feng shui* (see box opposite) – presumably deliberately – by interrupting the line from the palace to Qianmen and by facing north. Mao himself wanted to be cremated, and the erection of the mausoleum was apparently no more than a power ploy by his would-be successor, Hua Guofeng. In 1980 Deng Xiaoping, then leader, said it should never have been built, although he wouldn't go so far as to pull it down again.

After depositing your bag at the offices over the road to the east (¥10), join the orderly queue of Chinese – almost exclusively lower-class out-of-towners – on the northern side. The queue advances surprisingly quickly, and takes just a couple of minutes to file through the chambers in silence. Mao's pickled **corpse**, draped with a red flag within a crystal coffin, looks unreal, which it may well be; a wax copy was made in case the preservation went wrong.

Chairman Mao

"A revolution is not a dinner party"
Mao Zedong

Mao Zedong, the son of a well-off Hunnanese farmer, believed social reform lay in the hands of the peasants. Having helped found the Chinese Communist Party, on the Soviet model, in Shanghai in 1921, he quickly organized a peasant workers militia – the Red Army – to take on the Nationalist government. A cunning guerrilla leader, Mao was a keen student of the tactics of the first tyrant Emperor Qin Shihuang, Sun Tzu (whose *Art of War*, the world's oldest military treatise, is popular today with macho Western office workers), and the game of Go. In 1934 Mao's army was encircled; the epic retreat that followed, the **Long March** – eighty thousand men walking ten thousand kilometres over a year – solidified Mao's reputation and spread the message of the rebels through the countryside. They joined another rebel force at Yan'an, in northern China, and set up the first soviets, implementing land reform and educating the peasantry.

In 1949, now at the head of a huge army, Mao finally vanquished the Nationalists and became the "Great Helmsman" of the new Chinese nation – and here the trouble started. The chain-smoking poet rebel indulged what appeared to be a personal need for permanent revolution in idiocies such as the **Great Leap Forward** of the Fifties and the **Cultural Revolution** of the Sixties (see p.178). His policies caused enormous suffering; some estimate Mao was responsible for the deaths of over 38 million people – mostly from famine as a result of incompetent agricultural policies. Towards the end of his life Mao became increasingly paranoid and out of touch, surrounded by sycophants and nubile dancers – a situation vividly described by his physician, Zhisui Li, in his book *The Private Life of Chairman Mao*.

Today the official Chinese position on Mao is that he was "seventy percent right". Although public images of him have largely been expunged, the personality cult he fostered lives on in taxis where his image is hung like a lucky charm from the rearview mirror, and he's often included among the deities in peasant shrines. The **Little Red Book**, source of political cracker slogans such as "power grows from the barrel of a gun", is still studied in schools, and English translations are widely available in Beijing – though from souvenir vendors rather than bookshops. His poetry is highly regarded; check it out at ⊛www.mzdthought.com.

Feng shui

Feng shui, literally "wind and water", is a form of geomancy, which assesses how objects must be positioned so as not to disturb the spiritual attributes of the surrounding landscape. This reflects Taoist cosmology, which states that the inner harmonies of the landscape must be preserved to secure all other harmonies. Buildings should be favourably oriented according to the compass – tombs for example, should face south – and protected from unlucky directions by other buildings or hills. Even the minutiae of interior **decor** are covered by *feng shui*. Some of its handy rules for the modern home include: don't have a mirror at the foot of the bed; don't have sharp edges pointing into the room; cover the television when it's not in use; and don't leave the toilet seat up.

Mechanically raised from a freezer every morning, it is said to have been embalmed with the aid of Vietnamese technicians who had previously worked on the body of Ho Chi Minh. Apparently 22 litres of formaldehyde went into preserving his body; rumour has it that not only did the corpse swell grotesquely when too much fluid was used, but that Mao's left ear fell off during the embalming process, and had to be stitched back on.

Much of the interest of a visit here lies in witnessing the sense of awe of the Chinese confronted with their former leader, the architect of modern China who was accorded an almost god-like status for much of his life. The atmosphere is one of reverence, and any joking will cause deep offence. Once through the marble halls, you're herded past a splendidly wide-ranging array of tacky Mao souvenirs. The flashing Mao lighter that plays the national anthem on opening is a perennial favourite (¥10).

The Great Hall of the People

Taking up almost half the west side of the square is the monolithic **Great Hall of the People** (daily 8.30am–3pm when not in session; ¥20; buy tickets and leave bags at the office on the southern side), one of ten Stalinist wedding-cake-style buildings constructed in 1959 to celebrate "ten years of liberation" (others include Beijing Zhan and the Military Museum). This is the venue of the National People's Congress (the Chinese legislature), and the building is closed to the public when the Congress is in session – you'll know by the hundreds of black Audis with darkened windows parked outside. What you see on the mandatory, roped-off route through the building is a selection of its 29 cavernous, dim reception rooms, decorated in the same pompous but shabby style seen in the lobbies of cheap Chinese hotels – badly fitted red carpet, lifeless murals and armchairs lined up against the walls. Each room is named after a part of China; one is called "Taiwan Province". The route ends at the massive five-thousand-seater banqueting hall where you can buy a canteen lunch (¥10).

When Mrs Thatcher came here in 1982 she tripped on the steps – this was seen in Hong Kong as a terrible omen for the negotiations she was having over the territory's future. In 1989, the visiting Mikhail Gorbachev had to be smuggled in through a side entrance to avoid the crowds of protesters outside. However, if you're not a national leader on a meet-and-greet, you'll be better rewarded elsewhere; the Russian-built Exhibition Hall (see p.91) is a more pleasing example of monumental communist architecture.

The museums

On the east side of the square are two museums (both Tues–Sun 8.30am–5pm; last entry 4.15pm; exhibitions ¥10–20), housed in the same building but with separate ticket offices. The **Museum of the Revolution** covers China in the nineteenth and twentieth centuries. It's full of propaganda, and, in practice, seems almost always to be closed for refits (during the Cultural Revolution it was shut for twelve years) as its curators are constantly having to reinvent the displays according to the latest Party line. The exhibits from the twentieth century – mostly photos of politicians – are dull (and the coverage terminates at 1949, post-liberation history being just too contentious), but those from the nineteenth century, including such oddments as a contract signed by a peasant selling his wife, and "Weapons used by the British against the Tibetan People", are fascinating. There are copious English captions, full of terms like "foreign aggression" and "colonial oppressors". At the time of writing the museum was closed yet again (presumably to be spruced up in time for the 2008 Olympics) and those halls that were open held for the most part uninteresting temporary exhibitions. One worthwhile permanent exhibition is the **historical waxworks show** (¥10), which displays 35 figures (more are promised), including heroes of the people such as devoted Party member Lei Feng, Norman Bethune (the only foreigner, a Canadian surgeon who worked with the Red Army), the historian Sima Qian, Confucius and, of course, Mao, whose figure here looks more realistic than the one in the tomb. Sadly there are no English captions, but the figure of the little girl staring up in homage at the red flag at the entrance drives home the point well enough – this is art to inspire patriotism, the latest incarnation of Socialist Realism.

The south side of the building holds the **Museum of Chinese History**. This too was closed for a refit at the time of writing, but part of the permanent collection was displayed in two excellent shows – daily life in the Tang dynasty, and Shang Dynasty bronzes (each ¥10). The museum is intended more for the education of the Chinese masses rather than foreign tourists – it will be interesting to see whether, when it reopens, the exhibits are still divided according to a Marxist reading of history, into "primitive", "slave", "feudal" and "semi-colonial".

Tian'anmen

Tian'anmen (daily 8am–5pm; ¥15), the Gate of Heavenly Peace, is the main entrance to the Forbidden City (but don't buy a ticket here if that's where you're headed; the Forbidden City ticket office is further north on the right. An image familiar across the world, Tian'anmen occupies an exalted place in Chinese iconography, appearing on policemen's caps, banknotes, coins, stamps and indeed most pieces of official paper. As such it's a prime object of pilgrimage, with many visitors milling around waiting to be photographed in front of the large **portrait of Mao** (one of the very few still on public display), which hangs over the central passageway. Once reserved for the sole use of the emperor, but now standing wide open, the entrance is flanked by the twin slogans "Long Live the People's Republic of China" and "Long Live the Great Union between the Peoples of the World".

The ticket here affords you the chance to climb up onto the **viewing platform** above the gate. Security is tight: all visitors have to leave their bags, be frisked and go through a metal detector before they can ascend. Inside, the fact that most people cluster around the souvenir stall – which only sells official

△ Tian'anmen

The emperor speaks to his people

In the Ming and Qing dynasties, Tian'anmen was where the **ceremony** called "the golden phoenix issues an edict" took place. The minister of rites would receive an imperial edict inside the palace, and take it to Tian'anmen on a silver "cloud tray", he and his charge under a yellow umbrella. Here, the edict was read aloud to the officials of the court who knelt below, lined up according to rank. Next, the edict was placed in the mouth of a gilded wooden phoenix, which was lowered by rope to another cloud tray below. The tray was then put in a carved, wooden dragon and taken to the Ministry of Rites to be copied out and sent around the country.

Mao too liked to address his subjects from here; on October 1, 1949, he delivered the **liberation speech** to jubilant crowds below, declaring that "the Chinese people have now stood up"; in the 1960s, he spoke from this spot to massed ranks of Red Guards and declared that it was time for a "cultural revolution" (see p.178).

certificates to anyone who wants their visit here documented – reflects the fact that there's not much to look at.

The parks

The two parks either side of Tian'anmen, **Zhongshan** to the west and the grounds of the **People's Culture Palace** to the east, are great places to escape the square's rigorous formality (both open daily 6am–9pm; ¥3).

Zhongshan park boasts the ruins of the Altar of Land and Grain, a site of biennial sacrifice during the Qing and Ming dynasties, with harvest-time events closely related to those of the Temple of Heaven (see p.60). There's a new concert hall here too (see p.131). The People's Culture Palace – symbolically named in deference to the fact that only after the communist takeover in 1949 were ordinary Chinese allowed within this central sector of their city – has a number of modern exhibition halls, often worth checking for their temporary art shows, and a scattering of original fifteenth-century structures, most of them Ming or Qing ancestral temples.

The Forbidden City

Lying at the heart of the city, the Imperial Palace, Gugong, or, most evocatively, the **Forbidden City**, is Beijing's finest monument. To do it justice, you should plan to spend a whole day here, though you could wander the complex for a week and keep discovering new aspects. The central halls, with their wealth of imperial pomp, may be the most magnificent buildings, but for many visitors it's the side rooms, with their displays of the more intimate accoutrements of court life, that bring home the realities of life for the inhabitants in this, the most gilded of cages.

Although the earliest structures (none of which survive today) on the site of the Forbidden City began with Kublai Khan during the Mongol dynasty, the **plan** of the palace buildings is essentially Ming. Most date back to the fifteenth century and the ambitions of the **Emperor Yongle**, the monarch responsible for switching the capital from Nanjing back to Beijing in 1403 (see p.175). His programme to construct a complex worthy enough to house the Son of

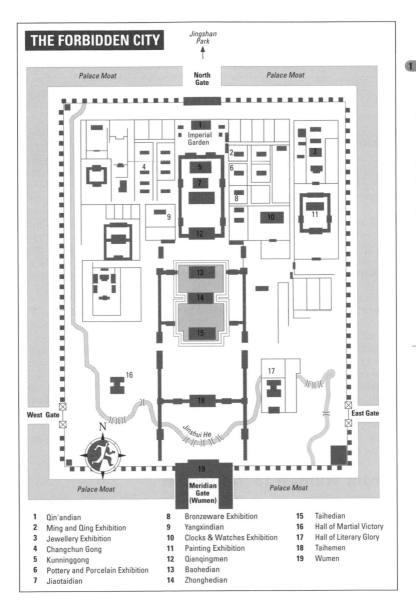

THE FORBIDDEN CITY

Jingshan Park

Palace Moat — North Gate — Palace Moat

Imperial Garden

West Gate

East Gate

Jinshui He

N

Meridian Gate (Wumen)

Palace Moat — Palace Moat

1	Qin'andian	**8**	Bronzeware Exhibition	**15**	Taihedian
2	Ming and Qing Exhibition	**9**	Yangxindian	**16**	Hall of Martial Victory
3	Jewellery Exhibition	**10**	Clocks & Watches Exhibition	**17**	Hall of Literary Glory
4	Changchun Gong	**11**	Painting Exhibition	**18**	Taihemen
5	Kunninggong	**12**	Qianqingmen	**19**	Wumen
6	Pottery and Porcelain Exhibition	**13**	Baohedian		
7	Jiaotaidian	**14**	Zhonghedian		

Heaven was concentrated between 1407 and 1420, involving up to ten thousand artisans and perhaps a million labourers.

All the halls of the Forbidden City were laid out according to geomantic theories – in accordance with the balance between *yin* and *yang*, or negative and positive energy. The buildings, which are signposted in English, face south in order to benefit from the invigorating advantages of *yang* energy, and as a protection against harmful *yin* elements from the north, both real and imagined – cold winds, evil spirits and steppe barbarians. Ramparts of compacted earth and a fifty-metre-wide moat isolated the complex from the commoners outside, with the only access being through four monumental gateways in the four cardinal directions. The layout is the same as that of any grand Chinese house of the period; pavilions are arranged around courtyards, with reception rooms and official buildings at the front (south), arranged with rigorous symmetry, and a labyrinthine set of private chambers to the north.

Visiting the Forbidden City

You can get to the Forbidden City on **bus** #5 from Qianmen, or #54 from Beijing Zhan, or you could use #1, which passes the complex on its journey along Chang'an Jie; all three buses drop you at the north end of Tian'anmen Square. The nearest **subways** are Tian'anmen Xi and Tian'anmen Dong, each about 300m away. Once through Tian'anmen, you find yourself on a long walkway, with the moated palace complex and massive main gate, Wumen, directly ahead; this is where you buy your ticket. If you're in a taxi, you can be dropped right outside the ticket office. The complex is **open** daily from 8.30am to 4.30pm (last admission 4pm April–Sept, 3.30pm Oct–March) and **tickets** cost ¥40 (clock and jewellery exhibitions ¥20 each, combined ticket ¥60).

Note that as well as the main gate, you can enter the complex through the smaller north and east gates (there are ticket offices just inside both gates). You can get to the north gate on bus #101, #103, or #109, which pass right by, and to the east gate on bus #819.

Visitors have the freedom of most of the one-square-kilometre site, though not of all the buildings. If you want detailed explanations of everything you see, you can tag along with one of the numerous tour groups, buy one of the many specialist books on sale at Wumen, or take the **audio tour** (¥40), also available at the main gate. On the audio tour, you're provided with a cassette player and headphones, and suavely talked through the complex by Roger Moore. If you take this option, it's worth retracing your steps afterwards for an untutored view. There are plenty of toilets inside the complex, and a *Starbucks* coffee shop at the back.

From Wumen to Taihemen

A huge building, whose central archway was reserved for the emperor's sole use, **Wumen** (Meridian Gate) is the largest and grandest of the Forbidden City gates. From its vantage point, each lunar new year the Sons of Heaven would announce to their court the details of the forthcoming calendar, including the dates of festivals and rites, and, in times of war, inspect the army. It was customary for victorious generals returning from battle to present their prisoners here for the emperor to decide their fate. He would be flanked, as on all such imperial occasions, by a guard of elephants, the gift of Burmese subjects. In the Ming dynasty, this was also where disgraced officials were flogged or executed.

In the wings on either side of the Wumen are two drums and two bells; the drums were beaten whenever the emperor went to the Temple of the Imperial Ancestors, the bells rung when he visited the temples of Heaven (see p.60) and Earth (see p.89).

Passing through Wumen, you find yourself in a vast paved court, cut east–west by the **Jinshui He**, or Golden Water Stream, with its five marble bridges, one for each Confucian virtue (see p.89). They're decorated with carved torches, a

Imperial symbolism

Almost every colour and image in the palace is richly **symbolic**. Yellow was the imperial colour; only in the palace were yellow roof tiles allowed. Purple was just as important, though used more sparingly; it symbolized joy and represented the pole star, centre of the universe according to Chinese cosmology (the implication of its use – usually on wall panels – was that the emperor resided in the earthly equivalent of the celestial zenith). The sign for the emperor was the dragon, for the empress, the phoenix; you'll see these two creatures represented on almost every building and stairway. The crane and turtle, depicted in paintings, carved into furniture or represented as freestanding sculptures, represent longevity of reign. The numbers nine and five crop up all over the complex, manifested in how often design elements are repeated; nine is lucky and associated with *yang*, or male energy, while five, the middle single-digit number, is associated with harmony and balance. Nine and five together – power and balance – symbolize "the heavenly son" – the emperor.

symbol of masculinity. Beyond is a further ceremonial gate, **Taihemen**, the Gate of Supreme Harmony, its entrance guarded by a magisterial row of lions, and beyond this a larger courtyard where the principal imperial audiences were held. Within this space the entire court – up to a hundred thousand people – could be accommodated. They made their way in through the lesser side gates – military men from the west, civilian officials from the east – and waited in total silence as the emperor ascended his throne. Then, with only the Imperial Guard remaining standing, they prostrated themselves nine times.

The galleries running round the courtyard housed the imperial storerooms. The buildings either side are the Hall of Martial Victory to the west and Hall of Literary Glory to the east; the latter, under the Ming emperors, housed the 11,099 volumes of the encyclopedia Yongle commissioned.

The ceremonial halls

The three main **ceremonial halls** stand directly north of Taihemen, dominating the court. In accordance with tradition, the main halls are built all on the same level – on a raised stone platform – and made of wood. Their elegant roofs, curved like the wings of a bird, are supported entirely by pillars and beams; the weight is cleverly distributed by ceiling consoles, while the walls beneath are just lightweight partitions. Doors, steps and access ramps are always odd in number, with the middle passageway reserved for the emperor's palanquin.

Raised on a three-tiered marble terrace is the first and most spectacular of the halls, the **Taihedian**, Hall of Supreme Harmony. The vast hall, nearly 38m high, was the tallest in China during the Ming and Qing dynasty – no civilian building was allowed to be taller. Taihedian was used for the most important state occasions: the emperor's coronation, birthday or marriage; ceremonies marking the new lunar year and winter solstice; proclamations of the results of the imperial examinations; and the nomination of generals at the outset of a military campaign. During the Republic, it was proposed that parliament should sit here, though the idea wasn't put into practice.

Decorated entirely in red and gold, Taihedian is the most sumptuous building in the complex. In the central coffer, a sunken panel in the ceiling, two gold-plated dragons play with a huge pearl. The gilded rosewood chair beneath, the dragon throne, was the exact centre of the Chinese universe. A

Dining, imperial style

The emperor ate twice a day, at 8am and around noon. Often meals consisted of hundreds of dishes, with the emperor eating no more than a mouthful of each. According to tradition, no one else was allowed to eat at his table, and when banquets were held he sat at a platform well above his guests. Such occasions were extremely formal and not to everyone's tastes. A Jesuit priest invited to such a feast in 1727 complained, "A European dies of hunger here; the way in which he is forced to sit on the ground on a mat with crossed legs is most awkward; neither the wine nor the dishes are to his taste . . . Every time the emperor says a word which lets it be known he wishes to please, one must kneel down and hit one's head on the ground. This has to be done every time someone serves him something to drink." If you're curious about the kind of food he was given, you should try imperial cuisine at the *Fangshan* or *Yushan* restaurants (see p.120 & p.119).

marble pavement ramp, intricately carved with dragons and flanked by bronze incense burners, marks the path along which the emperor's sedan chair was carried whenever he wanted to be taken somewhere. The grain measure and sundial just outside are symbols of imperial justice.

Moving on, you enter the **Zhonghedian**, Hall of Middle Harmony, another throne room, where the emperor performed ceremonies of greeting to foreign dignitaries and addressed the imperial offspring (the progeny of his several wives and numerous concubines). It owes its name to a quote from the *I-Ching* (see p.182), a Chinese tome dating back to 200 BC: "avoiding extremes and self control brings harmony" – the idea being that the middle course would be a harmonious one. The hall was also where the emperor examined the seed for each year's crop; it was used, too, as a dressing room for major events held in the Taihedian.

The third of the great halls, the **Baohedian**, or Preserving Harmony Hall, was the venue for state banquets and imperial examinations; graduates from the latter were appointed to positions of power in what was the world's first recognizably bureaucratic civil service. Huge ceremonies took place here to celebrate Chinese New Year; in 1903, this involved the sacrifice of ten thousand sheep. The hall's galleries, originally treasure houses, display various finds from the site, though the most spectacular, a vast marble block carved with dragons and clouds, stands at the rear of the hall. A Ming creation, reworked in the eighteenth century, it's among the finest carvings in the palace and certainly the largest – the 250-tonne chunk of marble was slid here from well outside the city by flooding the roads in winter to form sheets of ice.

The imperial living quarters

To the north, repeating the hierarchy of the ceremonial halls, are the three principal palaces of the **imperial living quarters**. Again, it's the first of these, the **Qianqinggong**, or Palace of Heavenly Purity, that's the most extravagant. Originally the imperial bedroom, its terrace is surmounted by incense burners in the form of cranes and tortoises. It was here in 1785 that Qianlong presided over the famous "banquet of old men" that brought together three thousand men of over sixty years of age from all corners of the empire. The hall was also used for the lying in state of the emperor, and played a role in the tradition, begun by Qing Emperor Yongzheng, which finally sorted out the problem of **succession** (hitherto fraught with intrigue and uncertainty, as the principle of

Eunuchs and concubines

For much of the imperial period, the Forbidden City was home to members of the royal household. Around half of these were **eunuchs**, introduced into the imperial court as a means of ensuring the authenticity of the emperor's offspring and, as the eunuchs would never have any family, an extreme solution to the problem of nepotism. As virtually the only men allowed into the palace, they came into close contact with the emperor and often rose to positions of considerable power. Their numbers varied greatly from one dynasty to the next – the Ming court is supposed to have employed twenty thousand, but this is probably an overestimate; the relatively frugal Qing Emperor Kangxi reduced the number to nine thousand.

Most of the eunuchs (or "bob-tailed dogs" as they were nicknamed) came from poor families, and volunteered for their emasculation as a way of acquiring wealth and influence. The operation cost six silver pieces and was performed in a hut just outside the palace walls. Hot pepper-water was used to numb the parts, then after the blade had flashed the wound was sealed with a solder plug. The plug was removed three days later – if urine gushed out, the operation was a success. If it didn't, the man would die soon, in agony. Confucianism held that disfiguration of the body impaired the soul, so in the hope that he would still be buried "whole", the eunuch carried his severed genitalia in a bag hung on his belt. One problem eunuchs were often plagued with was bed-wetting; hence the old Chinese expression, "as stinky as a eunuch".

Eunuchry was finally banned in 1924, and the remaining 1500 eunuchs were expelled from the palace. An observer described them "carrying their belongings in sacks and crying piteously in high pitched voices".

Scarcely less numerous than the eunuchs were the **concubines**, whose role varied from consorts to whores. At night, the emperor chose a girl from his harem by picking out a tablet bearing her name from a pile on a silver tray. She would be delivered to the emperor's bedchamber naked but for a yellow cloth wrapped around her, and carried on the back of one of the eunuchs, since she could barely walk with her bound feet. Favoured wives and concubines were the only women in dynastic China with power and influence; see the box on Cixi (p.98) for a telling example of just how far a concubine could get.

primogeniture was not used). Keeping an identical document on his person, Yongzheng and his successors deposited the name of his chosen successor in a sealed box hidden in the hall. When the emperor died, it was sufficient to compare the two documents to proclaim the new Son of Heaven.

Beyond, echoing the Zhonghedian in the ceremonial complex, is the **Jiaotaidian**, Hall of Union, the empress's throne-room, where the 25 different imperial document seals were kept. The ceiling here is possibly the finest in the complex, a gilt confection with a dragon surrounded by phoenixes at the centre; also here is a fine, and very hefty, water clock. The two characters *wu wei* at the back of the hall mean "no action" – a reference to the Taoist political ideal of not disturbing the course of nature or society.

Lastly, the **Kunninggong**, or Palace of Earthly Tranquillity, was where the emperor and empress traditionally spent their wedding night. By law the emperor had to spend the first three nights of his marriage, and the first day of the Chinese New Year, with his first wife. On the left as you enter is a large sacrificial room, its vats ready to receive offerings (1300 pigs a year during the Ming dynasty). The wedding chamber is a small room, off to one side, painted entirely in red, and covered with decorative emblems symbolizing fertility and joy. It was last pressed into operation in 1922 for the wedding of 12-year-old

Pu Yi, the last emperor, who, finding it "like a melted red wax candle", decided that he preferred the Mind Nurture Palace and went back there.

One of a group of palaces to the west, the Mind Nurture Palace, or **Yangxindian**, was where emperors spent most of their time. Several of these palaces retain their furniture from the Manchu times, most of it eighteenth-century; in one, the **Changchungong** (Palace of Eternal Spring), is a series of paintings illustrating the Ming novel, *The Story of the Stone*.

The museums

To the east of the Palace of Earthly Tranquillity is a group of palaces, once residences of the emperor's wives and now adapted as **museum galleries** (see box). The atmosphere here is much more intimate than in the state buildings, and you can peer into well-appointed chambers full of elegant furniture and ornaments, including English clocks decorated with images of English gentle-folk, which look very odd among the jade trees and ornate fly whisks.

The Imperial Garden

From the Inner Court, the Kunningmen opens north onto the **Imperial Garden**, by this stage something of a respite from the elegant buildings. There are a couple of **cafés** here (and toilets) amid a pleasing network of ponds, walkways and pavilions, designed to be reminiscent of southern Chinese landscapes.

Exhibitions in the Forbidden City

Many of the outlying residences within the Forbidden City now host **exhibitions** of art and traditional artefacts. Below we list some of the main displays and the buildings – all signposted in English – in which they're housed; most are on the eastern side. They're all free unless specified otherwise.

Ming and Qing crafts. In Jingyanggong, to the east of the Imperial Garden. Exquisite lacquerware, and carvings of jade, wood, bamboo and ivory.

Pottery and porcelain. In Chenqiangong and Yonghegong, south of the Ming and Qing crafts exhibition. Seven hundred pieces of pottery and porcelain from the Stone Age to the Qing dynasty.

Bronzeware. In Jingrengong, Zhaigong and Chengshudian, south of the pottery and porcelain exhibition. Five hundred pieces of bronzeware from the Shang dynasty to the Warring States period (sixteenth century BC to 200 BC).

Painting. In Huangjidian, Ningshougong and adjacent houses in the east part of the palace. Thousands of magnificent paintings from the Jin to the Qing dynasties are on show, with the displays changing monthly.

Jewellery (¥20). In Yangxindian and Leshoutang, north of the painting exhibition. The first hall mostly houses gold, silver and jade tableware and tea and wine utensils. There are also gold chimes, seals, books and a pagoda that was used to store any hair which fell out, on brushing, from the imperial head of Emperor Qianlong's mother. The second hall holds the costumes and utensils the emperor and empress used. Particularly impressive is a huge jade carving illustrating a Taoist immortal taming the waves. It weighs over five tonnes and reputedly took ten years to carve.

Clocks and watches (¥20). In Fengxiandian, the eastern palace quarters. This hall displays the result of one Qing emperor's passion for liberally ornamented Baroque timepieces, most of which are English and French, though the rhino-sized water clock by the entrance is Chinese. Some clocks are wound to demonstrate their workings at 11am and 2pm.

In the middle of the garden, the **Qin'andian**, or Hall of Imperial Tranquillity, was where the emperor came to worship a Taoist water deity, Xuan Wu, who was responsible for keeping the palace safe from fire. You can exit here into Jingshan Park, which provides an overview of the complex – see p.82.

2

South of the centre

Most visitors head south to sample the glorious Temple of Heaven, but it's worth taking your time to get there: just south of Tian'anmen Square, the **Qianmen district** offers a tempting antidote to the square's formality and grandeur – and a quick change of scale. The lanes and *hutongs* here comprise a **traditional shopping quarter**, full of small, specialist stores which, to a large extent, remain grouped according to their particular trades. It's a part of the city that lends itself to browsing and wandering, and a good place to eat, with one of the best selections of snacks available in the capital.

Down Qianmen Dajie, once the Imperial Way, now a clogged road, lies ravishing **Tiantan**, the Temple of Heaven. An example of imperial architecture at its best, it's perfectly set in one of Beijing's prettiest parks. Another site of Imperial ritual nearby, the Temple of Agriculture, has become an engrossing **Museum of Architecture**. Also in the area is the rather less glamorous **Museum of Natural History**, which contains a gruesome surprise. West of here, **Niu Jie** – at the heart of the city's Muslim quarter – and the **Museum of Ancient Architecture** are both worth a diversion. A very different sort of large-scale project is on show back near Qianmen in the **Underground City**, a shabby relic of communist paranoia.

Qianmen and around

The northern entrance to this quarter is marked by the imposing, fifteenth-century, double-arched **Qianmen**, the gate just south of Tian'anmen Square. Before the city's walls were demolished, this controlled the entrance to the inner city from the outer, suburban sector. Banned from the former in imperial days, shops and places of entertainment became concentrated around Qianmen. The quarter's biggest street, **Qianmen Dajie**, runs immediately south from the gate; off to either side are commercial streets and *hutongs*, with intriguing traditional pharmacies and herbalists' shops, dozens of clothes shops and silk traders (the Beijing Silk Shop sells gorgeous dresses; see p.138), and an impressive array of stalls and cake shops selling fresh food and cooked snacks.

As well as plenty of street food and fast food available opposite Qianmen gate, there are some great restaurants in this area – try the *Quanjude Roast Duck* for a slap-up meal or *Duyichu* for a snack. Vegetarians should head south to *Gongdelin*. See chapter 8 for reviews of these places.

A good way to sample the *hutongs* is on a **hutong tour**, during which you'll be ridden around on a rickshaw to guild halls, opera houses, shops and markets.

Dazhalan Jie	大栅栏街	dàzhàlán jiē
Fayuan Si	法源寺	fǎyuán sì
Liulichang Jie	琉璃厂街	liúlíchǎng jiē
Museum of Ancient Architecture	古代建筑博物馆	gǔdài jiànzhù bówùguǎn
Natural History Museum	自然博物馆	zìrán bówùguǎn
Niu Jie	牛街	niújiē
Qianmen	前门	qiánmén
Temple of Heaven	天坛	tiāntán
Tiantan Park	天坛公园	tiāntán gōngyuán
Underground City	地下城	dìxià chóng

The tours leave at 9am and 2pm from a point 50m west of the Laoshe Tea House on Qianmen Xi Dajie (☎010/63027010, ⓦwww.hutongtourinxuanwu.com). Only go on the official rickshaws, which have "Hello Beijing" written on them.

Dazhalan Jie

The oldest and most interesting of the Qianmen lanes is the cramped **Dazhalan Jie**, which leads west off Qianmen Dajie; the lane's entrance is marked by a white arch, opposite the *Qianmen Quanjude Roast Duck* restaurant on the east side of the road. Once where theatres were concentrated, it's now a hectic pedestrianized shopping district, its genteel old buildings mostly occupied by tea merchants and clothing stores.

Go down the first alley on the left, and one of the first shops you'll pass on the right is the Liubiju, a **pickle shop** that's more than 100 years old. It looks quaint, with pickled vegetables sold out of ceramic jars, but smells awful. Back on Dazhalan Jie, you'll find the Ruifuxiang, a venerable **fabric shop**, a little further down on the right – look for the storks on its facade, above the arched entrance. This is the place to get silk and satin fabrics, and *qipaos* (see p.201); whether or not you're buying, take a look at the exhibition, on the top floor, of old photos of the street. On the other side of the road at no. 24, the Tongrengtang is a famous **traditional Chinese medicine store**, whose reputation has spread as far as Korea and Japan. The place even has its own foreign-exchange counter, opposite a booth where a resident pharmacist offers on-the-spot diagnoses.

At the end of the pedestrianized area, the street narrows and you enter a district of **hutongs**. A stroll here offers a glimpse of the bustle and decay that's typical of Chinese metropolitan life but vanishing from central Beijing; you'll come across cobblers and knife sharpeners and dubious hairdressers, stone lions flanking sagging courtyard doors, and furtive fruit vendors with an eye out for the police. The prevalence of public toilets hints at one reason why the locals don't care much that the *hutongs* are being ripped up – the buildings have terrible plumbing. If you keep going straight, you'll pass the *Yuandong Hotel* and eventually rejoin the traffic at Nanxinhua Jie. Getting lost is likely but not unpleasant; Liulichang (see below) is a good destination to ask for.

Liulichang Jie

Turn north at the western end of Dazhalan, then head west along a *hutong*, then north and west again, to reach **Liulichang Jie**, parallel to Dazhalan Jie. If you're approaching from Hepingmen subway stop, you can get here by heading south down Nanxinhua Jie, which cuts Liulichang Jie at right angles – look for the marble bridge over the road. Liulichang, whose name literally means

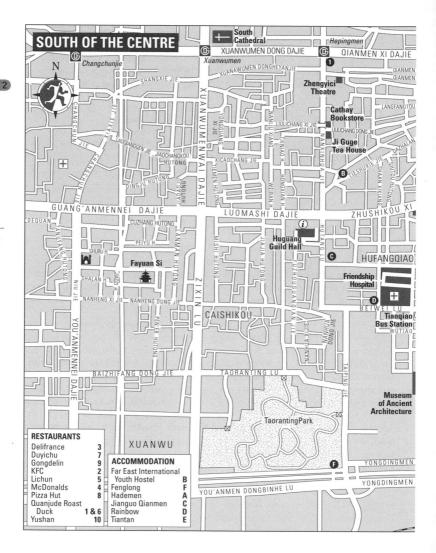

SOUTH OF THE CENTRE

South Cathedral

Hepingmen

XUANWUMEN DONG DAJIE
QIANMEN XI DAJIE

Changchunjie
Xuanwumen
XUANAWUMEN DONGHEYANJIE
QIANMEN
QIANMEN

SHANGXIE JIE
Zhengyici
Theatre
LANGFANGTOU

Cathay
Bookstore

LIULICHANG XI JIE
LIULICHANG DONG JIE

JIAOQIANGGEN JIE
XI JIE
YONGGUANG
NANLU XIANG
YENJAO H
Ji Guge
Tea House

JIAOCHANGKOU HUTONG
XICAOCHANG JIE
TIEMEN H
NANXINHUA JIE
TIESHUXIE JIE
SHAAN XIXIANG
SHITOU HUTONG
DAZHALAN

QINGJU HUTONG
TOUFANG HUTONG
HONGXIAN H
WEIRAN H

GUANG'ANMENNEI DAJIE
LUOMASHI DAJIE
ZHUSHIKOU XI

DEQUAN
CUZHANG HUTONG
TANGFANG HUTONG
Huguang
Guild Hall
HUFANGQIAO

SHURU H
PEIYU H
MISHI HUTONG
Friendship
Hospital

Fayuan Si
SHALAN H
LANNAN HUTONG
ZHOUGUANJIA HUTONG
BEIWEI LU

NIU JIE
NANHENG XI JIE
NANHENG DONG JIE
ZIXIN LU
CAISHIKOU LU
NANHUA JIE
Tianqiao
Bus Station
WUTIAO

YOU'ANMENNEI DAJIE
PENTI HUTONG

BAIZHIFANG DONG JIE
TAORANTING LU
NANXINHI JIE YI'NAN L
TAIPING JIE

Museum
of Ancient
Architecture

XUANWU
TaorantingPark
YONGDINGMEN

YOU'ANMEN DONGBINHE LU
YONGDINGMEN

RESTAURANTS
Delifrance   3
Duyichu   7
Gongdelin   9
KFC   2
Lichun   5
McDonalds   4
Pizza Hut   8
Quanjude Roast
  Duck   1 & 6
Yushan   10

ACCOMMODATION
Far East International
  Youth Hostel   B
Fenglong   F
Hademen   A
Jianguo Qianmen   C
Rainbow   D
Tiantan   E

"glaze factory street", after the erstwhile factories here making glazed tiles for the roofs of the Forbidden City, has been rebuilt as a heritage street, using Ming-style architecture; today it's full of curio stores (remember to bargain hard, and assume everything is fake) and bookshops. The Ji Guge **tea house** at no. 136 offers a welcome respite for shoppers. The area's best **bookshop** is the Cathay Bookstore at the north corner of Nanxinhua Jie, which has plenty of picture books in English.

Underground City

In yet another giant and impractical Chinese engineering project (the Great Wall and the brand new Three Gorges Dam on the Yangzi River also come to

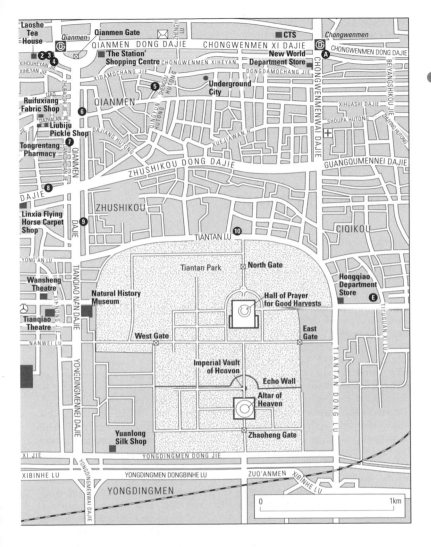

mind) Mao had "volunteers" construct a warren of **bunkers** under the city in the 1960s. A response to the nuclear threat from the Soviet Union, the tunnel network had entrances all over the city, a control centre in the western hills, and supply arteries big enough for trucks to drive down. Fortunately it was never put to use; it was too close to the surface to be protection against any but the smallest conventional bombs.

Today the tunnels are falling into disrepair and most of the entrances are sealed. You can get in using an entrance sunk deep in the *hutongs* southeast of Qianmen (daily 8.30am–5pm; ¥20). Maps of the *hutongs* aren't reliable, but one foolproof approach is to head east from Qianmen along the north side of Qianmen Dong Dajie. When you reach Zhengyi Lu, which leads north off the road, cross to the south side of Qianmen Dong Dajie and head down the narrow *hutong* here, then take the first left past a sign in English for the *Liyun Duck* restaurant. Head left at the end of this *hutong*, and the entrance is 300m down here on the right. The staff are quite taken aback by visitors, and to be honest there's really not much to see. From the entrance, stairs lead down to a claustrophic, dimly lit, arched tunnel that echoes with your footsteps. It's all rather sad and spooky and a grim monument to state paranoia. Rusty metal doors, labelled with landmarks, lead off to the rest of the network; rather disconcertingly, no one comes down to make sure you don't wander off into the labyrinth.

Tiantan and around

Set in its own large and tranquil park about 2km south of Tian'anmen, **Tiantan**, the Temple of Heaven, is widely regarded as the high point of Ming design. For five centuries it was at the very heart of imperial ceremony and symbolism, and for many modern visitors its architectural unity and beauty remain more appealing – and on a much more accessible scale – than the Forbidden City.

Construction of the sumptuous temple was begun during the reign of Emperor Yongle and completed in 1420. It was conceived as the prime meeting point of earth and heaven, and symbols of the two are integral to its design. Heaven was considered round, earth square; thus the round temples and altars stand on square bases, while the park has the shape of a semicircle beside a square.

The intermediary between earth and heaven was of course the **Son of Heaven**, the emperor, and the temple was the site of the most important ceremony of the imperial court calendar, when the emperor prayed for the year's harvests at the **winter solstice**. Purified by three days of fasting, he made his way to the park on the day before the solstice, accompanied by his court in all its magnificence. On arrival at Tiantan, the emperor would meditate in the Imperial Vault, ritually conversing with the gods on the details of government, before spending the night in the Hall of Prayer for Good Harvests. The following day he sacrificed animals before the Altar of Heaven. It was forbidden for commoners to catch a glimpse of the great annual procession to the temple, and they were obliged to bolt their windows and remain, in silence, indoors. Indeed, the Tiantan complex remained sacrosanct until it was thrown open to the people on the first Chinese National Day of the Republic, in October 1912. The last person to perform the rites was General Yuan Shikai, the first president of the republic, on December 23, 1914. He planned to declare himself emperor but died a broken man, his plans thwarted by opponents, in 1916.

Tiantan Park (daily 8.30am–7pm; ¥10 low season, ¥15 high season) is possibly the best in the city, and worth a visit in its own right; it's easy to find peaceful seclusion away from the temple buildings. Old men gather here with their pet birds and crickets, while from dawn onwards, *tai ji* practitioners can be seen lost in concentration among the groves of 500-year-old thuja trees. A variety of buses pass by: #106 from Dongzhimen (for the north gate); bus #17 or #54 from Qianmen (west gate); bus #41 from Qianmen (east gate); and bus #120 from Beijing Zhan or #803 from Qianmen (south gate).

The temple buildings

Although you're more likely to enter the park from the north or the west, to appreciate the temple buildings (daily 9am–5pm; combined ticket ¥30 low season, ¥35 high season, or individual building tickets ¥20), it's best initially to skirt round onto the ceremonial route up from the **Zhaoheng Gate**, the park's south entrance. This main pathway leads straight to the circular **Altar of Heaven**, consisting of three marble tiers representing (from the top down) heaven, earth and man. The tiers are comprised of blocks in various multiples of nine, cosmologically the most powerful number, representing both heaven and emperor. The centre of the altar's bare, roofless top tier, where the Throne of Heaven was placed during ceremonies, was considered to be the middle of the Middle Kingdom – the very centre of the earth. Various acoustic properties are claimed for the altar; from this point, it is said, all sounds are channelled straight upwards to heaven. To the east of the nearby fountain, which was reconstructed after fire damage in 1740, are the ruins of a group of buildings used for the preparation of sacrifices.

Directly ahead, the **Imperial Vault of Heaven** is an octagonal tower made entirely of wood, with a dramatic roof of dark blue glazed tiles, supported by eight pillars. This is where the emperor would change his robes and meditate. The shrine and stone platforms inside held stone tablets representing the emperor and his ancestors, and the two chambers either side held tablets representing the elements. The tower is encircled by the **Echo Wall**, said to be a perfect whispering gallery, although the unceasing cacophony of tourists trying it out makes it impossible to tell.

△ The Hall of Prayer for Good Harvests

The principal temple building – the **Hall of Prayer for Good Harvests**, at the north end of the park – amply justifies all this build-up. Made entirely of wood, without the aid of a single nail, the circular structure rises from another tiered marble terrace and has three blue-tiled roofs. Four compass-point pillars, representing the seasons, support the vault, enclosed in turn by twelve outer pillars (one for each month of the year and the hour of the day). The dazzling colours of the interior, surrounding the central dragon motif on the coffered ceiling, make the hall seem ultramodern; it was in fact rebuilt, faithful to the Ming design, after the original was destroyed by lightning in 1889. The official explanation for this appalling omen was that it was divine punishment meted out on a sacrilegious caterpillar, which was on the point of reaching the golden ball on the hall's apex when the lightning struck. Thirty-two court dignitaries were executed for allowing this to happen.

The museums

Two museums are worth combining with a visit to Tiantan. Just north of Tiantan Park's western gate, the **Natural History Museum** (daily 8.30am–4.30pm; ¥15) has recently improved its displays, and includes a terrific room full of dinosaur skeletons. One display that you won't find in a similar Western museum is held in a separate building on the right before the main entrance. Pickled legs, arms, brains and foetuses are arranged around the stars of the show, two whole adult corpses: a woman wearing socks, gloves and a hood; and a man with all his skin removed, leaving just the fingernails and lips. Few foreigners emerge from here unshaken, shown up by the Chinese kids who take it all in their stride.

A short walk to the southwest is the former **Xiannong Temple**, recently reconverted from a school into a rather fine little **Museum of Ancient Architecture** (daily 9am–5pm; ¥15). Look for the red arch south off Beiwei Lu; the ticket office is just beyond here and the museum itself is further down the road on the right. The temple, twin of the nearby Temple of Heaven, was dedicated to the god of earth, and every year the emperor ritually ploughed a furrow to ensure a good harvest. The buildings and the flat altar are fine, though not spectacular. The **Hall of Worship** holds oddments such as the gold-plated plough used by the emperor, as well as a display explaining the building's history. More diverting is the main **Hall of Jupiter**, with its fantastically ornate ceiling and an enlightening collection of architectural exhibits, showing how China's tradition-al buildings were put together. There are wooden models, many with cutaways, of famous and distinctive buildings, including Yingxian's pagoda (west of Beijing in Shanxi province), and a stilt house of Yunnan province's Dong people. Also on hand are samples of **dougongs**, interlocking, stacked brackets, as complex as puzzle boxes. The giant floor model (1:1000 scale) of how Beijing looked in 1949 – before the communists demolished most of it – is extremely informative, revealing how all the surviving imperial remnants are fragments of an awesome grand design, with a precise north–south imperial axis and sites of symbolic sig-nificance at each of the cardinal points. For those who prefer spectacle, there's a great sinuous wooden dragon on show, once part of a temple ceiling.

Niu Jie and the Fayuan Si

Some 3km southwest of Qianmen, **Niu Jie** (Ox Street) is a cramped thor-oughfare in the city's **Muslim quarter**, in a rather shabby section of the city.

The street is a one-kilometre walk south along Changchun Jie from Changchun Jie subway stop, or you could get here on bus #6 from the north gate of Tiantan Park. Head under the arch at the north end of Niu Jie and you enter a chaotic street lined with offal stalls, steamy little restaurants and hawkers selling fried dough rings, rice cakes and *shaobing*, Chinese-style muffins with a meat filling. The white caps and the beards sported by the men distinguish these people of the Muslim **Hui minority** – of which there are nearly two hundred thousand in the capital – from the Han Chinese.

The street's focus is the **mosque** at its southern end (daily 8am–5pm; ¥10), an attractive and colourful marriage of Chinese and Islamic design, with abstract and flowery decorations and text in Chinese and Arabic over the doorways. You won't get to see the handwritten copy of the Koran, dating back to the Yuan dynasty, without special permission, or be allowed into the main prayer hall if you're not a Muslim, but you can inspect the courtyard, where a copper cauldron, used to cook food for the devotees, sits near the graves of two Persian imams who came here to preach in the thirteenth century. Also in the courtyard is the "tower for viewing the moon", which allows imams to ascertain the beginning and end of Ramadan, the Muslim period of fasting and prayer.

Head south from the mosque, take the second *hutong* on the left, and after a few hundred metres you'll come to the **Fayuan Si**. This is one of Beijing's oldest temples, though the present structures are in fact Qing and thus relatively recent. It's appealingly ramshackle, with the well-worn prayer mats and shabby fittings of a working temple. Monks sit outside on broken armchairs counting prayer beads or bend over books in halls that stink of butter – burnt in lamps – and incense. There are two great Ming bronze lions in the first courtyard, looking like armoured were-puppies, and more fine bronzes of the four Heavenly Guardians and a chubby Maitreya in the hall beyond. The halls behind are home to a miscellany of Buddhist sculpture, the finest of which is a five-metre-long wooden reclining Buddha in the back hall.

West of the centre

eading west from Tian'anmen Square along **Chang'an Jie**, the giant freeway which runs dead straight east–west across the city, you pass a string of grandiose buildings, the headquarters of official and corporate power. Architectural styles are jumbled together here, with International Style, Postmodern whimsy and brute Stalinism all in evidence. Though most of the sites and amenities are elsewhere, and the area has not modernized as fast as the rest of the city, western Beijing has enough of interest tucked away to entertain the curious for a few days. Along Chang'an Jie itself, there's a pretty decent shopping district, **Xidan**, where you can rub shoulders with locals, and the surprisingly good **Military Museum**. Just off Chang'an Jie is the pleasant **Baiyun Guan**, a Taoist temple that seems worlds away from its surroundings.

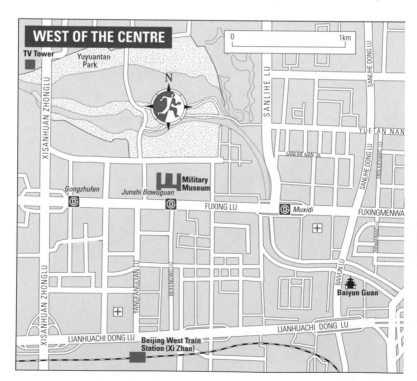

Baiyun Guan	白云观	*báiyún guàn*
Cultural Palace of National Minorities	民族文化宫	*mínzú wénhuàgōng*
Military Museum	军事博物馆	*jūnshì bówùguǎn*
TV tower	电视塔	*diànshìtǎ*
Xidan	西单	*xīdān*
Yuyuantan Park	玉渊潭公园	*yùyuāntán gōngyuán*
Zhongnanhai	中南海	*zhōngnán hǎi*

Zhongnanhai to Xidan

As you head west from Tian'anmen Square along Xichang'an Jie, the **Communist Party Headquarters** is the first major structure you pass. Named **Zhongnanhai**, the walled complex isn't hard to spot, as armed sentries stand outside the gates, ensuring that only invited guests actually get inside. Once home to the Empress Dowager Cixi (see p.98), since 1949 it's been the base of the Communist Party's Central Committee and the Central People's Government; Mao Zedong and Zhou Enlai both worked here. In 1989, pro-democracy protesters camped outside hoping to petition their leaders, just as commoners with grievances waited outside the Forbidden City in imperial times. A similar protest came from an unexpected source in 1999, when the practitioners of **Falun Gong**, a quasi-religious sect followed mostly by the aged in search of health and longevity, organized a mass protest to com-

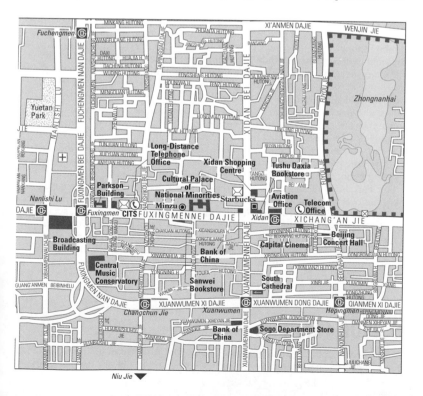

plain against government harassment of the group. Ten thousand devotees assembled around Zhongnanhai and sat down cross-legged on the pavement for the afternoon. Religious groups and secret societies have always flourished in China – the Boxers (see p.98) are a particularly prominent example – and governments have tended to treat them warily, as potential sources of organized dissent. Falun Gong have been ruthlessly suppressed ever since.

After the next junction, the **Beijing Telecom Office** rears above you – like the buildings around Tian'anmen Square, it's another of the "ten years of liberation" construction projects (see p.45), similarly grand and uninviting. Just to the west, the **Aviation Office**, the place to buy tickets for internal flights (see p.141) and catch the airport bus, stands on the site of Democracy Wall. In 1978, as part of the so-called "Beijing Spring", posters questioning Mao and his political legacy, and calling for political freedoms, were pasted up here. The movement was suppressed the following year.

The next major junction is **Xidan**, site of some of the capital's most ambitious modern buildings, the most successful of which is I.M. Pei's Bank of China at the northwest corner. Inside, the giant atrium leads the eye up to his signature glass pyramids in the ceiling. The shopping district of **Xidan Bei Dajie**, the street running north of here, is worth exploring, at least along its initial few blocks (though not at a weekend when it's heaving with people). This is where trendy Beijingers shop, and the area is a dense concentration of **department stores and stalls**, selling everything the burgeoning middle class requires. The sixth and seventh floors of the Xidan Shopping Centre (the ugly brown glass building) are the in place for adolescent consumption, and the taste – at least at the time of writing – was for a Japanese-influenced sartorial excess. When you've had enough of feeling trapped in a pop video, head upstairs to the giant food court and games arcade. A more upmarket (but just as claustrophobic) shopping experience is on offer at the Xidan CVIK Store, a couple of hundred metres further north of here on the west side of the street.

West of here, Xichang'an Jie continues into Fuxingmennei Dajie. On the north side of the street, 400m west of Xidan intersection, the **Cultural Palace of National Minorities** was once a museum and exhibition centre. It's now full of cheap stalls, which is a shame, as it is quite striking architecturally, with some grand Socialist-Realist wall reliefs of minority peoples and Tibetan and Islamic elements incorporated into the decoration. Plans are afoot to convert it back to its original function, as a centre for minority culture. Across the road nearby is the pleasant **Sanwei Bookstore**, which has its own tea house where evening performances of jazz and Chinese folk music are staged (see p.127).

The Parkson Building, at the next large intersection, is an upmarket mall. Skip the overpriced clothes and head for the sixth floor, which holds an **arts and crafts exhibition** of showpieces – most of them in jade but with ceramics and ivory too – by contemporary masters. The aesthetic is often dubious – a meeting of cadres in ivory, for instance – but the craftsmanship is undeniable. Look out for the four renowned jade pieces, each over a metre high: a dragon relief, a mountain, a vase with chains on the handles and a two-eared cup. Begun in 1985, each piece took forty or so craftsmen four years to make.

Baiyun Guan

A kilometre south of Fuxingmenwai Dajie, **Baiyun Guan** (White Cloud Temple; daily 8am–5.30pm; ¥10) is well worth hunting out; it's signposted in

Taoism

Humans model themselves on earth
earth on heaven
heaven on the way
and the way on that which is naturally so

Lao Zi, *Daodejing*

Taoism is a religion deriving from the *Daodejing* or "Way of Power", an obscure, mystical text (see p.182) comprising the teachings of the semi-mythical Lao Zi, who lived around 500 BC. The Tao (spelt *dao* in *pinyin*), which literally means "Way", is defined as being indefinable; accordingly the book begins: "The Tao that can be told/is not the eternal Tao/The name that can be named/is not the eternal name." But it is the force that creates and moves the natural world, and Taoists believe that the art of living lies in understanding it and conforming to it. Taoism emphasizes contemplation, meditation, non-committedness to dogma, and going with the flow. Its central principle is that of *wu wei*, literally non-action, perhaps better understood as "no action which goes against nature".

In part Taoism developed in reaction to the rigour and formality of state-sponsored Confucianism (see p.89). Taoism's holy men tend to be artisans and workmen rather than upright advisers, and in focusing on the relationship of the individual with the natural universe, Taoism represents a retreat from the political and social. The communists, accordingly, regard Taoism as fatalistic and passive.

English from Baiyun Lu, whose northern end is not far from Muxidi subway stop, and can also be reached on bus #212 from Qianmen or #40 from Nansanhuan Zhong Lu. Once the most influential Taoist centre in the country, the temple has been renovated after a long spell as a barracks during communist times, and now houses China's national Taoist association, as well as being home to thirty monks. A popular place for pilgrims, with a busy, thriving feel, it's at its most colourful during the Chinese New Year temple fair (see p.33).

Though laid out in a similar way to a Buddhist temple, Baiyunguan has a few distinctive features, such as the three gateways at the entrance, symbolizing the three states of Taoism – desire, substance and emptiness. Each hall is dedicated to a different deity, whose respective domains of influence are explained in English outside; it's from the hall to the gods of wealth that the thickest plumes of incense emerge. The eastern and western halls hold a great collection of Taoist relics, including some horrific paintings of hell showing people being sawn in half and the like. An attached bookshop has plenty of tapes of devotional music and lucky charms, though only one text in English, the *I-Ching* (see p.182). In the western courtyard, a shrine houses twelve deities, each linked with a different animal in the Chinese version of the zodiac; here, visitors light incense and kowtow to the deity that corresponds to their birth year. Also in the courtyard is a shrine to **Wen Cheng**, the deity of scholars, with a three-metre bronze statue of him outside. Rubbing his belly is supposed to bring success in academic examinations.

Three **monkeys** depicted in relief sculptures around the temple are believed to bring you good luck if you can find, and stroke, them all. One is on the gate, easy to spot as it's been rubbed black, while the other two are in the first courtyard. Another playful diversion is trying to ding the bell under the courtyard bridge by throwing a coin at it. In the back courtyard, devotees amuse themselves by closing their eyes and trying to walk from a wall to an incense burner.

The layout of Chinese temples

Whether Buddhist, Taoist or Confucian, Chinese **temples** follow the same basic **layout**: like cities and houses, they face south and are surrounded by walls. Gates are sealed by heavy doors, usually guarded by paintings or statues of warrior deities to chase away approaching evil spirits. The doors open into a courtyard, where further protection is provided by a **spirit wall**, which has to be walked around (evil spirits are thought unable to turn corners). Beyond you'll find a succession of halls arranged around ornamental courtyards. In case evil spirits do get in, the least important buildings are positioned at the front.

Buddhist temples usually use bright red pillars, while **Taoist** temples use black. Just inside a Buddhist temple you'll be flanked by the four Heavenly Kings of the Four Directions, and faced by portly Maitreya, the laughing Buddha. The main hall is dominated by three large statues sitting on lotus flowers – the Buddhas of the past, present and future – while the walls are lined with often rather outlandish looking **arhats**, or saints. Around the back of the Buddhist trinity is a statue of **Guanyin**, the multi-armed goddess of mercy. **Taoist** temples are similar, but their halls might be dedicated to any number of legendary figures (for more on Taoism, see p.67). The Taoist holy trinity is made up of the **three immortals** who each ride different animals (a crane, tiger and deer) and represent the three levels of the Taoist afterlife. You're also likely to see Guanyin represented in Taoist temples – her help in childbirth makes her universally popular. Animal carvings are more popular with the animist Taoists, who use good luck and longevity symbols such as bats and cranes. Other figures in Taoist temples include the Yellow Emperor and another eight immortals. **Guan Yu**, the red-faced god of war and healing, and **Zhuge Liang** are also popular choices – both are characters in the old story the *Three Kingdoms*, and are based on historical figures.

Confucian temples, though now restored, generally function as museums or libraries, having received a serious battering in the "criticize Confucius" campaign once launched by China's communist leaders. Nonetheless, you'll usually find a surviving statue of the great sage somewhere on site (for more on Confucianism, see p.89).

Yuyuantan Park and around

Back on Fuxingmenwai Dajie, a good ten-minute walk west from the intersection with Baiyun Lu, past Muxudi subway stop and onto Fuxing Lu, brings you to the **Military Museum** (daily 8am–4.30pm; ¥5). Now that all the communists have been to marketing school, it's almost refreshing to be confronted with the old-fashioned Soviet-style brutalism of this stern building, subtle as a jackboot. The entrance hall is full of big and very bad art, photo-collages of Mao inspecting his army and soldiers performing an amphibious landing (a hint at Taiwan's fate perhaps) and the like. The last Chinese public image of Marx hung here until 1999. The hall beyond has a wealth of Russian and Chinese weaponry on show, including tanks and rockets, and – in case martial feelings have been stirred – there's an air-rifle shooting gallery at the back. In the rear courtyard a group of miscellaneous old aircraft includes the shells of two American spy planes (with Nationalist Chinese markings) shot down in the 1950s. Upstairs, you'll find plaster copies of statues of military and political leaders.

Head back to the lobby, turn west and climb the unsignposted, dim staircase to the much more engaging **upper halls**. The exhibition on the third floor commemorates the Korean War, whose chief interest for foreign visitors lies in the fact that it's one of those places that isn't meant for them – captions are only in Chinese and there is much crowing over what is presented as the defeat

△ Baiyun Guan

of American power. There's also more bad art, paintings of lantern-jawed soldiers charging machine-gun posts and the like. The fourth floor holds a large exhibition on historical warfare, this time with English captions. Arranged in chronological order, it presents Chinese history as a series of bloody conflicts between rival warlords – which is, in fact, not far from the truth. The suits of armour worn by Qing soldiers and Japanese pirates are intimidating even when empty. Also on display are mock-ups of ingenious Chinese siege weapons, Ming dynasty gunpowder-driven devices for firing eighty arrows at a time, and the world's earliest handgun, from the fifteenth century. Opposite this hall lies another treat for the connoisseur of kitsch – the "Friendship Hall", containing gifts given to representatives of the Chinese military abroad. Competition for the most tasteless item is fierce, but the gold sub-machine gun from Lebanon and the silver model tractor from Romania certainly deserve a mention.

Behind the museum, **Yuyuantan Park** offers respite from the traffic. It's low on trees and grass, but the large lake is pleasant to walk around or ride a pedal boat on (¥10/hr). In the southwest corner stands the dome-shaped China Millenium Monument, a sterile public work and "Centre for Patriotic Education". The Communist Party's version of Chinese history is inscribed on bronze plates that form a walkway leading up to a flat altar, and worthy statuary and murals abound.

The TV tower

Northwest of the military museum, a three-kilometre walk away through Yuyuantan Park, lies Beijing's **TV tower** (daily 8am–5pm; ¥50). A giant, needle-like structure on the third ring road, the tower stands on the foundation of the Altar of the Moon, a Ming-dynasty sacrificial site. You ride up to the top in a lift and are given a Coke and a helping of cake once you get there. Though these don't justify the steep price of admission, the outdoor viewing platform 400m above ground does offer stunning views of the city on a clear day. Telescopes are dotted around for closer examination – unfortunately the view into Zhongnanhai is blocked by some judiciously placed buildings.

East of the centre

If you head east from Tian'anmen, the first thing you encounter, setting the tone for the rest of this cosmopolitan sector of the city, is the incongruously European architecture of the **legations quarter**, once home to foreign diplomats. Just to the north, the eastern section of **Chang'an Jie** is glamorous and commercial, with heavy lashings of shopping – the best in China outside Shanghai and Hong Kong – plus flashy hotels and plenty of restaurants and amenities. It's Beijing's most fashionable area; for anyone who's been in China for a while it's the place to come to stock up on luxuries, and for newcomers it offers the chance to experience the new realities of life for privileged locals. The most obvious landmark here is the **Beijing Hotel**, on the corner where **Wangfujing Dajie**, Beijing's most famous shopping street, leads north off Dongchang'an Jie. However, a better marker for the abrupt transition from the political zone of Tian'anmen to the commercialism of this sector is the street's first large billboard, to be found over the road from Wangfujing Dajie. Now used for advertisements, for years it denounced corruption, and policemen used to prevent foreigners from taking pictures of it.

Beyond the intersection with Dongdan Bei Dajie and Chongwenmennei Dajie, about 1500m east of Tian'anmen Square, Dongchang'an Jie becomes **Jianguomen Dajie**. The strip around here is a ritzy area given much of its international flavour and atmosphere of casual affluence by its large contingent of foreigners, comprising staff from the Jianguomen embassy compound as well as upmarket tourists. Eating and staying here will soon sap many tourists' budgets (first-time visitors here can be heard expressing disappointment that China is as expensive as New York), but the wide variety of shopping on offer – cheap clothes markets, the best Friendship Store in China and plazas that wouldn't look out of place in Hong Kong – will suit all pockets. Jianguomen Dajie is about as far away from traditional China as you can get, but the **Ancient Observatory** halfway along, and the bizarre **Dongyue Temple** to the north, offer respite from rampant modernity.

The Ancient Observatory	古观象台	*gǔguānxiàng tái*
Chaoyangmen	朝阳门	*cháoyángmén*
Dongyue Temple	东岳庙	*dōngyuè miào*
Jianguomen	建国门	*jiànguómén*
Police Museum	警察博物馆	*jǐngchá bówùguǎn*
Ritan Park	日坛公园	*rìtán gōngyuán*
St Michael's Church	东交民巷天主堂	*dōngjiāomínxiàng tiānzhǔtáng*
Sanlitun Lu	三里屯路	*sānlǐtún lù*
Wangfujing	王付井	*wángfùjǐng*

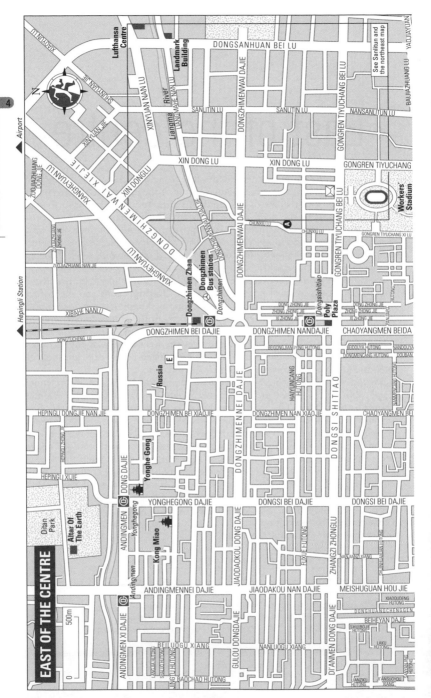

EAST OF THE CENTRE

0   500m

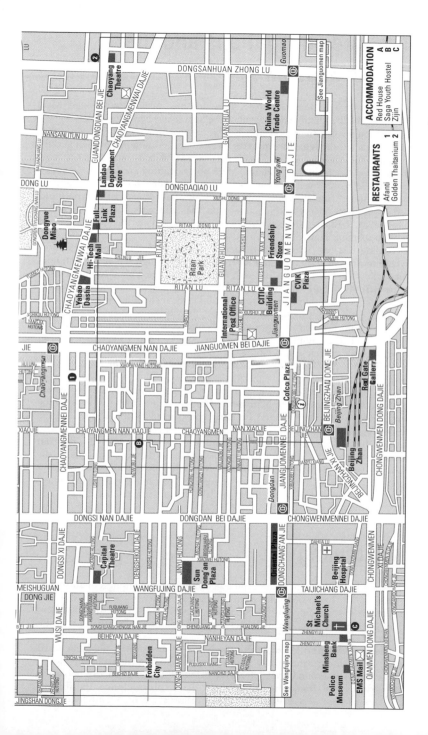

ACCOMMODATION
Red House A
Saga Youth Hostel B
Zijin C

RESTAURANTS
Afanti 1
Golden Thaitanium 2

See Jianguomen map

DONGSANHUAN ZHONG LU

Guomao

Chaoyang Theatre

China World Trade Centre

GUANGHUA LU

CHAOYANGMENWAI DAJIE

GUANDONGDIAN BEI JIE

NANSANLITUN LU

BAIJIAZHUANG LU

Yong'ani

DONGDAQIAO LU

Landao Department Store

XIUSHUI DONG JIE

DONG LU

Full Link Plaza

RITAN BEILU

RITAN DONG LU

Friendship Store

Dongyue Miao

DONGHUANBEI ZHIJIAO NANLU

Hi-Tech Mall

CHAOYANGMENWAI DAJIE

SHENLU JIE

Ritan Park

GUANGHUA LU

XIUSHUI NAN JIE

Yabao Dasha

JIANHUA LU

XIUSHUI BEI JIE

CVIK Plaza

SHIKOU HUTONG

YANGCA HUTONG

RITAN LU

RITAN LU

CITIC Building

JIANGUOMENWAI DAJIE

International Post Office

XIUSHUJIE

Jianguomen

JIE

HUTONG

CHAOYANGMEN NAN DAJIE

JIANGUOMEN BEI DAJIE

Chao'yangmen

XIAOPAIFANG HUTONG

Cofco Plaza

BEIJINGZHAN DONG JIE

Beijing Zhan

Red Gate Gallery

CHAOYANGMENNEI DAJIE

XIAOJIE

CHAOYANGMEN NAN XIAOJIE

CHAOYANGMEN NAN XIAOJIE

WUDINGHOU HUTONG

JIANGUOMENNEI DAJIE

Beijing Zhan

Beijing Zhan

CHONGWENMEN DONG DAJIE

Dongdan

JIANGUOMENNEI DAJIE

XIANGZIKANG JIE

BEIJINGZHAN XI JIE

DONGSI NAN DAJIE

DONGDAN BEI DAJIE

CHONGWENMENNEI DAJIE

DONGSI XI DAJIE

Capital Theatre

JINYU HUTONG

DENGSHIKOU HUTONG

BAOCHAO HUTONG

Sun Dong an Plaza

Oriental Plaza

DAHUA LU

CHONGWENMEN

CHONGWENMEN XI DAJIE

MEISHUGUAN

DONG JIE

WANGFUJING DAJIE

DONGCHANG'AN JIE

TAIJICHANG DAJIE

Beijing Hospital

WUSI DAJIE

FUQIANG HUTONG

DONGCHANG

DONG'ANMEN DAJIE

CAICHANG HUTONG

HUALONG JIE

Wangfujing

BEI JIE

BEIHEYAN DAJIE

DONGHUANG CHENGGE NAN JIE

CHENGUANG JIE

NANHEYAN DAJIE

See Wangfujing map

St Michael's Church

ZHENGYI LU

Minsheng Bank

EMS Mail

Forbidden City

DONGHUAMEN DAJIE

PUDUSIXI XIANG

NANCHIZI DAJIE

QIANMEN DONG DAJIE

Police Museum

JINGSHAN DONGJIE

The foreign legations and the Police Museum

Head east down Dongjiaomin Xiang, the first alley opposite the Mao Memorial Hall, and, still within sight of the Soviet-inspired symbols of Chinese power, you'll come to an odd stretch of street that shows very different influences. This was the **legation quarter**, created at the insistence of foreign officials in 1861, and run as an autonomous district with its own postal system, taxes and defences; initially, Chinese were not permitted entry without a pass. By the 1920s over twenty countries had legations here, most built in the style of their home countries, with imported fittings but using local materials, and today you'll see plenty of Neoclassical facades and wrought-iron balconies. Most of the buildings are now used by the police and are therefore politically sensitive – the area used to be left blank on maps.

Heading east past what used to be the French and Russian concession – where most of the buildings have been destroyed (though the old French hospital, the first building on the left, still stands), you come to the **Police Museum** (Tues–Sun 9am–4.30pm; ¥5). Anything vaguely related to crime or public order is exhibited on its four small floors, including murder weapons, forensics tools, uniforms and an ingenious Qing dynasty fire engine, as well as details of notorious crimes captioned in excited prose – the "forces of the law" always catch the "despicable ruffians", of course. There's plenty of English labelling, and, interestingly, some of it is very critical of the Cultural Revolution – probably the first public display of such sentiments, at least in English.

Keep heading east, over Zhengyi Lu, and you'll find the best-preserved concession architecture. The **Minsheng Bank**, just after the crossroads on the north side, is a Gothic Revival building constructed by the Japanese in the 1930s. Much of the opulent interior, including the chandeliers, tiled floor and balustrades, is original. You can't miss the steep yellow roofs of the **Belgian Concession** – now the *Zhengyi Hotel* – a little further on. Opposite it, the Gothic Revival **St Michael's Church** is worth a poke about if you find it open. In a concession to local taste, the pillars are painted red as in Chinese temples, and the statues of the saints are labelled in Chinese characters.

Wangfujing

Wangfujing Dajie is where the capital gets down to the business of **shopping** in earnest. The haunt of quality stores for over a century, it was called Morrison Street before the communist takeover. The western side of the street has plenty of department stores, small clothes shops and photo studios; the eastern side holds two giant malls.

The new **Oriental Plaza**, at the south end of the street, is the biggest mall in Asia, stretching east for nearly a kilometre. Among interminable clothes stores (fancy on ground level, affordable below) there's a good arty bookshop, the Oriental Arts Bookstore. Also here is the **Explorascience Exhibition**, a series of interactive displays at the plaza's western end (Mon–Fri

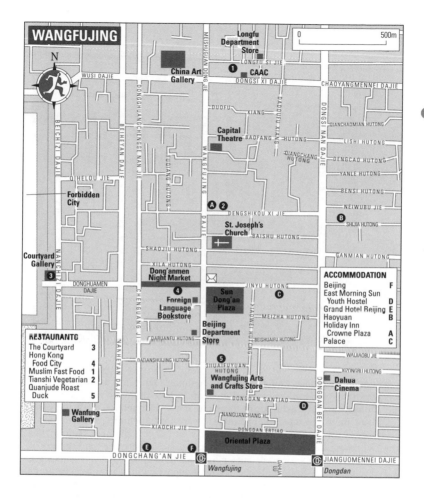

WANGFUJING

China Art Gallery

Longfu Department Store

CAAC

Capital Theatre

Forbidden City

St. Joseph's Church

Courtyard Gallery

Dong'anmen Night Market

Foreign Language Bookstore

Sun Dong'an Plaza

Beijing Department Store

Wangfujing Arts and Crafts Store

Dahua Cinema

Wanfung Gallery

Oriental Plaza

ACCOMMODATION
Beijing	F
East Morning Sun Youth Hostel	D
Grand Hotel Beijing	E
Haoyuan	B
Holiday Inn Crowne Plaza	A
Palace	C

RESTAURANTS
The Courtyard	3
Hong Kong Food City	4
Muslim Fast Food	1
Tianshi Vegetarian	2
Quanjude Roast Duck	5

9.30am–5.30pm, Sat & Sun 10am–7pm, closed second Mon & Tues of each month; ⓦwww.explorascience.com). For "shock the folks back home" food – scorpions and sparrows on skewers and the like – visit **Xiaochi Jie**, an alley leading west at the south end of the street. It's lined with small stalls run by Muslim Uigurs from northwest China, who compete fiercely, haranguing passers-by. As well as exotica, plenty of stalls do tasty bowls of noodles for a few yuan. Back on the main street, the store most frequented by visitors is the Foreign Language Bookstore at no. 235, the largest bookshop of its kind in China (see p.138). Opposite is the **Sun Dong'an Plaza**, another glitzy mall, convenient for a snack – the place is home to a food court and several fast-food chain restaurants – as well as a cinema, a games arcade and a paintballing court. The tacky dioramas of old city life in the basement are best avoided. Continue heading north up Wangfujing for 1km and you'll come to the **China Art Gallery**, a huge exhibition hall showcasing state-approved works (see p.133).

△ Chang'an Jie

A number of *hutongs* lead east from Wangfujing Dajie into a quiet area well away from the bustle of the main street. If you're here in the evening, don't miss the **Donghuamen Yeshi night market**, at the intersection of Wangfujing Dajie and Jinyu Hutong, where simple, cheap food, including many regional delicacies, is sold at the rows of stalls. At the end of Shuaifuyuan Hutong, the graceful medical college building is a former palace where the ten brothers of a Ming-dynasty emperor were once persuaded to live, so that he could keep a wary eye on them. Today, only the ornate flying eaves hint at its former function. Continuing east for about 300m through the *hutongs*, you'll reach Dongdan Bei Dajie, parallel to Wangfujing, which is rapidly rivalling it as a shopping area full of boutiques, mostly selling Western imports.

Jianguomen

Another cluster of lustrous buildings hoves into view around the Beijing Zhan subway stop, the most striking being the *International Hotel* on the north side of the street, which resembles a toy robot in all but scale. Opposite, just north of Beijing Zhan, the Henderson Centre is yet another glossy mall, which never achieved full occupancy and seemed to be closing down at the time of writing. On the north side of Chang'an Jie, the grand new **Chang'an Theatre** has nightly performances of Beijing opera (see p.127).

JIANGUOMEN DAJIE

RESTAURANTS, CAFÉS BARS & CLUBS

The Elephant	1
Lemongrass	7
Makye Ame	6
Mexican Wave	4
Pizza Hut	9
Rotary Sushi	10
Sammies	11
Starbucks	8
Sichuan Government	5
Subway	12
Phrik Thai	2
Xiheya Ju	3

ACCOMMODATION

International	C
International Youth Hostel	A
Jianguo	D
New Otani	E
St Regis	B

Jesuit missionaries began to arrive in China in the seventeenth century. Though they weren't allowed to preach freely at first, they were tolerated for their scientific and astronomical skills, and were invited to stay at court: precise astronomical calculations were invaluable to the emperor who, as master of the calendar, was charged with determining the cycle of the seasons in order to ensure good harvests, and observing the movement of celestial bodies to harmonize the divine and human order. Some Jesuits rose to high positions in the imperial court, and in 1692 they finally won the right to preach in China. The missionaries made little headway in spreading Catholicism, however, as a Vatican edict forced them to condemn all Chinese rites and rituals, such as sacrifices to ancestors, as anti-Christian.

Matteo Ricci (1552–1610) was the most illustrious of the early Jesuit missionaries to China. A keen Chinese scholar, he translated the Confucian analects into Portuguese and created the first system for romanizing Chinese characters. He began studying the Chinese language in 1582, when he arrived in Macau. In 1603 he moved to Beijing and won the respect of the local literati with his extensive knowledge of cartography, astronomy, mathematics and the physical sciences.

The **journals** Ricci kept offer a rare outsiders' view of the country at a time when China was closed to all but a select few foreign visitors. His eye is perceptive and his insights are acute. He compares European and Chinese civilizations thus: "They [the Chinese] are quite content with what they have . . . in this respect they are much different from the peoples of Europe who are frequently discontent with their own governments and covetous of what others enjoy. While the nations of the West seem to be entirely consumed with supreme domination, they cannot even preserve what their ancestors have bequeathed them, as the Chinese have done through a period of some thousands of years."

The Ancient Observatory

Beside the concrete knot that is the intersection between Jianguomennei Dajie and the second ring road, the **Ancient Observatory** (Wed–Sun 9–11.30am; 1–4.30pm; ¥15), an unexpected survivor marooned amid the high-rises, comes as a delightful surprise. The first observatory on the site was founded on the orders of Kublai Khan, the astronomers commissioned to reform the inaccurate calendar then in use. Subsequently the observatory was staffed by Muslim scientists, as medieval Islamic science enjoyed pre-eminence, but, strangely, in the early seventeenth century it was placed in the hands of Jesuit missionaries, a small group of whom arrived in Beijing in 1601. Led by one Matteo Ricci (see box above), they proceeded to astonish the emperor and his subjects by making a series of precise astronomical forecasts. The Jesuits re-equipped the observatory and remained in charge through to the 1830s.

Today the squat, unadorned building is empty, and visitors aren't allowed inside. The best features of the complex are, however, accessible: its garden, a placid retreat; and the eight Ming-dynasty **astronomical instruments** sitting on the roof – stunningly sculptural armillary spheres, theodolites and the like, all beautifully ornamented with entwined dragons, lions and clouds. The small museum attached, displaying pottery decorated with star maps, as well as navigational equipment dating from the Yuan dynasty onwards, is a bonus.

Jianguomenwai Dajie

Beyond the observatory and the second ring road, the **International Club** is the first sign that you're approaching the capital's diplomatic sector. A restrained building, it's dwarfed by the multistorey monolith of the CITIC building just to the east. Turn left at the International Club up Ritan Lu and you'll come to the **Jianguomenwai diplomatic compound**, the first of two embassy complexes (the other is at Sanlitun, well northeast of here). It's an odd place, a giant toy-town with neat buildings in ordered courtyards and frozen sentries on plinths.

Ritan Park is just one block north from the International Club, a five-minute walk from Jianguomen Dajie. The park was one of the imperial city's original four, one for each cardinal direction; Tiantan (to the south; see p.60), Ditan (north) and Yuetan (west) were the others. Each park was the location for a yearly sacrificial ritual performed by the emperor. Today, Ritan Park is popular with embassy staff and courting couples, who make use of its numerous secluded nooks. The place has been much renovated of late, and is now very attractive, with paths winding between groves of cherry trees, rockeries and ponds. A road leading west from the park, **Yabao Lu**, is home to stalls and markets which sell cheap clothes and fashion accessories, mostly designer fakes aimed at Russians.

Back on Jianguomenwai Dajie, beyond the CITIC building, you reach the Friendship Store (see p.135). On the south side of the street, the CVIK Plaza (daily 9am–9pm) is a more modern shopping centre with five floors of clothes and accessories.

The main reason to continue beyond here is to head for the **Silk Market** just north of Yong'an Li subway stop, where there are some bargains to be had among the stacks of inexpensive clothes on sale. From here, it's a dull couple of kilometres to the **World Trade Centre** just before the intersection with the third ring road. Dedicated consumers who make it here are rewarded with Beijing's most exclusive mall, boasting four gleaming storeys of pricey goods, as well as a basement skating rink.

Chaoyangmenwai Dajie and Sanlitun

North of Jianguomenwai Dajie, the **Dongyue Temple** (Tues–Sun 8am–5pm; ¥10, a short walk from Ritan Park or Chaoyangmen subway stop, is an intriguing place, in pointed contrast to all the shrines to materialism outside. Dating back to the Ming dynasty, it's recently been restored, and today the large, very new-looking complex is busy with devotees. Pass under the Zhandaimen archway – originally constructed in 1322 – and you enter a courtyard holding around thirty annexes, each of which deals with a different aspect of Taoist life, the whole making up a sort of surreal spiritual bureaucracy. There's the "Department of Suppressing Schemes", "Department of Wandering Ghosts", even a "Department for Fifteen Kinds of Violent Death". In each, a statue of Taoist deity Lao Zi holds court over weird, brightly painted figures which wouldn't look out of place in *Dr Who*. The temple shop sells red tablets which worshippers sign and leave outside the annexes as petitions to the spiritual officials. Departments dealing with longevity and wealth are unsurprisingly popular, but so, tellingly, is the "Department for Official Morality".

It's not too far north of here to **Sanlitun**, the city's largest bar district (see p.122 for more). By night it's raucous and gaudy, but during the day oddly civilized, and the many small cafes and restaurants are good for people-watching. As well as drinking, there are plenty of opportunities to eat well and shop here.

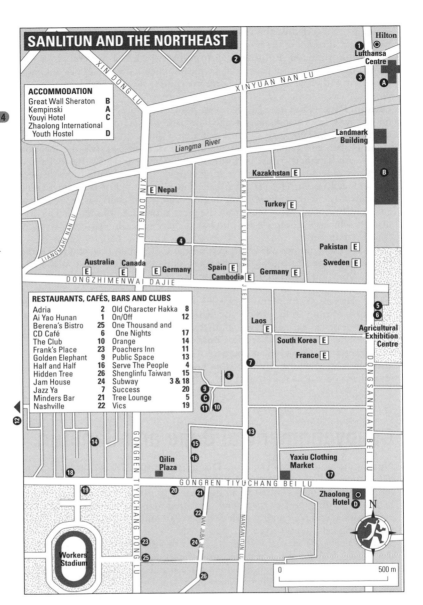

SANLITUN AND THE NORTHEAST

Hilton
Lutthansa
Centre

ACCOMMODATION
Great Wall Sheraton **B**
Kempinski **A**
Youyi Hotel **C**
Zhaolong International
Youth Hostel **D**

XIN DONG LU

XINYUAN NAN LU

Liangma River

LIANGMAHE NAN LU

Landmark
Building

Kazakhstan **E**

Turkey **E**

E Nepal

XIN DONG LU

SANLITUN LU LUBA

Pakistan **E**

Sweden **E**

Australia Canada
E **E** **E** Germany

Spain **E**
Cambodia **E**

Germany **E**

DONGZHIMENWAI DAJIE

RESTAURANTS, CAFÉS, BARS AND CLUBS

Adria	2	Old Character Hakka	8
Ai Yao Hunan	1	On/Off	12
Berena's Bistro	25	One Thousand and	
CD Café	6	One Nights	17
The Club	10	Orange	14
Frank's Place	23	Poachers Inn	11
Golden Elephant	9	Public Space	13
Half and Half	16	Serve The People	4
Hidden Tree	26	Shenglinfu Taiwan	15
Jam House	24	Subway	3 & 18
Jazz Ya	7	Success	20
Minders Bar	21	Tree Lounge	5
Nashville	22	Vics	19

Laos **E**

South Korea **E**

France **E**

Agricultural
Exhibition
Centre

DONGSANHUAN BEI LU

Yaxiu Clothing
Market

Qilin
Plaza

GONGREN TIYUCHANG BEI LU

GONGREN TIYUCHANG DONG LU

NAN JIU JIE

NANSANLITUN LU

Zhaolong
Hotel **D**

N

Workers'
Stadium

0   500 m

EAST OF THE CENTRE | Chaoyangmenwai Dajie and Sanlitun

4

80

North of the centre

The area north of the Forbidden City has a good collection of sights you could happily spend a few days exploring. Just outside the Forbidden City are **Beihai and Jingshan parks**, two of the finest in China; north of here, the area around the Shicha Lakes is fast attaining a left-bank feel as laid-back bars and cafés open along the lakesides. Around the lakes you'll find Beijing's best-preserved **hutongs**, once the home of princes, dukes and monks. The alleys are a labyrinth, with something of interest around every corner; some regard them as the last outpost of a genuinely Chinese Beijing. Buried deep within them is **Prince Gong's Palace**, with the **Bell and Drum towers**, once used to mark dawn and dusk, standing on the eastern edge of the district.

Three subway stops east of here, a Tibetan lamasery, the **Yonghe Gong**, is one of Beijing's most colourful (and popular) attractions. While you're in the vicinity, don't miss the peaceful, and unjustly ignored, **Confucius Temple** and the quiet **Ditan Park**, all within easy walking distance of one another. If you head west instead, you'll finds a number of good little **museums** – the homes of two twentieth-century cultural icons, **Lu Xun** and **Xu Beihong**, now hold exhibitions of their works, and the **Baita Si** functions as a museum of religious relics as well as a place of pilgrimage.

Baita Si	白塔寺	*báitǎ sì*
Beihai Park	北海公园	*běihǎi gōngyuán*
Beijing aquarium	北京海洋馆	*běijīng hǎiyángguǎn*
Bell Tower	钟楼	*zhōnglóu*
Confucius Temple	孔庙	*kǒngmiào*
Ditan Park	地坛公园	*dìtán gōngyuán*
Drum Tower	鼓楼	*gǔlóu*
Exhibition Centre	展览馆	*zhǎnlǎn guǎn*
Guangji Si	广济寺	*guǎngjì sì*
Houhai	后海	*hòuhǎi*
Jingshan Park	景山公园	*jǐngshān gōngyuán*
Lu Xun Museum	鲁迅博物馆	*lǔxùn bówùguǎn*
Prince Gong's Palace	恭王府	*gōngwáng fǔ*
Qianhai	前海	*qiánhǎi*
Song Qingling's residence	宋庆龄故居	*sòngqìnglíng gùjū*
Wanshou Si	万寿寺	*wànshòu sì*
Wuta Si	五塔寺	*wǔtǎ sì*
Xu Beihong Museum	徐悲鸿纪念馆	*xúbēihóng jìniànguǎn*
Yonghe Gong	雍和宫	*yōnghé gōng*
Zizhuyuan Park	紫竹院公园	*zǐzhúyuàn gōngyuán*
Zoo	北京动物园	*běijīng dòngwùyuán*

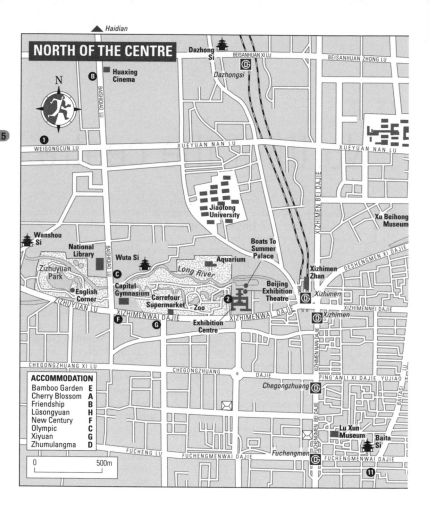

▲ Haidian

NORTH OF THE CENTRE

Dazhong Si

BEISANHUAN XI LU

BEISANHUAN ZHONG LU

B Huaxing Cinema

Dazhongsi

N

1

WEIGONGCUN LU

BAISHIQIAO LU

XUEYUAN NAN LU

XUEYUAN NAN LU

XIZHIMEN BEI DAJIE

Jiaotong University

Xu Beihong Museum

Wanshou Si

National Library

Wuta Si

Boats To Summer Palace

Aquarium

Zizhuyuan Park

Long River

Xizhimen Zhan

DESHENGMEN XI DAJIE

English Corner

Capital Gymnasium

Carrefour Supermarket

Beijing Exhibition Theatre

Xizhimen

ZIZHUYUAN LU

F

G

XIZHIMENWAI DAJIE

Zoo

XIZHIMENWAI DAJIE

2

XIZHIMENNEI DAJIE

Xizhimen

Exhibition Centre

XIZHIMEN NAN DAJIE

CHEGONGZHUANG XI LU

CHEGONGZHUANG

DAJIE

PING'ANLI XI DAJIE YUJIAO H

Chegongzhuang

FUCHENGMEN BEI DAJIE

Lu Xun Museum

Baita Si

FUCHENG LU

FUCHENGMENWAI DAJIE

Fuchengmen

FUCHENGMENWAI DAJIE

11

ACCOMMODATION

Bamboo Garden	E
Cherry Blossom	A
Friendship	B
Lüsongyuan	H
New Century	F
Olympic	C
Xiyuan	G
Zhumulangma	D

0   500m

Northwest of here, around the transport hub of Xizhimen and easy to reach on the subway, are a couple of architectural oddities – the new **Exhibition Centre** and the old **Wuta Si** – plus the **zoo** and a good museum, the **Wanshou Si**, housed in a grand temple complex.

Jingshan and Beihai parks

Jingshan Park (daily 6am–9pm; ¥3) is a natural way to round off a trip to the Forbidden City, as most visitors exit from the north gate, just across the road from the park. Otherwise you can get here on bus #101 from Fuchengmen or Chaoyangmen subway stops. An artificial mound, the park was the byproduct of the digging of the palace moat, and served as both a windbreak and a barrier to keep malevolent spirits (believed to emanate from the north) from

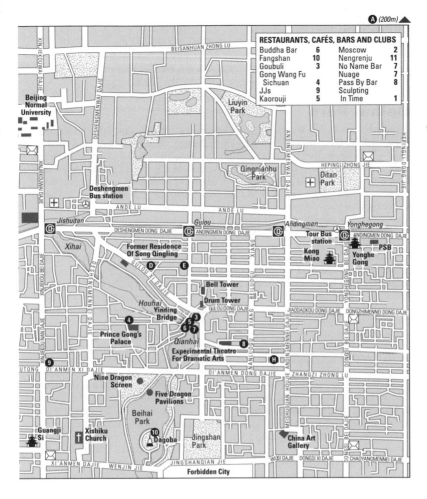

RESTAURANTS, CAFÉS, BARS AND CLUBS

Buddha Bar	6	Moscow	2
Fangshan	10	Nengrenju	11
Goubuli	3	No Name Bar	7
Gong Wang Fu		Nuage	7
Sichuan	4	Pass By Bar	8
JJs	9	Sculpting	
Kaorouji	5	In Time	1

entering the imperial quarter of the city. Its history, most momentously, includes the suicide in 1644 of the last Ming emperor, Chong Zhen, who hanged himself here from a locust tree after rebel troops broke into the imperial palace. The spot, on the eastern side of the park, is easy to find as English-language signs for it appear everywhere (beneath those pointing the way to a children's playground), though the tree that stands here is not the original. Though he was a dissolute opium fiend, the suicide note pinned to his lapel was surprisingly noble:

> **My own insufficient virtue and wretched nature has caused me to sin against heaven above. I die knowing I am wholly unworthy to stand before my sacred ancestors . . . let the rebels tear my miserable body to pieces but let them touch not a single hair on the head of the least of my subjects.**

Afterwards, the tree was judged an accessory to the emperor's death and as punishment was manacled with an iron chain.

It's the **views** from the top of the hill that make this park such a compelling target. They take in the whole extent of the Forbidden City – affording a revealing perspective – and a fair swath of the city outside, a deal more attractive than seen from ground level. To the west is a lake, Beihai; to the north the Drum and Bell towers; and to the northeast the Yonghe Gong.

Beihai Park

Almost half of Beihai Park (daily 6am–8pm, park buildings till 4pm; ¥5 for the park, ¥10 for the park and entry to all buildings) only a few hundred metres west of Jingshan Park, is lake, and it's a favourite skating spot in winter. Supposedly created by Kublai Khan, long before any of the Forbidden City structures were conceived, the park is on a suitably ambitious scale: the lake was man-made, the island in its midst created with the excavated earth. Qing Emperor Qianlong oversaw its landscaping into a classical Chinese garden in the eighteenth century. Most of the buildings here lie on the island, its hill crowned by a white dagoba, a suitable emblem for a park which contains a curious mixture of religious constructions, storehouses for cultural relics and imperial garden architecture. Today its elegance is marred by funfairs and souvenir shops among the willows and red-columned galleries (though *KFC* was ordered to close its branch here for lowering the tone); still, it's a grand place to retreat from the city and recharge. Bus #101 passes Beihai Park's south gate en route between Fuchengmen and Chaoyangmen subway stops, while you can get to the park's north gate on bus #13 from Yonghe Gong subway stop.

Just inside the main gate, which lies on the park's southern side, the **Round**, an enclosure of buildings behind a circular wall, has at its centre a courtyard which holds a large jade bowl, said to have belonged to Kublai Khan. The white-jade Buddha in the hall behind was a present from Burmese Buddhists. From here, a walkway provides access to the island, dotted with religious architecture – which you'll come across as you scramble around the rocky paths – including the **Yuegu Lou**, a hall full of steles (stone slabs carved with Chinese characters); and to the giant **dagoba** sitting on top, built in the mid-seventeenth century to celebrate a visit by the Dalai Lama. Nestling inside is a shrine to the demon-headed, multi-armed Lamaist deity, Yamantaka. An exclusive restaurant, the *Fangshan* (see p.120), where the decor and the food are imperial, sits off a painted corridor running round the base of the hill. The island has a pier where you can rent a rowing boat or duck-shaped pedal boats for ¥10 an hour – also available from a pier near the south gate (same price).

On the north side of the lake stands the impressive **dragon screen**, its purpose to ward off evil spirits. An ornate wall of glazed tiles, depicting nine stylized, sinuous dragons in relief, it's one of China's largest, at 27m in length, and remains in good condition. Nearby are the five **Dragon Pavilions**, supposedly in the shape of a dragon's spine. It's easy to see why the gardens and rockeries over on the other side of the lake were popular with Qianlong: the atmosphere remains tranquil even when the place is crowded at weekends. The park's north exit brings you out at the south end of the Shicha lakes.

Around the Shicha lakes

The area north of Beihai Park has been subject to very little modernization, and the street plan here remains a tangle of narrow **hutongs**. These cluttered, grey alleyways show Beijing's other, private, face: here you'll see poky courtyards and converted palaces, and come across small open spaces where old men sit with caged pet birds. The network of *hutongs* centres on the two artificial **Shicha lakes**, Qianhai and Houhai. Created during the Yuan dynasty, they were once the terminus for a canal network that served the capital. Two giant old buildings, the Bell and Drum towers, are half hidden away to the east of the area.

The best way to get around the area is by bike. Traffic within the hutongs is light, and you're free to dive into any alley you fancy, though you're almost certain to get lost – in which case cycle around until you come to the lake. You could walk here from Jishuitian or Gulou subway stop, though the best point of entry is opposite the northern entrance to Beihai Park – to get here by bus, take trolleybus #111 from Dongdan Bei Dajie, or bus #13 from the Yonghe Gong.

In response to the appeal of this area, regular **hutong tours** leave from 200m west of the north entrance to Beihai Park (daily at 9am & 2pm, May–Oct also 7pm; ¥180; ☎010/66159097, ⓦwww.hutongtour.com for more information and booking). More imaginative than most tours (visitors are biked about in rickshaws), it's very popular with tour groups. Beware hustlers offering the same

Courtyard houses

Beijing's *hutongs* are lined with *siheyuans*, single-storey **courtyard houses** that are home to about a fifth of the city's population. These traditional Chinese dwellings follow a plan that has hardly changed since the Han dynasty, in essence identical to that of the Forbidden City.

A typical courtyard house has its entrance in the south wall. Just outside the front door stand two flat stone blocks, sometimes carved into lions, for mounting horses and to demonstrate the family's wealth and status. Step over the threshold and you are confronted with a freestanding wall; this is to keep out evil spirits, which can only travel in straight lines. Behind it is the outer courtyard, with the servants' quarters to right and left. The entrance to the inner courtyard, where the family lived, would be in the north wall. The most important rooms, used by the elders, are those at the back, facing south.

With the government anxious to turn Beijing into a showcase for Chinese modernity, however, it seems unlikely that many of these houses will survive, and there are only around 300,000 courtyard houses left. Most are in the working-class district of Qianmen, where each holds several families. A wander around the *hutongs* here shows the houses in their worst light; the dwellings are cramped and poorly maintained, the streets dirty, the plumbing and sanitation inadequate; it's surely only a matter of time before their inhabitants are rehoused in the new suburbs. But in the *hutongs* you'll also see how the system creates a neighbourliness absent from the new high-rises – here, you can't help knowing everyone else's business.

City planners have responded to increasingly vocal complaints about the destruction of Beijing's architectural heritage by pointing out that *hutongs* full of courtyard houses are unsuitable for contemporary living: besides the difficulty of providing them with proper plumbing, the houses are very cold in winter, and with only one storey they're an inefficient use of land. Anyway, they argue, the population of a modern city ought to live outside the centre. Ironically though, the area around the Shicha lakes, where most of the city's other remaining courtyard houses are to be found, has become a fashionable area for high-ranking cadres to live. The majority of the houses here are in much better condition than in Qianmen, and many are earmarked for protection. And recently a number of new luxury housing estates have been built in courtyard-house style – the best examples are around Deshengmen in the north of the city. They're very popular with foreigners.

tours – the official rickshaws have "Beijing Hutong Tourist Agency" written on them.

Qianhai and Houhai

Just north of Beihai Park and across Di'anmen Xi Dajie is the pretty lake, **Qianhai**. It has been dredged and cleaned up recently, and the lakeside is rapidly becoming rather fashionable, thanks to the bars and restaurants clustered around it. Certainly it's an appealing place, removed from the traffic and with an easygoing feel. Look out for the hardy folk who swim here every day, all year round, cutting a hole in the ice in winter. You can hire pleasure boats from a jetty on the western bank (¥10/hr). Head north around either side of the lake and you'll come to the cute humpback **Yinding Bridge** spanning the narrowest point and marking the divide between Qianhai and **Houhai**. From the top of its hump you can see the western hills on (very rare) clear days. This is a great place to sit outside over a coffee at one of the bars (see p.124) and enjoy the scenery, something that can't be said about too many public places in Beijing. There's also a famous restaurant just north of the bridge, the *Kaorouji* (see p.120), that's been here for centuries.

Prince Gong's Palace

The best-kept courtyard house in the city, this mansion on Liuyun Jie (daily 8.30am–5pm; ¥5) was once the residence of Prince Gong, who was the brother of Emperor Xianfeng and father of the last Qing emperor, Pu Yi. Its nine courtyards, joined by covered walkways, have been restored to something like their former elegance, and the landscaped gardens are attractively leafy. The largest hall now hosts performances of **Beijing opera**, at around 11am and 4pm (for tour groups), and also at 7.30pm. Just north of the exit lies the excellent *Sichuan Restaurant* (see p.120).

You can get to Prince Gong's palace from Beihai Park by following the curving alley north that starts opposite the park's north entrance – Qianhai will be on the right as you walk along – then taking the first left onto Qianhai Xi Jie. Follow this as it curves round, until you reach an intersection with the music conservatory on your right; here you turn right into Liuyun Jie. There are plenty of other old palaces in the area, as this was once something of an imperial pleasure ground and home to a number of high officials and distinguished eunuchs. Head north up Liuyin Jie and you pass the former **Palace of Tao Beile**, now a school, after about 200m. It's one of a number of converted buildings in the area, some of which are identified by plaques.

Song Qingling's residence

On the northern shore of Houhai, Song Qingling's former residence at no. 46 Houhai Beiyan (Tues–Sun 9am–4.30pm; ¥10) is another Qing mansion, with a pleasant, spacious garden. The wife of Sun Yatsen, who was leader of the short-lived republic which followed the collapse of imperial China (see p.176), Song commands great respect in China, and the exhibition inside details her busy life in a dry, admiring tone. More interesting is the opportunity to see the interior of a Chinese mansion from the beginning of the twentieth century – all the furnishings are as they were when she died, and her personal effects, including effects such as letters and cutlery, are on display. It's not much of a diversion from here to head west to the Xu Beihong museum (see opposite), about 1km from Deshengmennei Dajie.

The Drum and Bell towers

The formidable two-storey **Gulou** (Drum Tower; daily 9am–4.30pm; ¥10), a squat, fifteenth-century Ming creation, sits at the eastern end of Gulou Xi Dajie, about 1km southeast of the Song Qingling residence. The drums were banged to mark the hours of the day (every Chinese city had a similar tower) and to call imperial officials to meetings. Every half-hour between 10am and noon and from 2pm to 4pm a troupe of drummers in traditional costume whack cheerfully away at the giant drums inside. They're not, to be blunt, terribly artful, but it's still an impressive sight.

The building's twin, the **Zhonglou** (Bell Tower; same times and prices), at the other end of the small plaza, was originally Ming. Destroyed by fire and rebuilt in the eighteenth century, it still has its original iron bell which, until 1924, was rung every evening at 7pm to give an indication of the time.

It's easy to reach the lakes from the towers: take the first *hutong* you see on the right as you walk south along Di'anmenwai Dajie from the Drum Tower, then turn left for Yinding Bridge.

Xu Beihong Museum

Just outside the quarter of *hutongs*, but easily combined with a visit to the Shicha lakes, the **Xu Beihong Museum** at 53 Xinjiekou Bei Dajie (Tues–Sun 9–11am & 1.30–4.30pm; ¥1) is worth the diversion and not hard to get to – it's 500m south of the Jishuitan subway stop. The son of a wandering portraitist, Xu Beihong (1895–1953) did for Chinese art what his contemporary Lu Xun did for literature. Xu had to look after his entire family from the age of 17 after his father died, and spent much of his early life labouring in semi-destitution and obscurity before receiving the acclaim he deserved. His extraordinary facility is well in evidence here in seven halls which display a huge collection of his works. These include many of the ink paintings of horses, for which he was most famous, and also oil paintings in a Western style, which he produced while studying in France (and which are now regarded as his weakest works); the large-scale allegorical images also on display allude to events in China at the time. However, the pictures it is easiest to respond to are his delightful sketches and studies, in ink and pencil, often of his son.

Yonghe Gong and around

Though it is a little touristy, **Yonghe Gong** is well worth a visit (daily 9am–4pm; ¥25) – you won't see many bolder or brasher temples than this, built towards the end of the seventeenth century as the residence of Prince Yin Zhen. In 1723, when the prince became Emperor Yong Zheng and moved into the Forbidden City, the temple was retiled in imperial yellow and restricted thereafter to religious use. It became a lamasery in 1744, housing monks from Tibet and Inner Mongolia. The temple even had a presiding role over the latter territory, supervising the election of the Mongolian Living Buddha (the spiritual head of Mongolian Lamaism), who was chosen by drawing lots out of a gold urn. After the civil war in 1949, Yonghe Gong was declared a national monument and closed for the following thirty years. Remarkably, it escaped the ravages of the Cultural Revolution (see p.178), when most of the city's religious structures were destroyed or turned into factories and warehouses.

The temple couldn't be easier to reach, as the Yonghe Gong subway stop is right next to it. There are five main **prayer halls**, arranged in a line from south to north, and numerous side buildings housing bodhisattva statues and paintings, where monks study scripture, astronomy and medicine. Visitors are free to wander through the prayer halls and pretty, ornamental gardens, the experience largely an aesthetic rather than a spiritual one nowadays. As well as the amazing mandalas hanging in side halls, the temple contains some notable statuary. The statues in the third hall, the **Pavilion of Eternal Happiness**, are nandikesvras, representations of Buddha having sex. Once used to educate emperor's sons, the statues are now completely covered by drapes. The chamber behind, the **Hall of the Wheel of Law**, has a gilded bronze statue of the founder of the Yellow Hats (the largest sect within Tibetan Buddhism) and paintings which depict his life, while the thrones next to it are for the Dalai Lama (each holder of the post used to come here to teach). In the last, grandest hall, the **Wanfu Pavilion**, stands an eighteen-metre-high statue of the Maitreya Buddha, the world's largest carving made from a single piece of wood – in this case, the trunk of a Tibetan sandalwood tree. Gazing serenely out, the giant reddish-orange figure looms over you; details, such as his jewellery and the foliage fringing his shoulders, are beautifully carved. It took three years for the statue, a gift to Emperor Qianlong from the seventh Dalai Lama, to complete its passage to Beijing.

The lamasery also functions as an active Tibetan Buddhist centre. It's used basically for propaganda purposes, to show that China is guaranteeing and respecting the religious freedom of minorities. Nonetheless, it's questionable how genuine the monks you see wandering around are; at best, they're state-approved. After all, this was where the Chinese state's choice for Panchen Lama – the Tibetan spiritual leader, second only to the Dalai Lama in rank – was officially sworn in, in 1995. Just prior to that, the Dalai Lama's own choice for the post, the then 6-year-old Gedhum Choekyi Nyima, had "disappeared" – he remains the youngest political prisoner in the world.

If the temple leaves you hungry for more things Tibetan, visit the *Makye Ame* restaurant (see p.117).

Confucius Temple

On the west side of Yonghegong Dajie, opposite the alley by which you enter Yonghe Gong, is a quiet *hutong* lined with shops selling incense, images and tapes of religious music. Down the alley and on the right, on Guozijian Dajie, the **Confucius Temple** (daily 8.30am–5pm; ¥10) is as restrained as the Yonghe Gong is gaudy. Perhaps the best thing to do here is sit on a bench in the peaceful courtyard among the ancient, twisted trees, and enjoy the silence, but there are also plenty of artefacts to seek out.

In the front courtyard, rows of **steles** record the names of those who studied here and passed the civil-service exams. The most recent steles – the ones furthest from the gate – are from the Qing dynasty, paid for by the scholars themselves as the emperor had refused to fund them. The dark, haphazard main hall is the **museum**, holding incense burners and musical instruments that the souvenir vendors will play on the slightest pretext. Another, new museum in the side hall to the north holds a diverse range of objects – the Tang pottery, which includes images of pointy-faced foreigners, is the most diverting. At the back, a warehouse-like building holds stele texts of the thirteen Confucian classics, calligraphy which once represented the standard to be emulated by all scholars.

Confucius

Confucius was born in 552 BC into a declining aristocratic family in an age of petty kingdoms where life was blighted by constant war and feuding. An itinerant scholar, he observed that life would be much improved if people behaved decently, and he wandered from court to court teaching adherence to a set of moral and social values designed to bring the citizens and the government together in harmony. Ritual and propriety were the system's central values, and great store was placed on the five **"Confucian virtues"**: benevolence, righteousness, propriety, wisdom and trustworthiness. An arch-traditionalist, he believed that society required strict hierarchies and total obedience: a son should obey his father, a wife her husband, and a subject his ruler.

Nobody paid Confucius much attention during his lifetime, and he died in obscurity. But during the Han dynasty, six hundred years after, Confucianism became institutionalized, underscoring a hierarchical system of administration which prevailed for the following two thousand years. Seeing that its precepts sat well with a feudal society, rulers turned Confucianism into the state religion, and Confucius became worshipped as a deity. Subsequently, officials were appointed on the basis of their knowledge of the Confucian texts, which they studied for half their lives.

The great sage only fell from official favour in the twentieth century with the rise of the egalitarian communists, and today there are no functioning Confucian temples left in China. Ironically, those temples that have become museums or libraries have returned to a vision of the importance of learning, which is perhaps closer to the heart of the Confucian system than ritual and worship.

Ditan Park

Just 100m north of Yonghe Gong is **Ditan Park** (daily 6am–9pm; ¥1), the northern member in the imperial city's original quartet of four parks (see p.79). As befits the park's name, this was where the emperor once performed sacrifices to the earth god (dì means "ground" or "earth"). The altar for these was the huge, tiered stone platform in the park's northwest corner. A small museum (¥5) next to it holds the emperor's sedan chair – covered, of course, so that no commoner could glimpse the divine presence on his journey here. Wandering among the trees is probably the most diverting way to spend time here, though; at weekends the place is busy with pensioners playing croquet, kids fishing for plastic toys in ponds and tai ji practitioners hugging trees. The park is at its liveliest during Chinese New Year, when it hosts a temple fair.

Around Fuchengmennei Dajie

East of Fuchengmen subway stop, **Fuchengmennei Dajie** is rather a pleasant street, treelined and with a diverse range of shops, and a few sights all within walking distance of each other. Accessed through an alley off Fuchengmennei Dajie, the massive white dagoba of the **Baita Si** (daily 9am–5pm; ¥10) is visible from afar, rising over the rooftops of the labyrinth of hutongs that surround it. Shaped like an upturned bowl with an inverted ice-cream cone on top, the 35-metre-high dagoba, designed by a Nepalese architect, was built in the Yuan dynasty. It's a popular spot with Buddhist pilgrims, who ritually circle it clockwise. The temple is worth a visit simply for the collection of thousands of small

△ The Confucius Temple

statues of Buddha – mostly Tibetan – housed in one of its halls, very impressive en masse. Another hall holds a collection comprising bronze *luohans* (Buddha's original group of disciples), including one with a beak; small bronze Buddhas; and other, weirder, Lamaist figures. The silk and velvet priestly garments on display here were unearthed from under the dagoba in 1978. A shop beside it sells religious curios, such as Buddha images printed on dried leaves.

About 250m east of here, on the north side of Fuchengmennei Dajie, is a temple that's been converted into a school – the spirit wall now forms one side of a public lavatory. It's a sad reminder of how temples were (mis)treated in Beijing, before the government realized they were a useful tourist resource. Nearby, at no. 133 you'll come across China's first sex shop, the Adam and Eve Health Store (now one of many), which opened in the 1990s and has separate entrances for men and women.

Nearly a kilometre east along Fuchengmennei Dajie is the **Guangji Si** (free admission), headquarters of China's Buddhist Association and a working Buddhist temple with an important collection of painting and sculpture. Visitors are free to look around, though only academics with a specialist interest in the art are normally allowed to see the collection. If you're in the area around meal time, seek out the excellent *Nengrenju* hotpot restaurant (see p.120).

Lu Xun Museum

Just east of the giant Fuchengmen Bei Dajie intersection, Xisantiao Hutong leads north off Fuchengmennei Dajie to the **Lu Xun Museum** (Tues–Sun 9am–4pm; ¥10). A large and extensively renovated courtyard house, this was where Lu Xun (1881–1936), widely accepted as the greatest Chinese writer of the modern era, once lived. He gave up a promising career in medicine to write books with the aim, so he declared, of curing social ills with his pithy, satirical stories. One of the most appealing and accessible of his tales is *The True Story of Ah Q*, a lively tragicomedy written in the plain style he favoured as an alternative to the complex classical language of the time. Set in 1911, during the inception of the ill-fated republic, it tells the life story of a worthless peasant, Ah Q, who stumbles from disaster to disaster, believing each outcome to be a triumph. He epitomized every character flaw of the Chinese race, as seen by his creator; Ah Q dreams of revolution and ends up being executed, having understood nothing.

Someone who abhorred pomp, Lu Xun might feel a little uneasy in his house now, now almost a shrine. His possessions have been preserved here like treasured relics, giving a good idea of what Chinese interiors looked like at the beginning of the twentieth century, and there's a photo exhibition on his life lauding his achievements. Unfortunately there are no English captions, though a bookshop on the west side of the compound sells English translations of his work.

The zoo and around

The area around **Xizhimen** is one of the city's transport hubs, and you're likely to pass through it on your way to the Summer Palaces or Haidian. If you head west from Xizhimen subway stop (buses #107 and #904, among others, pass by en route to Zizhuyuan Park), over the gargantuan traffic intersection, the first place of interest you come to on Xizhimenwai Dajie is the **Exhibition Centre**, easily distinguishable by its slim, star-topped spire. It's certainly worth inspection, and will stir anyone with a sense of historical irony. Built by the Russians in 1954, it's by far the city's best overtly communist construction, a work of grandiose Socialist Realism with great details, including heroic workers atop columns carved with acorns. Now the place is badly maintained – the electric chandeliers are unlit and the escalators flanking the grand staircases lie still – and is used, in thoughtless affront, for the most banal forms of capitalism: the arches of the colonnade outside are hung with billboards and its twelve magnificent, cavernous halls host tacky clothes markets. The road on the east side leads to the dock for boats to the Summer Palace (see p.97). Head up the alley on the west side and you'll come to the city's first Western restaurant, the *Moscow* (see p.120) – check out the crazy decor – more socialist grandiosity – if you're just passing.

Next along Xizhimenwai Dajie, the **zoo** (daily 7.30am–5.30pm; winter ¥15, summer ¥10), is worth visiting only for the panda house (¥5). Here you can join the queues to have your photo taken sitting astride a plastic replica of the creature, then push your way through to glimpse the living variety – kept in relatively palatial quarters and familiar through the much-publicized export of the animals to overseas zoos for mating purposes. While the pandas lie on their backs in their luxury pad, waving their legs in the air, other animals, less cute or less endangered, slink, pace or flap around their miserable cells. However, the new **Beijing Aquarium** (adults ¥100, kids ¥50, children under 1.2m free; Ⓦwww.bj-sea.com) in the northwest corner of the compound, is surprisingly good. As well as thousands of varieties of fish, including sharks, it has a dolphin show every day at 10am and 2.30 pm.

Past the zoo, head north up Baishiqiao Lu, take the first right and follow the canal, and ten minutes' walk will bring you to the **Wuta Si** (daily 9am–4.30pm; ¥10). If you've started to think that all old Chinese buildings look the same, the central hall here will come as a shock. Completed in 1424, it's a stone cube decorated on the outside with reliefs of animals, Sanskrit characters, and Buddha images – each has a different hand gesture – and topped with five layered, triangular spires. It's obviously Indian in influence, and it is said to be based on a temple in Bodhgaya, where Buddha gained enlightenment. You can enter and climb the 87 steps to the top (¥5), where you can inspect the spire carvings – including elephants and Buddhas, and, at the centre of the central spire, a pair of feet. The new halls behind the museum are home to statues of bulbous-eyed camels, docile-looking tigers, puppy-dog lions and the like, all rescued from spirit ways, tombs and long-destroyed temples. Outside is a line of seventeenth-century tombstones of Jesuit priests done in traditional Chinese style, with a turtle-like dragon at the base and text in Chinese and Latin.

From here it's a half-hour stroll following the river west back to Baishiqiao Lu, through the bamboo groves of **Zizhuyuan Park**, and out of the park's northwest exit to the **Wanshou Si** (days 9am–4.30pm; ¥10). This Ming temple, a favourite of Cixi's, was closed for intensive restoration at the time of writing, but should be open by the time you read this. It is to become a museum of ancient art, with exhibitions of jade seals, bronze statuary, ceramics, ivory figurines and the like, and should be worth a look.

The far northwest

I n the northwest corner of the city are a cluster of attractions, which improve the further out you go. The **Dazhong Si** (Great Bell Temple) and the pretty campus of **Beijing University** are worth a visit on the way to or from more alluring destinations, and the nearby districts of **Haidian** and **Zhongguancun** are known for hi-tech shopping and youth culture.

Though it is rather eclipsed by its newer neighbour, the old summer palace, **Yuanmingyuan**, is worth checking out all the same for the sobering history to which it attests. Nearby **Yiheyuan**, usually known in English as *the* **Summer Palace**, is an excellent place to get away from the smog of the city, its grounds large enough to have an almost rural feel. One of the loveliest spots in Beijing, it's now a vast public park, two thirds of which is taken up by Kunming Lake. During the hottest months of the year, the latter-day imperial court would decamp to this perfect location, the site surrounded by hills, cooled by the lake and sheltered by judicious use of garden landscaping. From here, it's not long by bus to Xiang Shan, the Botanical Gardens and other targets for excursions to the west of Beijing – see pp.152–154.

Dazhong Si

The **Dazhong Si** (Great Bell Temple; Tues–Sun 8am–4.30pm; ¥5) derives its name from the enormous bell hanging in the back; the other halls now house one of Beijing's most interesting little museums, showcasing several hundred bronze bells from temples all over the country. It's stuck out on Beisanhuan Lu, the north section of the third ring road, a long way from the centre; buses #302 and #367 go right past, or you can take the subway to Dazhongsi stop and walk 200m west. The best way to visit is on the way to or from the Summer Palace.

The bells here are considerable works of art, their surfaces enlivened with embossed texts in Chinese and Tibetan, abstract patterns, and images of storks and dragons. The odd, scaly, dragon-like creature shown perching on top of each bell is a *pulao*, a legendary animal supposed to shriek when attacked by a whale (the wooden hammers used to strike the bells are carved

Beijing University	北京大学	*běijīng dàxúe*
Dazhong Si	大钟寺	*dàzhōng sì*
Haidian	海淀	*hǎidiǎn*
Yiheyuan	颐和园	*yíhé yuán*
Yuanmingyuan	圆明园	*yuánmíng yuán*

6

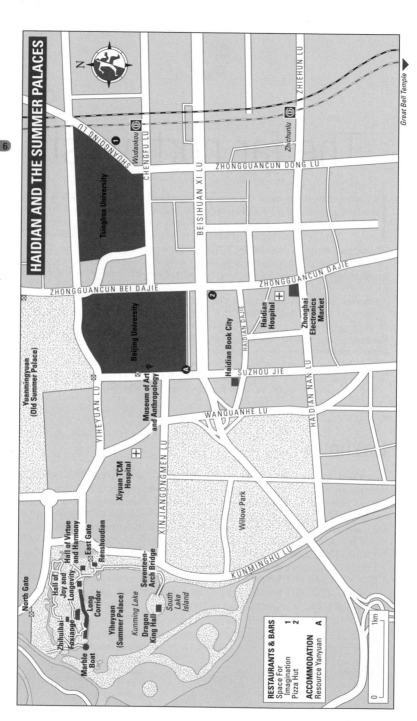

HAIDIAN AND THE SUMMER PALACES

N

Great Bell Temple ▶

ZHIEHUN LU

Zhichunlu

ZHONGGUANCUN DONG LU

BEISIHUAN XI LU

SHUANGQING LU

CHENGFU LU

Wudaokou

Tsinghua University

ZHONGGUANCUN BEI DAJIE

ZHONGGUANCUN DAJIE

Beijing University

Haidian Hospital

Zhonghai Electronics Market

HAIDIAN DAJIE

HAIDIAN NAN LU

Haidian Book City

SUZHOU JIE

Yuanmingyuan (Old Summer Palace)

YIHEYUAN LU

Museum of Art and Anthropology

WANGUANHE LU

XINJIANGONGMEN LU

Xiyuan TCM Hospital

Willow Park

KUNMINGHU LU

North Gate

Zhihuihai Foxiange

Marble Boat

Hall of Joy and Longevity

Hall of Virtue and Harmony

East Gate

Renshoudian

Long Corridor

Yiheyuan (Summer Palace)

Seventeen-Arch Bridge

Kunming Lake

Dragon King Hall

South Lake Island

RESTAURANTS & BARS
Space For Imagination   1
Pizza Hut   2

ACCOMMODATION
Resource Yanyuan   A

0   1km

to look like whales). The smallest bell here is the size of a goblet; the largest, a Ming creation called the King of Bells, is as tall as a two-storey house. Hanging in the back hall, it is, at fifty tonnes, the biggest and oldest surviving bell in the world, and can reputedly be heard up to 40km away. You can climb up to a platform above it to get a closer look at some of the 250,000 Chinese characters on its surface, and join Chinese visitors in trying to throw a coin into the small hole in the top. The method of its construction and the history of Chinese bell-making are explained by displays, with English captions, in side halls. Audio tapes and CDs on sale of the bells in action are more interesting than they might appear: the shape of Chinese bells dampens vibrations, so they only sound for a short time and can be effectively used as instruments.

Haidian

It's not an obvious tourist attraction – the only foreigners you're likely to see around here are students, and the area looks much like other parts of the city – but the **Haidian district** northwest of the Third Ring Road has a distinctive laidback atmosphere, courtesy of the cluster of universities and the students, artists and intellectuals who have taken advantage of the area's low rents. It's also in Haidian that you'll find plenty of Internet cafés, and, on Zhongguancun Lu, a hi-tech zone of **computer shops** for tempting if often warranty-free bargains (see p.140). You can get here using Wudaokou subway stop or on bus #320 from Xi Zhan or bus #332 from the zoo.

In the north of the area, on the way to the Summer Palace, you'll pass **Beijing Daxue** (Beida, as it's referred to colloquially), the most prestigious **university** in China, with a pleasant campus – old buildings and quiet, well-maintained grounds make it nicer than most of the city's parks. Bring your passport if you want to poke around, as you may be required to fill out a visitor's form by the guard at the gate. Originally established and administered by Americans at the beginning of the last century, the university stood on the hill in Jingshan Park before moving to its present site in 1953. Now busy with new contingents of students from the West, it was half-deserted during the Cultural Revolution (see p.178), when students and teachers alike, regarded as suspiciously liberal, were dispersed for "re-education". Later, in 1975–6, Beida was the power base of the radical left in their campaign against Deng Xiaoping, the pragmatist who was in control of the day-to-day running of the Communist Party's Central Committee during Mao's twilight years. The university's intake suffered when new students were required to spend a year learning Party dogma after 1989; now the place is once again a centre for challenging political thought. The **lake** is a popular place to skate in the winter – skates can be hired for ¥10 an hour.

Just inside the university west gate you'll find the diverting Arthur M. Sackler **Museum of Art and Anthropology** (daily 9.30am–4pm; ¥20; ⓦ www.sackler .org/china/amschina.htm). Used as a teaching museum, it holds a well-presented permanent collection of ceramics and tools from prehistory to the present, with English captions throughout; check the website for details of frequent temporary exhibitions.

You can meet China's new **intellectuals** by hanging out in the bars clustered around the university's gates. The Wudaokou District nearby is regarded as the home of Beijing's alternative culture; it's where most of the local punk bands originated, for example (see p.131). See "Drinking and nightlife", p.122, and "Entertainment and art", p.127, for more on Haidian.

Yuanmingyuan

Beijing's original summer palace, the **Yuanmingyuan** (daily 9am–6pm; ¥15), was built by the Qing Emperor Kangxi in the early eighteenth century. Once nicknamed China's Versailles for its elegant, European-influenced design, the palace boasted the largest royal gardens in the world, containing some two hundred pavilions and temples set around a series of lakes and natural springs. Today, however, there is little enough left in the 3.5-square-kilometre park upon which to hang your imagination. In 1860, the entire complex was burnt and destroyed by British and French troops, who were ordered by the Earl of Elgin to make the imperial court "see reason" during the Opium Wars (see p.176). The troops had previously spent twelve days looting the imperial treasures, many of which found their way to the Louvre and British Museum – their return undemanded as yet. This unedifying history is described in inflammatory terms on signs all over the park – the kind of signs that are absent from those many places where the vandalism was commited by the Chinese themselves.

The site is easily accessible on bus #375 from Xizhimen subway stop, or #322 from the zoo, but probably the quickest way here is to take the subway

△ Yuanmingyuan

to Wudaokou, then bus #331 or #375. If you happen to be visiting Beijing University (see p.95), the site is only a twenty-minute walk north. There are actually three parks here, the Yuanmingyuan (Park of Perfection and Brightness), Wanchunyuan (Park of Ten Thousand Springs) and Changchunyuan (Park of Everlasting Spring), all centred around the lake, Fuhai (Sea of Happiness), but all three are in a similar state, with dry ponds, crumbling walls and overgrown gardens. The best-preserved structures are the fountain and the **Hall of Tranquillity** in the northeastern section. The stone and marble fragments hint at how fascinating the original must once have been, with its marriage of European Rococo decoration and Chinese motifs.

Yiheyuan

There have been imperial summer pavilions at **Yiheyuan** (daily 8am–7pm, buildings close at 4pm; ¥40, plus additional charges of ¥5–10 to enter some buildings) since the eleventh century, although the present park layout is essentially eighteenth-century, created by the Manchu Emperor Qianlong. However, the key character associated with the palace is the **Empress Dowager Cixi** (see p.98), who ruled over the fast-disintegrating Chinese empire from 1861 until her death in 1908. Yiheyuan was very much her pleasure ground; it was she who built the palaces here in 1888 after Yuanmingyuan was destroyed, and determinedly restored them after another bout of European aggression in 1900.

The palace buildings, many connected by a suitably majestic gallery, are built on and around **Wanshou Shan** (Longevity Hill), which fills most of the space north of the lake and west of the main gate. Many of these edifices are intimately linked with Cixi – anecdotes about whom are the stock output of the numerous tour guides. To enjoy the site, however, you need know very little of its history: like Beihai (see p.84), the park, its lake and pavilions form a startling visual array, akin to a traditional Chinese landscape painting brought to life.

The fastest route to Yiheyuan is to get the subway to Wudaokou, then a taxi (¥10) or bus #375 the rest of the way. Alternatively, bus #322 from the zoo terminates here; or you could take luxury bus #808 from Qianmen. There's also a promising new **boat service** to Yiheyuan taking the old imperial approach, along the now dredged and prettified Long River, the trip embarking from a new dock at the back of the Exhibition Centre (see p.91). You ride in either one of the large, dragon-shaped cruisers or in one of the smaller speedboats which hold four, passing the Wuta Si, Zizhuyuan Park, and a number of attractive bridges and willow groves en route. The boats operate daily between 9am and 3pm, leaving when they are full; the trip takes an hour and costs ¥40 one way, ¥70 return.

The palace compound

The East Gate, by which most visitors enter, and where buses stop, is overlooked by the main palace compound. A path leads from the gate, past several halls (all signposted in English), to the lakeside. The strange bronze animal in the first courtyard is a *xuanni* or kylin, with the head of a dragon, deer antlers, a lion's tail and ox hooves. It was said to be able to detect disloyal subjects. The building behind is the **Renshoudian** (Hall of Benevolence and Longevity), a majestic, multi-eaved hall where the empress and her predecessors gave audience; it retains much of its original nineteenth-century furniture, including an imposing red sandalwood throne carved with nine dragons and flanked by peacock feather fans. The inscription on the tablet above reads "Benevolence in rule leads to long life". Look out, too, for the basket of flowers studded with precious stones.

A little way further along the main path, to the right, the **Deheyuan** (Palace of Virtue and Harmony) is dominated by a three-storey theatre, complete with trap doors in the stage for surprise appearances and disappearances by the actors. Theatre was one of Cixi's main passions – she even took part in performances sometimes, playing the role of Guanyin, the goddess of mercy. Today some of the halls function as a museum of theatre, with displays of costumes and props and waxworks of Cixi and attendants. The most unusual exhibit is a vintage Mercedes Benz, a gift to the warlord Yuan Shikai (see p.176) in the early twentieth century and the first car to appear in China.

The next major building along the path is the lakeside **Yulangtang** (literally, Jade Waves Palace). With a neat touch of irony, it's where the Emperor Guangxu, then still a minor, was kept in captivity for ten years while Cixi exercised his powers. A pair of decorative rocks in the front courtyard, supposed to resemble a mother and her son, were put there by Cixi to chastise Guangxu for insufficient filiality. Another monstrous hypocrisy is perpetrated in the hall, which contains a tablet of Cixi's calligraphy reading "The magnificent palace inspires everlasting moral integrity." One character has a stroke missing; apparently no one dared tell her.

North of here, behind Renshoudian, are Cixi's private quarters, three large courtyards connected by a winding gallery. The largest of these is the **Leshoutang** (Hall of Joy and Longevity), which houses Cixi's hardwood throne. The large table in the centre of the main hall was where she took her notorious meals of 128 courses. The chandeliers were China's first electric lights, installed in 1903 and powered by the palace's own generator.

The Dowager Empress Cixi

The notorious Cixi entered the imperial palace at 15 as the **Emperor Xianfeng's concubine**, quickly becoming his favourite and bearing him a son. When the emperor died in 1861 she became regent, ruling in place of her infant boy. For the next 35 years she, in effect, ruled China, displaying a mastery of intrigue and court politics. When her son died of syphilis, she installed another puppet infant, her nephew, and retained her authority. Her fondness for extravagant gestures (every year she had ten thousand caged birds released on her birthday) drained the state's coffers, and her deeply conservative policies were inappropriate for a time when the nation was calling for reform.

With foreign powers taking great chunks out of China's borders on and off during the nineteenth century, Cixi was moved to respond in a typically misguided fashion. Impressed by the claims of the xenophobic **Boxer movement** (whose Chinese title translated as "Righteous and Harmonious Fists") that their members were invulnerable to bullets, in 1899 Cixi let them loose on all the foreigners in China. The Boxers laid siege to the foreign legation's compound in Beijing for nearly two months before a European expeditionary force arrived and, predictably, slaughtered the agitators. Cixi and the emperor only escaped the subsequent rout of the capital by disguising themselves as peasants and fleeing the city. On her return, Cixi clung on to power, attempting to delay the inevitable fall of the dynasty. One of her last acts, the day before she died in 1908, was to order the murder of her puppet regent, which was duly carried out.

> ## Boating and skating on Kunming Lake
>
> **Boating** on Kunming Lake is a popular pursuit – with the locals as much as foreign visitors – and well worth the money (boats can be hired at any of the jetties for ¥10/hr). Apart from the jetty by the marble boat, you can dock over below Longevity Hill, on the north side of the lake by the gallery. Getting out on the lake affords the chance to row out to the two bridges spanning narrow stretches of water – the gracefully bowed Jade Belt on the western side and the long, elegant seventeen-arch bridge on the east. In winter, the Chinese **skate** on the lake here, a spectacular sight as some of the particpants are really proficient; skates are available for rent at the main entrance (¥10/hr).

The north shore of Kunming Lake

From Leshoutang, the **Long Corridor** runs to the northwest corner of **Kunming Lake**. Flanked by various temples and pavilions, the corridor is actually a seven-hundred-metre covered way, its inside walls painted with more than eight thousand recently restored images of birds, flowers, landscapes and scenes from history and mythology. Near the west end of the corridor is Cixi's ultimate flight of fancy, a magnificent lakeside pavilion in the form of a 36-metre-long **marble boat**, boasting two decks. Completed by Cixi using funds intended for the Chinese navy, it was regarded by her acolytes as a characteristically witty and defiant snub to her detractors. Her misappropriations helped speed the empire's decline, with China suffering heavy naval defeats during the 1895 war with Japan. Close to the marble boat is a jetty – the tourist focus of this part of the site – with rowing boats for rent (see box above).

Wanshou Shan

About halfway down the long gallery, you'll see an archway and a path that leads uphill away from the lake. Heading up the path, through two gates, brings you to the **Paiyundian** (Cloud Dispelling Hall), which was used by Cixi as a venue for her infamously extravagant birthday parties. The elegant objects on display here are twentieth-birthday presents to her from high officials (the rather flattering oil painting of her was a present from the American artist Hubert Vos). The largest building here, near the top of the hill, is the **Foxiangge** (Tower of Buddhist Incense), a charming three-storey octagonal pagoda built in 1750, that commands a panoramic view of the whole park. Deservedly, the area around it is a popular picnic spot.

The **Zhihuihai** (Sea of Wisdom) **hall**, on top of the hill, is strikingly different in style from the other buildings, as it has not a single beam or column and is tiled in green and yellow ceramic tiles. It's dotted with niches holding Buddha statues. At the foot of the hill on the far (north) side lies a souvenir market and the little visited but very pleasant back lake. Walk along the side of this lake for half a kilometre and you arrive at the **Garden of Harmonious Interests**, a pretty collection of lotus-filled ponds and pavilions connected by bridges. Cixi used to fish from the large central pavilion, and to ensure her satisfaction, eunuchs dived in and attached fish to her hook. The bridge up to the pavilion is called "know the fish bridge" after an argument that took place here between two Ming dynasty philosophers: one declared that the fish he could see were happy; the other snorted, "How could you know? You're not a fish", whereupon the first countered, "You're not me, so how do you know I don't know?"

The south of the park

It's a long, but very pleasant, walk to the southern part of Kunming Lake, where the scenery is wilder and the crowds are thinner. Should you need a destination, the main attraction to head for is the white **seventeen-arch bridge**, 150m long and topped with 544 cute, vaguely canine lions, each in a slightly different posture. The bridge leads to **South Lake Island**, where Qianlong used to review his navy, and which holds a brace of fine halls, most striking of which is the **Yelu Chucai Memorial Temple**. Yelu, an adviser to Genghis Khan during the Yuan dynasty, is entombed next to the temple, in the company of his wives and concubines, slaughtered for the occasion. The small, colourful **Dragon King Hall** nearby was used to pray for rain.

Listings

Listings

Accommodation

eijing does not have the plethora of small, family-run guesthouses that
you find in the rest of Asia. Hotels are large and generally impersonal
concerns, with standardized, rather nondescript, modern interiors. Your
choice of accommodation is restricted by the law dictating that foreigners can stay only in certain government-designated hotels, which renders
many inexpensive places off limits (though now that China is a member of the
World Trade Organization, this provision will need to be amended as it contravenes the organization's regulations). For information on finding long-term
accommodation in the city, see p.37.

Central Beijing – anywhere within or just off the second ring road – has
plenty of luxury and a few mid-range hotels, and budget options have recently
blossomed, with a number of good youth hostels having opened in the centre
and near the Sanlitun bar district. Beijing being the size it is, proximity to a
subway stop is a big advantage, so hotels on or near the second ring road – and
therefore the loop line – are often the most convenient. **Out of the centre**,
the vast majority of hotels are on or near the third ring road, a long way out
in what is usually a dull area, though there are usually good transport connections to the centre. These hotels are mainly mid-range and comfortable
without many frills; all have a business centre.

Outside the budget category, the best hotels are in or around the **Chaoyang**
district, in the **east** of the city. Though rather anonymous architecturally, it's a
cosmopolitan area with most of the nightlife and some of the best restaurants.
The **north** of the city has some charming areas, notably around the Drum
Tower, but there aren't many good places to stay here. The **west** and **south** of
the city are, on the whole, less interesting, and though there are plenty of
accommodation options here, few are included below for this reason. That said,
we've made a point of reviewing some places in the **far south** of the city,

Accommodation price codes

The accommodation in this book has been graded according to the price codes
below, representing the price of the **cheapest double room** available to foreigners.
Most places have a range of rooms, however, and staff will usually offer you the
more expensive ones – it's always worth asking if they have anything cheaper.
Some upmarket establishments have separate high- and low-season rates, in
which case the price code represents the cost in high season (April–Sept).

❶ Up to ¥100	❹ ¥200–300	❼ ¥650–900
❷ ¥100–150	❺ ¥300–450	❽ ¥900–1400
❸ ¥150–200	❻ ¥450–650	❾ Over ¥1400

临时住宿登记表
REGISTRATION FORM FOR TEMPORARY RESIDENCE

请用正楷填写　PLEASE WRITE IN BLOCK LETTERS

英文姓 Surname	英文名 First name	性别 Sex
中文姓名 Name in Chinese	国籍 Nationality	出生日期 Date of birth
证件种类 Type of certificate (eg passport)	证件号码 Certificate No.	签证种类 Type of visa
签证有效期 Valid date of visa	抵店日期 Date of arrival	离店日期 Date of departure
由何处来 From	交通工具 Carrier	往何处 To
永久地址 Permanent address		停留事由 Object of stay
职业 Occupation		
接待单位 Received by		房号 Room No.

which is where you should head if you absolutely must have the cheapest beds, or if more central places are full.

At all but the very cheapest hotels, rack rates should not be taken seriously; it's almost always possible to **bargain** the rate down, sometimes by as much as two-thirds in the off season. If you're on a really tight budget, a little searching around should turn up a bed in a clean dorm for about ¥50 a night, or an en-suite double room for less than ¥250.

Reservations can be made by phone – generally someone on reception will speak English – but aren't usually necessary, even at expensive places. You can reserve rooms from a counter at the airport (on the left as you exit customs), and they will usually offer a small discount – though you'll get a much better deal if you sort out the same room yourself. **Online** reservations are simple, don't require a credit-card payment and often offer a sizeable discount: try Ⓦwww.hotelschina.net, Ⓦwww.asia-hotels.com or Ⓦwww.sinohotel.com.

Checking in involves filling in a tiresome form (an example appears above) and paying a deposit. At old-style places, you won't be given your own room key; instead you'll get a chit to take to the floor attendant, who will give you a plastic card to keep that identifies your room number. Remember to grab a few hotel business cards when you check in; these are vital when you want to let taxi drivers know where you're staying. Whatever type of place you stay in, you can rely on the presence of plastic slippers for you to use around your room, and a giant thermos flask of hot water that the attendant will refill for you any time.

All hotels have **tour offices** which offer trips to the obvious tourist sights – the Great Wall, acrobatics and Beijing opera shows. These trips aren't necessarily as expensive as you might expect, and are the most convenient way to get to remote destinations such as Simatai Great Wall. Some hotels also offer a booking service for train and plane tickets.

Youth hostels

Beijing's **hostels** have vastly improved of late: they're generally very clean, and feature a lounge, kitchen, use of their washing machine (typically for ¥5), bike rental (around ¥20 a day) and Internet access (for ¥10/hr or so). Don't be put off if you don't fit the backpacker demographic; most of these places also have simple double rooms, usually with shared facilities.

Note that any place billing itself a "youth hostel" will give you a ¥10 per night discount if you have a youth-hostel card, which they will sell you for ¥50. Note also that two hotels, the excellent *Lüsongyuan* (see p.110) and the pretty decent *Red House* (see p.106), also have dorms, and that the otherwise mid-range *Rainbow* (see p.109) has some inexpensive rooms.

ACCOMMODATION | Youth hostels

7

Eastern Beijing

East Morning Sun Youth Hostel
东方晨光青年旅馆
dōngfāngchénguāng qīngnián lǚguǎn
8–16 Dongdan San Tiao ☏010/65284347,
℻65284350
This place claims it will soon be able to accept foreigners, so call to check before turning up. It's worth considering thanks to its central location, round the back of the Oriental Plaza (see the Wangfujing map on p.75 for the location). Single, double and triple rooms available, though no dorms. ❷

International Youth Hostel
国际青年旅舍
guójìqīngnián lǚshè
9 Jianguomennei Dajie ☏010/65126688 ext 6146, ℻65229494.
This place should have reopened by the time this reads (if not, head up the road to the *Saga*). It's just north of Beijing Zhan subway stop, on the tenth floor of the building behind and just to the east of the *International Hotel* – look for the "youth hostel" sign (and see the map on p.77). Very centrally located and with great views. No private rooms; dorm beds ¥60.

Saga Youth Hostel
实佳国际青年旅舍
shíjiā guójìqīngnián lǚshè
9 Shijia Hutong, off Chaoyangmen Nan Xiao Jie,
☏010/65272773, ✉sagayangguang@yahoo.com.
In a quiet *hutong* off a busy street, and walkable from the airport bus stop (the terminus of Route B) and the main train station. It's signposted off Chaoyangmen Nan

Xiao Jie, just beyond the stop for bus #24. The hostel is clean and utilitarian, with a tour office, bike rental, Internet access, a kitchen and a washing machine. Unusually, some of the otherwise plain dorms have TVs. For the location, see the map on pp.72–73. Dorm beds ¥40–60, ❸

Zhaolong International Youth Hostel
兆龙青年旅舍
zhàolóngqīngnián lǚshè
2 Gongrentiyuchang Bei Lu ☏010/65972299,
℻65972288, ⊛www.zhaolonghotel.com.cn.
Behind the swanky *Zhaolong Hotel* – follow the cars right round from the glitzy facade to the shabby car park behind. Staying so near to glamour isn't likely to sap morale in this excellent new hostel, clean and ably managed, a short stumble from the bars on Sanlitun Lu. Offers laundry, tours, bike rental and Internet access. Dorm beds ¥60–70, ❷

Southern Beijing

Far East International Youth Hostel
远东国际青年旅舍
yuǎndōng guójìqīngnián lǚshè
90/113 Tieshuxie Jie ☏010/63018811,
℻63018233.
Easily the best budget place, consisting of two buildings opposite each other deep in the *hutongs* of Qianmen, off Nanxinhua Jie. Both have been recently renovated and are clean and bright. The building on the west side is a lovely traditional courtyard house, converted into dorms, and of the two is a nicer place to stay, though use the facilities in the newer building as the showers aren't

105

very good. There are more dorms in the basement of the new building, and en-suite double rooms on the upper floors. There are two tour offices (the one run in the western building is private, and much better than the hotel's own, in the eastern building), plus Internet access, bike rental, a kitchen, and a washing machine. Staff are generally friendly if bumbling. It's tough to find first time (see the map on pp.58–59), and cab drivers never know where it is – the simplest way to get here is to walk south from Hepingmen subway stop and take the second alley on the left after Liulichang's pedestrian overpass. Then it's left at the T-junction, first right, left, and the hotel is 50m up here. Dorm beds ¥60 in the courtyard house, ¥50 in the new building, **❹**

Hotels

The capital's **upmarket** hotels (**❼–❾**) are legion, and more are being thrown up all the time. They're usually managed by foreigners, and offer facilities such as gyms, saunas, and business centres. These establishments are comparable to their counterparts anywhere in the world, though the finer nuances of service might be lacking. Even if these hotels are beyond your budget, you can still avail yourself of their lavish facilities, such as the lobby toilets featuring uniformed attendants who wipe the seat for you. If nothing else, these hotels make useful landmarks, and some have restaurants that are neither bad nor, by Western standards at least, expensive. Some of the hotels in this bracket offer **off-season discounts** of up to 70 percent.

Mid-range hotels (**❹–❻**) are well equipped and comfortable, offering spacious double rooms, but are generally anonymous and unstylish – except for a few hotels converted from old courtyard houses, which have quiet gardens, period furniture, and an ambience that is recognizably Chinese. Breakfast apart, meals are generally better eaten outside rather than in the hotel restaurant, as hotel food is mediocre and expensive at this level.

Budget hotels (**❶–❸**) are clean but spartan, boast little in the way of facilities and invariably have a small contingent of clueless or sulky staff. The bathrooms, though clean, may be a little worn.

Most hotels have few **single rooms**; if you're on your own you might be able to persuade the receptionist to let you have a double room for half price. **Breakfast** is not usually included in the rate except in the classier places, where a choice of Western and Chinese fare is available.

Eastern Beijing

The two establishments reviewed at the start of this section are marked on the map on pp.72–73.

Red House
瑞秀宾馆
ruìxiù bīnguǎn
10 Chunxiu Jie ☎010/64167500, ℻64167600, ⊛www.redhouse.com.cn.
A good, newish hotel/hostel with one-bedroom and shared two-bedroom apartments, plus six- and eight-bed dorms. Discounts available for long-term guests. To get there from Dongzhimen subway stop, head east along Dongzhimenwai Dajie and take the turning opposite *Pizza Hut*, and you can't miss the place – it's a deep red. Dorm beds ¥70 including breakfast, one-room apartments ¥200–400, two-room ¥400–600.

Zijin
紫金宾馆
zǐjīn bīnguǎn
9 Chongwenmen Xi Dajie ☎010/651360016, ℻65249215.
In the grounds of the former Belgian legation, though the rooms are in a new building east of the original and built to emulate it, with faux period fittings. Very close to Tian'anmen Square, but quiet and offering decent service. Qianmen subway stop. Recommended, especially if you can

get a discount (not uncommon). **❻**

Wangfujing

See the map on p.75 for the locations of the places reviewed here.

Beijing
北京饭店
běijīng fàndiàn
33 Dongchang'an Jie ☎010/65137766,
🖷65137703, 🌐www.chinabeijinghotel.com.cn.
One of the most recognizable buildings in Beijing, this mansion just east of Tian'anmen Square was built in 1900 and has recently been renovated. The view from the top floors of the west wing, over the Forbidden City, is superb. After the addition of a new wing in 1974, an office block had to be constructed nearby so that top-floor guests couldn't see into Zhongnanhai.
Unfortunately the hotel rested on its laurels for decades, and even though it's now trying to catch up with the competition, this is still more the home of cadres on junkets than businessmen. Wangfujing subway stop. **❽**

Grand Hotel Beijing
北京贵宾楼饭店
běijīng guìbīnlóu fàndiàn
36 Dongchang'an Jie ☎010/65130057,
🖷65130050, 🌐www.grandhotelbeijing.com.cn.
A new, central, five-star palace next to the *Beijing*, also with views over the Forbidden City. Rooms feature period rosewood furniture and there's plenty of elegant calligraphy around. Wangfujing subway stop. Doubles start at $275. **❾**

Haoyuan
好园宾馆
hǎoyuán bīnguǎn
53 Shijia Hutong ☎010/6512 5557, 🖷6525 3179.
Down a quiet alley off Dongsi Nan Dajie – look for the gates with two red lanterns hanging outside. This converted courtyard house has personality, the rooms kitted out with imitation Qing furniture, including four-poster beds. Recommended, but it's very small and often booked up. Beijing Zhan subway stop. **❺**

Holiday Inn Crowne Plaza
国际艺苑皇冠饭店
guójìyìyuàn huángguān fàndiàn
48 Wangfujing Dajie ☎010/65133388,
🌐www.crowneplaza.com.
Well-established hotel with artsy pretensions (there's an on-site gallery) and handy for the shops. The best of a number of

pricey hotels in the area. Wangfujing subway stop. Doubles from $220. **❾**

Palace
王府饭店
wángfǔ fàndiàn
Jingyu Hutong ☎010/6512 8899, 🖷6512 9050,
🌐www.peninsula.com.
A discreet, very upmarket place (doubles start at $300) with a good reputation among business travellers. It's well located, within walking distance of the Forbidden City, but if you need to get around quickly by taxi, be aware of the traffic snarls around here during rush hour. Wangfujing subway stop. **❾**

Jianguomen

The places reviewed here are marked on the map on p.77.

International
北京国际饭店
běijīng guójì fàndiàn
9 Jianguomenwai Dajie ☎010/65126688,
🖷65129972.
Just north of the train station, and next to the airport bus stop, this stern-looking black edifice gets a lot of tired travellers checking in. It's a little old-fashioned, with dim, cavernous rooms, and as they don't need to try very hard for custom, it's overpriced, and the staff are slack. Staying here is useful, however, for the airport bus and the CITS ticket office on the ground floor. **❻**

Jianguo
建国饭店
jiànguó fàndiàn
5 Jianguomenwai Dajie, ☎010/65002233,
🖷65002871, 🌐www.hoteljianguo.com.
Deservedly very popular, as it's well run and attractive, with many of the rooms arranged around cloistered gardens. The restaurant, *Justine's*, has the best French food in the city. Yong'an Li subway stop. Doubles start at $190. **❾**

New Otani
长富宫饭店
chángfúgōng fàndiàn
26 Jianguomenwai Dajie ☎010/65125555,
🖷65139810.
You can get seriously pampered in this five-star Japanese-managed modern mansion, though the fee for the privilege is hefty. There's a good-sized swimming pool, saunas and a squash court. Jianguomen subway stop. Doubles from $250. **❾**

St Regis
国际俱乐部饭店
guójìjùlèbù fàndiàn
21 Jianguomen Wai Dajie, ☏010/64606688,
Ⓕ64603299, ⓦ www.luxurycollection.com.
The plushest hotel in the city, though with
double rooms from $225, it's not the most
expensive. The choice of visiting notables
such as President George W. Bush, with
(for example) real palm trees in the lobby,
and a personal butler to unpack your suit-
case. ❾

Sanlitun and the northeast

The places reviewed here are shown
on the map on p.80.

Great Wall Sheraton
长城饭店
chángchéng fàndiàn
6 Dongsanhuan Bei Lu ☏010/65005566,
Ⓕ65001919, ⓦ www.sheraton.com.
A modern compound out on the third ring
road towards the airport. Built around a
seven-storey atrium, it's not only architecturally impressive but also very comfortable, with a good ground-floor tea house
that has jazz performances. Plenty of
excellent restaurants and some lively bars
lie nearby. Doubles from around $260. ❾

Kempinski
凯宾斯基饭店
kǎibīnsījī fàndiàn
Lufthansa Centre, 50 Liangmaqiao Lu
☏010/64653388, Ⓕ64653366.
On the third ring road, this luxurious business hotel is a little out of the way, though
the huge shopping complex attached
means there's no shortage of diversions on
site. Doubles from $270. ❾

Youyi
友谊饭店
yóuyí fàndiàn
Off Sanlitun Lu ☏010/64172632 or 64156866,
ⓦ www.poachers.com.cn.
A tempting prospect, this new hotel is tidy
and well run, and abuts the city's best
inexpensive bar. The location is great:
Sanlitun's bars and some classy restaurants are within short walking distance, and
it's not as noisy as you might expect. To
find it, head north up Sanlitun Lu and turn
left after 200m, at the sign for *Cross Bar*.
Take the first left and the hotel will be on
the right, next to the *Poachers Inn* (see
p.124). There are a few four-bed dorms but

most of the rooms are doubles. The bathrooms, all communal, are spotless, and
there's also Internet access and free
laundry service. Rate includes breakfast.
Dorm beds ¥70, ❸

Southern Beijing

The more central places here are
marked on the map on pp.58–59.

Fenglong
凤龙宾馆
fènglóng bīnguǎn
5 You'anmen Dong Jie ☏010/63536413,
Ⓔsuyuling@etang.com.
Best of the old-style backpacker mother-
ships, with a wide range of dorms and
rooms – ask to see a selection, as quality
varies widely. Rooms on the second floor
are generally best. Offers bike rental,
Internet access and even photo developing. Staff are slack but the tour office is
good – this is the nerve centre from which
the tours offered by most of the other
budget places are run. The proximity of
Taoranting Park is a pleasant bonus. Bus
#122 from Beijing Zhan. Dorm beds
¥25–50, ❷

Hademen
哈德门饭店
hādémén fàndiàn
2a Chongwenmenwai Dajie ☏010/67012244,
Ⓕ67016865.
This place is a little rambling and the staff
don't speak much English, but given that
it's close to Chongwenmen subway and
the train station, it's worth considering.
Rooms are en suite and quite comfy. ❺

Jianguo Qianmen
建国前门饭店
jiànguó qiánmén fàndiàn
175 Yong'an Lu ☏010/63016688, Ⓕ63013883.
This cavernous old hotel has improved
after recent renovation, and has at least a
glimmer of character. The architecture is
po-faced Soviet style, but the interiors are
stylishly decorated. It's well located, close
to the Temple of Heaven, but overall quite
pricey for what you get, perhaps because
it's a long-standing favourite of tour
groups. The theatre, where nightly performances of bastardized Beijing opera are
shown (see p.127), is to be avoided. Bus
#14 south from Hepingmen subway stop
comes here – get off at the third stop. ❻

Rainbow
新北纬饭店
xīnběiwěi fàndiàn
Xijing Lu ☏010/63012266, ⒻＰ63011366,
ⓦwww.rainbowhotel.com.cn.
This efficiently run Sino-Japanese joint venture consists of two buildings, to separate the riffraff from the high rollers: the budget building to the west resembles a barracks, the eastern building a cruise liner. Facilities – open to guests in both buildings – include a gym and a large basement health centre, and there's a good Japanese restaurant as well as the novel *Health Food Restaurant* (see p.119). The cheapest rooms have shared bathrooms. Bus #20 from Beijing Zhan will get you to Yongdingmennei Dajie, from where the hotel is a one-kilometre walk west. Western building ❹, eastern building ❼

Tiantan
天坛饭店
tiāntán fàndiàn
1 Tiyuguan Lu ☏010/67012277, ⒻＰ67012279.
This comfortable hotel is located just east to Tiantan, though nothing else distinguishes this area. ❻

The far south

Jinghua
京华饭店
jīnghuá fàndiàn
Nansanhuan Xi Lu ☏010/67222211.
Once the hub for budget travellers, this has been overtaken by the competition – only stay here if you absolutely must have the cheapest dorm bed in town. It's very far from the centre, badly run, sleazy, and, quite literally, stinks – it's next door to a fetid canal. To get here, take bus #66 from the terminus at the southwest side of Tian'anmen Square, get off at the Yang Qiao intersection on the third ring road, then walk east (past *McDonald's*) for 200m. Dorm beds ¥20–45, ❸

Qiaoyuan
侨园饭店
qiáoyuán fàndiàn
135 You'anmen Dongbinhe Lu ☏010/63012244.
Just west of Yongdingmen bus station and Beijing South train station, and near the third ring road, this has a wide range of rooms (some with private bathroom) and dorms in two buildings, the older one to the north, the newer to the south. Ask to see the room before you take it, as standards vary considerably. You probably won't make many friends here however, as the rather sterile compound has no restaurants, is miles from anywhere interesting, and occupancy is low. Buses #20 or #54 from Beijing Zhan both terminate at Yongdingmen bus station. Dorm beds ¥25–50, ❶

Northern Beijing

The places reviewed here are marked on the map on p.82–83, except for the *Resource Yanyuan* in Haidian, which appears on the map on p.94.

Bamboo Garden
竹园宾馆
zhúyuán bīnguǎn
24 Xiaoshiqiao Hutong, Jiugulou Dajie
☏010/64032299, ⒻＰ64012633.
This very pleasant hotel was converted from the residence of a Qing official, and the courtyards, elegant facades and gardens full of bamboo are its best feature. There's a wide range of rooms, the more expensive suites boasting period furniture. It's well located too, in a pleasant part of the city near Houhai. Head south from Gulou subway for about 250m down Jiugulou Dajie and take the fourth alley to the right; continue along for 100m, turn left and you're there. ❺

Cherry Blossom
樱花宾馆
yīnghuā bīnguǎn
17 Hepingli Dong Jie ☏010/64934455.
The main attraction of this newish hotel is its location in a lively part of the city, a university district with lots of good, inexpensive restaurants, notably Korean places in the alleys around. From Yonghe Gong subway stop, take bus #807 north or get a taxi the rest of the way (¥10). ❹

Friendship
北京友谊宾馆
běijīng yóuyí bīnguǎn
3 Baishiqiao Lu ☏010/68498888, ⒻＰ68498866,
ⓦwww.c-b-w.com/hotel/friendship.
Sprawling and sedate establishment set in large gardens on the third ring road. Built in 1954 for visiting Soviet dignitaries, it used to be a favourite among Beijing's foreign correspondents but is now rather old-fashioned. Each of the distinct compounds here is attractively designed, though, and there are outdoor and indoor swimming pools. ❻

109

Lüsongyuan

侣松园宾馆

lǔsōngyuán bīnguǎn

22 Banchang Hutong, off Jiaodaokou Nan Dajie ⊤010/64040436, ⓕ64030418, ⓔ lsyhotel@263.net.

A charismatic hotel converted from a Qing dynasty mansion, this is the city's best affordable accommodation, with a wide range of stylish, elegant rooms, as well as a basement dorm, pleasant gardens and even a tea house. It's popular with tour groups, so book ahead in season. To get there from Beijing Zhan, take bus #104 and get off at the Beibingmasi stop. Walk 50m south and you'll find a sign pointing you down an alley to the hotel. Dorm beds ¥60–100, **❹**

New Century

新世纪饭店

xīnshìjì fàndiàn

6 Xizhimenwai Dajie ⊤010/6846200, ⓕ6831110, ⓦ www.newcenturyhotel.com.cn.

A substantial, swanky, efficient business hotel with all mod cons, but in a rather noisy area by the Capital Gymnasium, 1km from Xizhimen subway stop. **❼**

Olympic

奥林匹克饭店

àolínpǐkè fàndiàn

52 Baishiqiao Lu ⊤010/62176688, ⓕ62174260.

It's hard to get too excited about this place, stuck out beyond the zoo and close to a lot of busy access roads, but it's clean, modern, and big discounts are possible. **❺**

Resource Yanyuan

资源燕圆宾馆

zīyuán yànyuán bīnguǎn

Haidian Lu ⊤010/62757199, ⓕ62750102.

Run by nearby Beijing University, this is a reasonably priced small hotel far from the centre in lively Haidian, on the route of bus #320 from Chegongzhuang subway stop. Besides rooms, they have one- to three-

bedroom apartments, which offer the best value (¥400–600). **❺**

Xiyuan

西苑饭店

xīyuàn fàndiàn

1 Sanlihe Lu ⊤010/68313388, ⓕ6355304.

A large, pleasant and fairly luxurious hotel which would be a lot more enticing if it wasn't stuck out near the zoo in an area that's most notable for heavy traffic. At least the staff try hard to please, and it's not too far to Xizhimen subway stop. **❽**

Zhumulangma

属穆朗玛宾馆

zhǔmùlǎngmǎ bīnguǎn

149 Gulou Xi Dajie ⊤010/64018822, ⓕ64011330.

Once a temple, though there's little evidence of that now. A good location, well inside the northern section of the second ring road and close to some of the nicest hutongs in the city, make this place worth investigating. Some rooms are shabby, though, so ask to look at the room before you commit yourself. Bus #5 from Qianmen Dajie passes by. **❹**

Western Beijing

Minzu

民族饭店

mínzú fàndiàn

51 Fuxingmen Dajie ⊤010/66014466, ⓕ66014849, ⓦ www.minzuhotel.com.

Built in 1959, this Chinese-run hotel has a slightly dated feel. There are more than six hundred rooms, plus a gym, a billiards room and a good first-floor restaurant, and the Sanwei tea house (see p.114) over the road is an added attraction. The hotel is midway between Fuxingmen and Xidan subway stops, and not too far from some attractive parts of the city – see the map on pp.64–65 for the location. **❼**

8

Eating

The Chinese love eating. Even pleasantries revolve around the subject; a way of asking "how are you?" – *nǐ chī fàn ma*? – translates literally as "have you eaten rice yet?. From market-stall buns and soup through to intricate varieties of regional cooking, China boasts one of the world's most complex cuisines.

Nowhere on the Chinese mainland has the culinary wealth of Beijing, with every style of Chinese food available, along with just about any Asian fare and most world cuisines. It's no surprise that, for some visitors, eating becomes the highlight of their trip. Prices are low compared with the West, and it's possible to eat well for less than ¥50 a head, although you can spend a lot more if you fancy dining lavishly in palatial surroundings. Meals are considered social events, and the Chinese like their restaurants to be *renao* – hot and noisy.

Restaurant hours are long, but the Chinese tend to eat early, sitting down to lunch at noon and dinner at six, so by 2pm most restaurants are empty and the staff impatient to begin their afternoon break. Late evening meals should present no problems, though some restaurants are closed by ten (those that see foreigners stay open much later). **Tipping** isn't expected; if there is a service charge, it will be on the bill. You don't have to eat with chopsticks; all restaurants have knives (*dāozi*) and forks (*chāzi*). Tofu dishes should be eaten with a spoon.

Among China's varied cuisines (see box, p.112), **Sichuan cooking** and **hotpot meals** are perhaps the most popular in Beijing. As for cuisines from elsewhere in Asia, Japanese and Korean food are widely available and well worth trying, and Thai food has recently become popular. You'll also find Indian, Russian and Middle Eastern cooking, generally in upmarket areas.

There's also ample opportunity to eat **Western food** in the city, though this generally costs around 20 percent more than a Chinese meal in a comparable restaurant. French and Italian food – though pretty mediocre and expensive – is fashionable with the nouveaux riches. If you really want the comforts of the familiar, try international fast-food chains, many of which are well established here.

Many visitors find the Chinese **breakfast** of dumplings and glutinous rice bland and unappealing, but the classic Beijing breakfast snack *jianbing guozi* (seasonal vegetables wrapped in an omelette wrapped in a pancake), deftly made in thirty seconds by street vendors, is definitely worth trying (¥2). Most large hotels offer some form of Western breakfast; alternatively, head to a branch of *Delifrance* for cheap croissants, *Dunkin' Donuts* for muffins or *Starbucks* for a cake and a caffeine jolt. Beijing is one of the few places in China where you can get a decent cup of coffee, but it's generally a drink of the Westernized elites – most Chinese can't stand it – so coffee shops tend to cluster in expensive areas.

Chinese cuisine

China has one of the most diverse and fascinating cuisines in the world, with four regional traditions; to help you order, we've included a useful menu reader on pp.194–199.

Northern food, encompassing the cuisine of the capital, is heavy and hearty, with lots of cabbage and potatoes; it's also a little less spicy and oily than food from elsewhere in China, and uses steamed buns and noodles as staples, rather than rice. **Beijing duck** (often called "Peking duck" in the West) and Mongolian hotpot are deservedly the two most famous northern dishes. Beijing duck – which can be sampled at one of the *Quanjude* chain of restaurants (see p.119) – consists of small pieces of meat which you dip in plum sauce, then wrap with chopped onions in a pancake. It's very rich and packs a massive cholesterol count. Mongolian **hotpot** – try this at *Neng Ren Ju* (see p.120) – is healthier, a poor man's fondue involving a large pot of boiling stock, usually heated by a gas burner under the dinner table. You dip strips of raw mutton, cabbage and noodles into the pot to cook them, then, when they're ready, dip them in a sauce before consuming. Also, don't leave Beijing without trying *jiāozi*, delicious meat-filled **dumplings**; something of a national institution and widely available, they're eaten especially during the Spring Festival.

The central coastal provinces produced **eastern-style** cooking, which delights in seasonal fresh seafood and river fish. Based around Shanghai, eastern cuisine emphasizes light, fresh, sweet flavours. The antithesis of the eastern style is the boisterous **Sichuan** cooking, hugely popular in the capital (the *Sichuan Restaurant* is a good place for it; see p.117) and often a favourite with visitors; it's characterized by the heavy use of chillis and pungent flavours. Though some Sichuan dishes are seriously spicy, there are still subtleties to enjoy in a cuisine which frequently uses less strident ingredients, such as orange peel, ginger and spring onions. Classic Sichuan dishes are *mápó dòufù*, bean curd with pork; *malà dòufu*, spicy beancurd; *gōngbào jīdīng*, stir-fried chicken with peanuts and peppers; and *suān cài yú*, fish with pickled vegetables

The joke that the Chinese will eat anything with four legs that's not a table refers in particular to **Cantonese** cooking. Snake liver, dog and guinea pig are among the more unusual dishes here, strange even to other Chinese, but more conventionally, there's huge consumption of lightly seasoned fresh vegetables. Dim sum (*diǎnxīn* in Mandarin), a meal of tiny flavoured buns, dumplings and pancakes, is very popular in the capital, where it tends to be taken at lunch (in Canton, it would generally be eaten in the morning). There are a lot of Cantonese restaurants in Beijing (*Fortune Garden* is regarded as the best; see p.116); they tend to be slightly more expensive than other Chinese restaurants.

When the Qing dynasty fell, many ex-imperial chefs set up restaurants, allowing the populace to sample **imperial cooking** – a sort of Chinese *haute cuisine* – for the first time. A good place to try imperial dishes, such as Mandarin sweet-and-sour fish (Empress Cixi's favourite) is the *Fangshan* restaurant (see p.120).

Chinese **vegetarian food**, which mostly comes from Shanghai, is developed from Buddhist principles that one should avoid killing. Beijing's vegetarian restaurants (*Tianshi* and *Gongdelin* among them; see p.116 and p.119) serve up luscious greens and cunning mock meats made of flavoured bean curd, with a taste and texture not far from the real thing.

Chinese **Muslim cooking**, found in restaurants run by members of the Hui minority community, eschews pork but otherwise isn't obviously different from what you'll find in other Chinese eating places. The beef dishes in the Muslim restaurants, such as the *Kaorouji* (see p.120) are often particularly good.

Beijing is well stocked with **supermarkets**, especially useful if you want to get a picnic together, or have the facilities to try some self-catering. See p.121 for details.

Fast food, street food and cafés

Fast food comes in two forms. The Chinese version, which you find in department stores or at street stalls, is usually a serving of noodles or dumplings, or rice with meat, in a polystyrene carton. Western imports such as *Pizza Hut, McDonald's* and *KFC* have made a considerable impact – there are over fifty branches of *McDonald's* in the city – and are now greatly imitated by local chains. Prices are cheaper than in the but expensive by Chinese standards (a Big Mac meal costs ¥18 - three times the price of a bowl of noodles). The best Asian fast-food are *Yoshinoya* (for noodles), *Dayang Dumplings (jiaozi)* and *Viva Curry* (fusion curries).

Street food, sold by stalls parked by the roadside, is widely available, though not right in the city centre, where vendors are shooed away by the police. The best place to try street fare is at one of the designated night markets (see below), which begin operating around 5pm and start to shut down around 10pm; they're at their busiest and best in the summer. Generally, what's on offer is hygienic – you can feel confident of food cooked in front of you. Most popular are the skewers of heavily spiced, barbecued meat, often served up by Uigurs from Xinjiang, China's far west. For cheap and filling suppers, try *huntun* (wonton) soup; *xianer bing*, savoury stuffed pancake; or the plentiful varieties of noodles. However, you should avoid anything that's eaten cold, such as the home-made wares of ice-cream vendors, which are often of a dubious standard.

It's also worth knowing that every shopping centre and plaza is also home to a **food court** – sometimes in the basement but usually on the top floor – which offers inexpensive meals from a cluster of outlets. Food courts are good places to start sampling simple Chinese food – the environment may not be very atmospheric but it's clean, and prices are fixed. Paying can be a little confusing at first; you have to buy a plastic card at a central booth (¥20 is the lowest denomination), which is debited at the food counters when you order. There's always a good range of dishes and as the food is all displayed on the counter it's easy to make your selection. Good, substantial food courts can be found at the Parkson Building on Fuxingmennei Dajie, in the Xidan stores (see p.65), and, on Wangfujing, on the sixth floor of the Sun Dong'an Plaza or the basement of the Oriental Plaza.

Baskin Robbins
Jianguomen Dajie, next to the Friendship Store.
This, the handiest branch, is open 24hr.
There's a sandwich section as well as all the usual ice creams. Other branches just do ice cream and close at 8pm; there's one just east of the zoo.
Delifrance
大磨坊面包
dàmòfáng miànbāo
Qianmen Xi Dajie; Level 2, Sun Dong'an Plaza, Wangfujing; east entrance of the Friendship Store, Jianguomenwai Dajie.

This little chain of French-style bakeries has pizza, croissants, cakes and decent coffee.
Dong'anmen night market
东安门夜市
dōng'ānmén yèshì
Dong'anmen Dajie, off Wangfujing Dajie.
Set up along the street, the stalls here offer *xiǎo chī* (literally, "little eats") from all over China. Nothing costs more than a few yuan, except the odd delicacy, such as chicken hearts.

Tea houses

For centuries, the tea house has been a meeting place in China, as central to the culture as the pub is in Britain. However, most tea houses were made to close during the Cultural Revolution, the regime viewing as dangerous their role as centres for debate and the exchange of ideas. Now tea houses are beginning to make a return, usually as upmarket tourist venues that also serve up Beijing opera (see p.127 and p.128) – there's an irony in all this, as the Chinese chattering classes now assemble in *Starbucks*.

Some tea houses are truer to the original concept, relaxed places for a snack and, of course, an endlessly refillable cup of Chinese green tea. The **Ji Guge Tea House** (daily 10am–9pm) at 136 Liulichang is a good spot to rest after browsing the street's curio shops (and itself sells attractively packaged tea and teapots, which make good gifts). The **Sanwei Bookstore** at 60 Fuxingmennei Dajie opposite the Minzu Hotel, has its own tea house that's deservedly popular with both locals and tourists; there are performances of traditional music or jazz here in the evenings (see p.127). For the traditional experience, try the **Purple Vine Tea House**, which has a branch at 2 Nanchang Jie, near the Forbidden City west gate, and 28 Sanlitun Bei Jie.

Duyichu
都一处烧麦馆
dōuyíchù shāomàiguǎn
36 Qianmen Dajie.
One of the best places in the Qianmen area for a light lunch, this cafeteria has been in business for over a century, though you'd never guess from the bland modern decor. The place has built up an enviable reputation for its steamed dumplings, which you can eat on the spot or take away.

Goubuli
狗不理包子铺
gōubùlǐ bāozipù
155 Di'anmenwai Dajie, just south of the Drum Tower.
A branch of the famous Tianjin dumpling restaurant (see p.161), this place sells delicious steamed buns with various fillings – the original fast food – for a few yuan. You can eat them here – the downstairs canteen is cheaper than upstairs – or take them home, as most of the customers do.

Kempi Deli
First floor, *Kempinski Hotel*, Lufthansa Centre, 50 Liangmaqiao Lu
Deserves a mention for producing the city's best bread and pastries. It's not cheap (a croissant is ¥12) but prices halve after 8pm. Daily 7am–11pm.

KFC
肯德基家乡鸡
kěndéjī jiāxiāngjī
Qianmen Xi Dajie, just south of Qianmen Gate;

Parkson Centre, Fuxingmenwai Dajie.
Opened in 1987, this was the first Western fast-food chain to colonize China, and has long been overtaken for verve and style by its other Western competitors. There's another branch in the Parkson Centre west of Xidan.

McDonald's
麦当劳餐厅
màidāngláo cāntīng
Qianmen Xi Dajie (by the *KFC*); Nansanhuan Xi Lu (200m west of the *Jinghua Hotel*); Jianguomenwai Dajie (opposite the CVIK Building); COFCO Plaza, Jianguomennei Dajie.
Always popular, and offering the standard menu with one variation – sweet red bean sweet pie. There are over fifty branches elsewhere in the city.

Pizza Hut
必胜客
bìshèngkè
33 Zhushikou Xi Dajie; Jianguomenwai Dajie (just west of the Friendship Store); 29 Haidian Lu; 27 Dongzhimenwai Dajie.
Relatively cheap pizzas and everything else you might expect from this chain. The quietest branch is the one on Zhushikou.

Sammies
秀水店
xiùshuǐ diàn
Jianguomenwai Dajie, just east of the silk market.
Imaginative sandwich menu and good smoothies (¥12). Open daily till midnight, and they deliver (☎010/65958708).

Starbucks Coffee Shop
First Floor, China World Trade Centre, Jianguomenwai Dajie; 1 Jianguomenwai Dajie (east side of the Friendship Store); COFCO plaza, 8 Jianguomennei Dajie; Chaoyangmenwai Dajie, opposite the Dongyue Temple; Forbidden City, near the north entrance; Sun Dong'an Plaza (basement) and Oriental Plaza (first floor, A307) on Wangfujing Dajie; north side of Xidan Plaza, Xidan.

Twenty years ago you'd have been pushed to find a cup of freshly brewed coffee in the capital; now a caffeine habit is *de rigueur*, and the coffee colonizers have overtaken *McDonald's* as the most potent symbol of Westernization. A medium coffee is ¥15; lattes, mochas, and other fancy variations are also available.

Subway
Jianguomenwai Dajie, just east of the *Jinglun Hotel*; China World Trade Centre Jianguomenwai Dajie; East side of the Henderson Centre, Jianguomennei Dajie (opposite the *International Hotel*); 52 Liangjiu Lu (opposite the *Kempinski Hotel*); opposite the north gate of the Workers' Stadium, Gongrentiyuchang Bei Lu.

An American chain offering filling if pricey sandwiches. Stays open till midnight.

Xiaochi Jie
小吃街
xiǎochī jiē
Xiagongfu Jie, running west off the southern end of Wangfujing.

This alley is lined with stalls where pushy vendors sell exotica at fixed prices. The ideal place to sample food to freak the folks back home – skewers of fried scorpions, silkworm pupae, goat's penises and crickets and sparrows are all available for less than ¥10 – though none of them, in truth, tastes of much. You can also get noodles and seafood for a few yuan.

Yoshinoya
Fourth floor of the Sun Dong'an Plaza, Wangfujing; outside the main gate of the Yiheyuan (Summer Palace); and in the New World Plaza, Jianguomennei Dajie.

A Japanese chain offering bowls of rice topped with slices of meat or fish and veg – fast food that's cheap, clean, pretty tasty and good for you.

Restaurants

Restaurants usually have two, sometimes more, dining rooms, with different prices – though the food comes from the same kitchen. The cheaper one is usually the open-plan area below. It's rarely worth phoning ahead to book a table except at popular places at weekends (our reviews include phone numbers where you might want to do so). The estimated prices for meals in the reviews are calculated on the basis of each person ordering a couple of dishes plus rice, or a main course and dessert. Note that in the smaller restaurants, such as those in the backstreets around Qianmen or Wangfujing, the prices on the English menu are around a third higher than in the Chinese version. You can tell if you're being surcharged by checking the price of *gongbao jiding* – spicy chicken with peanuts – which should be less than ¥10. If you don't order from the English menu, you won't get charged according to it, so in small restaurants you might want to order using the menu reader in this book (see p.194), or by pointing at dishes that take your fancy.

All the expensive **hotels** have several well-appointed restaurants, where the atmosphere is sedate and prices are sometimes not as high as you might expect. Look out for their special offers – set lunches and buffets, usually – advertised in the city's listings magazines.

Eastern Beijing

The two restaurants below are marked on the map on pp.72–73.

Afanti
阿凡提
āfántí

2A Houguaibang Hutong, off Chaoyangmennei Dajie ☎010/65272288.
A boisterous place serving Xinjiang food – kebabs, naan and such – and featuring belly dancing and a Uigur band. Popular with the kind of expat who feels impelled to dance on tables. Around ¥60 per person.

Golden Thaitanium
泰合金
tàihéjīn
Dongsanhuan Bei Lu, next to the Chaoyang Theatre.
Tasty, spicy and inexpensive Thai food in a relaxed setting. There's a picture menu to order from. For a pleasant evening out, combine a meal here with a trip to the acrobatics show at the theatre next door (see p.130); the restaurant stays open after the performance finishes at 9pm.

Wangfujing and around

The restaurants below are marked on the map on p.75.

Be There or Be Square
不见不散
bújiàn búsàn
Oriental Plaza, Wangfujing Dajie
☎010/85186518.
This fashionable place certainly has something going for it, with simple, fast Cantonese food, including lots of chicken and noodle dishes. The bean-under-glass patterns on the tables are amusing, as is the Western menu, which includes such items as "cream on toast" and is probably best avoided. Dishes labelled "homestyle" are all good, as are the crunchy noodles, deep-fried pork and aubergine and mince. It's popular with chic mobile phone toters, and the brown-shirted staff can be a bit saucy. Not expensive at about ¥40 per head, and open daily 24hr.

The Courtyard
四合院
sìhéyuàn
95 Donghuamen Dajie, outside the east gate of the Forbidden City ☎010/65268883.
Listed in *Condé Nast Traveller* as one of the world's fifty best restaurants, this elegant, modish place specializes in fusion cuisine – here, Continental food with a Chinese twist, such as "vegetable roulade wrapped with nori". A meal will set you back at least ¥250 a head. There's a contemporary art gallery downstairs (see p.133) and a cigar lounge upstairs. Daily 6pm–1am.

Fortune Garden
Palace Hotel, Jingyu Hutong ☎010/65128899.
See p.107 for the hotel's name in Chinese.
Upmarket Cantonese restaurant, popular with Cantonese businessmen. Try the *cha*

shao bao – barbecued pork buns. Eating here isn't cheap at around ¥150 per person, though at lunchtime there's a delicious *dim sum* buffet for ¥100 per person. Daily 11.30am–2.30pm & 6–10pm.

Green Tianshi Vegetarian Restaurant
绿色天食餐厅
lǜsè tiānshí cāntīng
57 Dengshi Xikou, just off Wangfujing Dajie
☎010/65242349, ⓦwww.greentianshi.com.
All dishes in this bright, modern restaurant are tuber-, legume- or grain-based, low in calories and cholesterol-free. Of course, this being China, most of this healthy veggie fare is presented as meat imitations. Try "chicken" or "eel" and wash them down with fruit juice – no booze is served. There's a picture menu. About ¥50 per head. The downstairs shop has pricey Western and Chinese health-food supplies. Daily 10am–10pm.

Hong Kong Food City
香港美食城
xiānggǎng měishí cāntīng
18 Dong'anmen Dajie ☎010/65136668.
A big, bright Cantonese restaurant with a good seafood menu. Popular with Chinese tourists, and can get noisy. Reasonably priced at around ¥60 per person – if you avoid the sharks' fin.

Muslim Fast Food
Off Dongsixi Dajie.
This tackily decorated canteen might not look like much, but it serves cheap and delicious food with lots of vegetarian options. Point to the dishes that take your fancy from the wide selection on display at the counters. The sticky sweets are especially good. Head north up Wangfujing Dajie and just past the crossroads with Wusi Dajie; you'll see a *hutong* full of clothes stalls on the east side of the road. Walk down here about 200m and you'll come to a little square. The restaurant is on the south side, opposite a *McDonald's* – look for the white lettering on a green background. Bus #102 from Chaoyangmen subway stop.

Wangfujing Quanjude Roast Duck
王府井全聚德烤鸭店
wángfǔjīng quánjùdé kǎoyādiàn
13 Shuaifuyuan Hutong ☎010/65253310.
Smaller than the others in the *Quanjude* chain (see p.119) – this one earned its unfortunate nickname, "Sick Duck", thanks

to its proximity to a hospital.
Daily 11am–1.30pm, 4.30–9pm

Jianguomen and around

See the map on p.77 for the locations of these restaurants.

The Elephant
大苯象
dàbènxiàng cāntīng
17 Ritan Bei Lu ☏010/65024013.
Bypass the dull Yugoslavian fare on offer on the ground floor, and head upstairs to this Russian restaurant, which has a wide variety of soups and salads, including the obligatory borscht. Each main dish comes with a generous side serving of mashed potato. Expect to pay about ¥80 per person, more if you hit the page-long vodka list.

Justine's
Jianguo Hotel, **5 Jianguomenwai Dajie. See p.107 for the hotel's name in Chinese.**
An exclusive French restaurant with the best wine list in the capital. Try the lobster soup or grilled lamb. Service is attentive. Around ¥150 per person.

Lemongrass
香兰叶餐厅
xiānglányè cāntīng
Just around the corner from the Friendship Store, Jianguomenwai Dajie.
Small Indian and Thai restaurant, with a great lunch buffet for only ¥38 – choose from a wide array of curries, soup, cold dishes and naan.

Makye Ame
玛吉阿米
mǎjí āmǐ
Second floor, A11 Xiushui Nan Jie ☏010/65069616.
Hale and hearty Tibetan food in a cosy atmosphere, considerably more upscale than anywhere in Tibet. Try the tashi delek (a meaty lasagne) and wash it down with butter tea. Tibetan singing and dancing on Wed & Fri nights. It's behind the Friendship Store – head north past the *Starbucks* and take the first alley to the left.

Mexican Wave
墨西哥风味餐
mòxīgē fēngwèicān
Dongdaqiao Lu ☏010/65063961.
With its relaxed atmosphere, this bistro is aimed at (and deservedly popular with) the expats from the embassy compounds nearby. The ambience is very Western; about the only thing to remind you that you're in China is the barman's accent. The set lunch menu, which changes daily, is tasty and good value (¥50), as are the many pizza options and the inevitable tapas and burritos.

Nadaman
中国大饭店（三层）
zhōngguó dàfàndiàn (sāncéng)
Third Floor, *China World Hotel*, China World Trade Centre ☏010/65052266.
Discreet, minimalist and seriously expensive Japanese restaurant with a three- or four-course set menu priced at ¥300 per person. Most of the ingredients are flown in from Japan. Take someone you want to impress.

Phrik Thai
泰辣椒餐厅
tàilàjiāo cāntīng
Gateway Building, 10 Yabao Lu ☏010/65925236.
Smart Thai restaurant popular with expats. Try the red curry and the chicken satay. Around ¥50 per person.

Rotary Sushi Restaurant
福助回转寿司
fúzhù huízhuǎn shòusī
Jianguomenwai Dajie
Cheap and idiot-proof Japanese fast-food restaurant just outside the Friendship Store. Choose dishes from the conveyor belt as they glide past (¥5–25, colour-coded according to price). Not a bad place for a light lunch.

Sichuan Government Restaurant
5 Gongyun Tou Tiao, off Jianguomennei Dajie.
A great find, serving homesick bureaucrats the best Sichuan food in the capital. Head north up the alley that passes the east side of the Chang'an Theatre and after 200m there's an alley to the right with a public toilet opposite. Fifty metres down the alley a set of green and gold gates on the left mark the entrance to the Sichuan government building. Pass through these into the compound and you'll see the restaurant on the left. No English menu, no concessions to wimpy palettes, no fancy decor, just fantastic, inexpensive food.

Xiheya Ju
義和雅居餐厅
xīhéyǎjū cāntīng
Ritan Park ☎010/65067643.
Food from all over China served in an imitation Qing-dynasty mansion. Try the *gan-
bian rou si* – dried beef fried with celery
and chilli, or the spicy Sichuan chicken or
shredded lamb. Deservedly popular with
locals and expats. ¥60 per head.

Sanlitun and the northeast

See the map on p.80 for the locations
of the places reviewed here.

Adria
阿得里亚
ādélīyà
**16 Xinyuan Jie. Bus #401 from Dongzhimen
subway stop.**
The best place in the capital for pizza, not
that that's saying much. The salmon steak
here is also recommended. Around ¥60
per person.

Ai Yao Hunan Restaurant
爱遥湘菜馆
àiyáoxiāng càiguǎn
9 Liangmaqiao Lu, opposite the *Hilton Hotel*.
An excellent little place that gets very busy,
so arrive early or late to be confident of
getting a table. It serves some of the best
shui zhu roupian, or boiled spicy pork, in
the capital; like many other Hunan dishes,
it's spicy, but with a sweet aftertaste. Other
dishes to try are Hunan favourites
luobogan larou, dried turnip with pork; and
rou mo chao suan dou jiao, sour green
beans with mince. Bus #18 from
Dongzhimen subway stop. ¥40 per head.

Berena's Bistro
**6 Gongrentiyuchang Dong Lu, at the southern
end of Sanlitun Nan Jiu Ba Jie
☎010/92262865.**
Foreigner-friendly but a little pricier than
elsewhere, serving Sichuan food the way
it's done in Western chinatowns. Try their
gongbao jiding or the sweet-and-sour
pork. Bus #118 from Dongsi Shitiao
subway stop. Reckon on ¥70 per head.

Golden Elephant
金象苑东方餐厅
jīnxiàngyuán dōngfāng cāntīng
**7 Sanlitun Bei Lu, off Sanlitun Lu
☎010/64171650.**
This pleasant place, the haunt of diplomats
from the Indian subcontinent (as well as

locals, for whom the food here is a bit of
an experiment) serves Indian and Thai
dishes. Try the *palak paneer, aloo gobi*,
tandoori chicken or garlic nan – which all
together will feed two. Around ¥50 per
person, though there's a lunchtime curry
buffet which is a bargain at ¥38. The beer
is cheaper than in the bars around. Daily
11am–10.30pm.

Old Character Hakka Restaurant
老汉子客家菜馆
lǎohànzi kèjiācàiguǎn
**Sanlitun Bei Jie, off Sanlitun Jie, next to the
Cross Bar** ☎010/64153376.
Harassed, shouty staff reveal how popular
this place is, and deservedly so – it's
cramped but atmospheric, and the food,
Hakka dishes from the south, is delicious
and not expensive. Head north up the west
side of Sanlitun, turn off after 200m and
follow the signs for the *Cross Bar*. Make sure
you don't end up in the pale imitation next
door – the real place has a black doorway.

One Thousand and One Nights
一千零一夜
yiqiān língyíyè
21 Gongrentiyuchang Bei Lu ☎010/65324050.
Beijing's first Middle Eastern restaurant, this
place is deservedly popular, a favourite both
with Western big noses who come here to
fill up on kebabs before or after hitting the
bars, and with homesick diplomats who puff
on hookahs on the pavement outside. Has
nightly belly dancing. It's open till very late
but some dishes sell out early on. Try the
hummus as a starter and the baked chicken
for a main course, and leave enough room
for some baklava (which can also be bought
separately at their sweet shop, 100m east
of the restaurant). Bus #118 comes here
from Dongsi Shitiao subway stop. About
¥60 per head. Daily11am–2am.

Paulaner Bräuhaus
**Lufthansa Centre, Beisanhuan Dong Lu.
☎010/64653388 ext 5732.**
German fare and great beer, brewed on
the premises. Their pork-and-sauerkraut
meal for two (¥135) is about as cheap a
meal as you'll get in the building, where
there are plenty of other upmarket restaurants: unsurprisingly, the *Trattoria*
(☎010/64653388 ext 5707) serves Italian
food and does pizza delivery, while in the
basement, *Sorabol* (☎010/64651845) specializes in Korean cuisine.

Serve the People

为人民服务

wèirénmínfúwù

1 Sanlitun Xiwujie ⊕010/64153242.

Hip and trendy Thai restaurant, going for a postmodern Soviet look, presumably ironically. Thai staples such as green curry, pork satay with peanut sauce and *tom yam* seafood soup are all worth trying, and you can ask them to tone down the spices. The stylish T-shirts worn by the staff are available to buy. About ¥70 per person.

Shenglinfu Taiwan Restaurant

盛林府

shènglínfǔ

18 Sanlitun Bei Lu, off Sanlitun Lu ⊕010/64159274.

This elegant and affordable little restaurant boasts classical Chinese decor and attentive service, and does a good clay-pot chicken in wine. You can also take part in a Taiwanese tea ceremony in an anteroom, though it's extremely expensive (at least ¥120) and the product is very bitter to most Westerners' tastes. To get here, head north up the west side of Sanlitun Lu and after 200m you'll see an English sign reading "orthodox Taiwan food", which points you down a *hutong*. Go down the alley, then turn right and look for the place with the red lanterns outside. Around ¥40 per person. Daily 10am–midnight.

Southern Beijing

See the map on p.58–59 for the locations of the places reviewed here.

Gongdelin

功德林素菜馆

gōngdélín sùcàiguǎn

158 Qianmen Nan Dajie.

This odd vegetarian restaurant serves Shanghai dishes with names like "the fire is singeing the snow-capped mountains". Try the imitation fish dishes, and the "dragons' eyes", made of tofu and mushrooms. It's partly owned by the government, so service is old-fashioned – meaning lacklustre at best – though meals are cheap at around ¥30 a head.

Health Food Restaurant

Rainbow Hotel, 13 Xijing Lu. See p.109 for the hotel's name in Chinese.

Recipes at this elegant, pricey place are guided by the principles of traditional Chinese medicine. The staff will explain which food is good for which part of the body – lamb and beef for the kidneys, fruit for the skin, sour food for the liver and sweet for the lungs. Meals cost around ¥100 per head, a lot more if you choose the ginseng or snake dishes.

Lichun

利群烤鸭店

lìqún kǎoyādiàn

11 Bei Xiang Hutong ⊕010/67025681.

Deep in a *hutong*, this place is tough to find but offers good duck at half the price of the chains (¥80). From Qianmen subway stop walk east along Qianmen Dong Dajie, take the first right into Zhengyi Lu, and turn right at the end. Then follow the English sign to the "Lijun Roast Duck Restaurant" and it's on the left. You'll probably have to ask. The restaurant is in an old courtyard house, and it's small, so you'd be wise to reserve beforehand.

Quanjude Roast Duck

全聚德烤鸭店

quánjùdé kǎoyādiàn

32 Qianmen Dajie ⊕010/67011379 **and 14 Qianmen Xi Dajie** ⊕010/63018833.

"The Great Wall and Roast Duck, try both to have a luck", says a ditty by the entrance to the Qianmen Dajie premises of this Beijing institution, operated by the same family since 1852 and sometime host to luminaries such as Fidel Castro. Though it's quite touristy, there's nothing inauthentic about the food, and the experience – the bustle and noise, the chef carving at your table – is a memorable one. At Qianmen Dajie, tour groups are herded upstairs, though the ground floor is livelier. Takeaway duck from the same kitchen can be bought next door. The branch on Qianmen Xi Dajie earned its local moniker, "Super Duck", thanks to its size – it seats over two thousand. Though it tends to be the haunt of large groups, there are more intimate side rooms with smaller tables. Prices are the same at both locations: a whole duck is ¥170. Not cheap, but worth doing once.

Yushan Restaurant

御膳饭店

yùshàn fàndiàn

87 Tiantan Lu, opposite the north gate of the Temple of Heaven ⊕010/67014263.

Empress Dowager Cixi was particularly fond of phoenix prawns and stuffed lotus root, both of which you can try at this branch of the famous *Fangshan Restaurant* (see below). The surroundings here are less grand though just as kitsch. It's also a little cheaper here, though you can still expect to pay well over ¥100 per head. Bus #60 from Chongwenmen subway stop to Hongqiao Market.

Northern Beijing

The map on pp.82–83 shows the places reviewed below.

Fangshan
仿膳饭店
fǎngshàn fàndiàn
Beijing Park, near the east gate
ⓣ010/64011879.
There is no better place than this, superbly situated on the central island in Beihai Park, to sample imperial cuisine in Beijing. It's all magisterially kitsch and good for a splurge. Arrive hungry; fixed-price meals start at ¥100 per person for fourteen courses. For ¥260 per head you get a different set of fourteen courses including chicken paté wrapped in seaweed and egg, and camel's paw with scallion. Staff in full costume are well versed in the history behind each dish. The place closes early in the evening; booking recommended. Daily 11am–1.30pm & 5–8pm.

Gong Wang Fu Sichuan Restaurant
恭王付四川饭店
gōngwángfǔ sìchuān fàndiàn
14 Liuyin Jie, just north of Prince Gong's Palace ⓣ010/66156924.
Fiery Sichuan food in a lavishly re-created traditional setting with bamboo chairs and a lot of rosewood. Sees plenty of tourist traffic, so there's an English menu and they'll tone down the spices if asked. Around ¥60 per head.

Kaorouji
烤肉季
kǎoròují

14 Qianhai Dong Yuan ⓣ010/64045921.
In the *hutongs* close to the Drum Tower, this Muslim place takes advantage of its great lakeside location with big windows and, in summer, balcony tables. Run by the same family for 150 years. The beef and barbecued lamb dishes are recommended. From the Drum Tower, continue south down Di'anmenwai Dajie, then take the first *hutong* on the right; the restaurant is a short walk down here, just before the lake bridge. Around ¥50 a head. Daily 11am–2pm & 5–8.30pm.

Moscow Restaurant
莫斯科餐厅
mòsīkē cāntīng
Off Xizhimenwai Dajie, 200m north up the first alleyway on the west side of the Exhibition Centre, by the zoo.
The best thing about this eccentric place is the decor – the main hall is a ballroom full of knobbly columns and chandeliers, which you'll have plenty of time to appreciate as service isn't speedy. The food is authentic, though, with borscht and stroganoff on the menu. Expect to pay at least ¥100 per head, so go for the experience rather than the food, and get there early as the hall is cleared for dancing at 8pm.

Nengrenju
能仁居饭庄
néngrénjü fànzhuāng
5 Taipingqiao Dajie, close to Baita Si.
A neat little place, perhaps the best in the capital to sample Mongolian hotpot. There's a lot on the menu, but stick to the classic ingredients – mutton, cabbage, potato and glass noodles – for a guaranteed good feed. With all those boiling pots, it gets quite hot and steamy here in the evening. The place is very popular with middle-class locals – you'll just have to tolerate the mobile phones. It's not geared around the portly banqueting crowd, so tables are small enough for conversation.

Koreatown

Beijing's large population of Korean expats are amply catered for in the strip of restaurants, shops and bars at "Koreatown", in Wudaokou, Haidian District, outside the Beijing Language and Culture Insititute. Prices are pretty inexpensive, around ¥30 per head. The other Koreatown, opposite the *Kempinski Hotel*, is a little more upmarket. At either, pick any restaurant that looks busy and order *nayng myon*, cold noodles; *bibimbap*, a clay pot of rice, vegetables, egg and beef; or *pulgoki* barbecued beef, which you cook yourself on the table grill.

From Fuchengmen subway stop, head east for about 500m, then turn right (south) down Taipingqiao Dajie.

Nuage

庆云楼

qìngyúnlóu

Just east of the Kaorouji, at 22 Qianhai Dong Zhao ☎010/64019581.

Deserves a mention not only as one of the few places to eat good Vietnamese food in Beijing, but also for the tropical fantasy that is the toilets. The upstairs bar-restaurant is smart and cosy. Try steamed garlic prawns and battered squid, and finish with super strong Vietnamese coffee if you don't intend to sleep any time soon. ¥100 per head. Daily 10am–9.30pm; bar stays open till 2am.

Sculpting In Time

雕刻时光

diāokèshíguāng

7 Weigongcun Lu, outside the southern gate of the Beijing Insititute of Technology.

A casual, attractive café with a largely student clientele. Fit in by drinking lattoo, browsing the book collection and gazing thoughtfully out of the window. They serve good muffins and pasta dishes here, too.

Supermarkets

These days, all the supermarkets sell plenty of Western food alongside all the Chinese, though few have a decent range of dairy products. The CRC Supermarket in the basement of the China World Trade Centre is impressive, though Western goods cost about twenty percent more here than they would at home. Park'n'Shop, in the basement of the COFCO Plaza on Jianguomen Dajie, is a little cheaper. The supermarket on the first floor of the Friendship Store, Jianguomenwai Dajie, is very pricey but a good place to find imported cheese and canned goods. The Parkson Store, Lufthansa Centre and CVIC Plaza also have large basement supermarkets, and Carrefour have opened stores at 6 Dongsanhuan Bei Lu, just west of the zoo, and on Xizhimenwai Dajie.

But for the best range of Western produce, including hard-to-find items such as oregano and hummus, head for **Jenny Lou's** outside the west gate of Chaoyang Park in the east of the city, where prices are half those of the Friendship Store.

Drinking and nightlife

Beijing's nightlife scene has recovered from the moral clampdown of the 60s and 70s, when "bourgeois" bars and tea houses disappeared. They were replaced by an artificial emphasis on traditional Chinese culture (especially opera and formal theatre), which was often worthy to the point of tedium, and at its worst when addressing the subject matter of the revolution. Nowadays nobody is much interested in this sort of stuff, and modern Beijingers, who suddenly find themselves with rising disposable incomes, living through comparatively liberal times, just want to have fun.

Today, Beijing offers much more than the karaoke lounges and bland hotel bars you'll find in many other Chinese cities. In the late 1980s the city was swept by a trend for huge **discos**, which are still popular today. The formula is always the same: a few hours of gentle dance music, followed by a slushy half-hour, when a singer comes on stage and dancers pair off, followed by a more raucous last hour or two when only the serious clubbers are left and the mood becomes much less restrained. Bizarrely, there's usually a raffle too – lucky winners walk off with perhaps a bicycle or a pair of sports shoes. More recently, more sophisticated, Western-style clubs have opened, which feature the latest DJs flown in from the West or Japan.

The fashion among modern urbanites, however, is for **bars**. In 1995, **Sanlitun Lu** in the east of the city had just one bar, and it was losing money. A new manager bought it, believing the place had potential but that the *feng shui* was wrong – the toilet was opposite the door and all the wealth was going down it. He changed the name, moved the loo, and – so the story goes – the city's bar scene, still clustered here, took off from there. Now the area is choked with drinking holes, a couple of new bar districts have sprung up, and new bars open all the time. Many are rip-offs of their popular neighbours; if one does well, soon four more will open around it, and before you know it, the original will have closed down. While many places can appear eerily familiar – pretty much everything is just like home, including the prices – you can still finds a cheap beer and a distinctly local ambience if you know where to look.

Bars

Beijing bars, like microbes, appear quickly, multiply, then die suddenly. For the latest information, check one of the expat magazines or Ⓦ www.beijingnights .com.

There's talk – there always is – of imminent demolition, but at the time of writing the biggest cluster of bars was around **Sanlitun Lu**. The establishments here all offer beer at Western prices and some have live music; cafés offer sobering blasts of coffee. A mellower scene exists around the attractive **Houhai**, where places are laid-back, with ambient music and no dancefloors. A small group of new expat-oriented bars around the west gate of **Chaoyang Park** in the far east of the city looks about to swell. Most other bars are close to universities, and the student clientele means these places tend to be cheaper and hipper, with a little more edge.

Bar **hours** are flexible – a bar tends to close only when its last barfly has lurched off – though all bars open till at least midnight (well into the early hours at weekends). We've listed the phone numbers of bars that can be tough to find (just get your cabbie to ring them) or have regular gigs; usually there's a cover charge to get in of around ¥30 when a band is playing (¥100 if it's the legendary Cui Jian; see p.131).

Though Chinese beer can be cheaper than bottled water if bought in a shop, a 350ml bottle of Tsingtao or the local Yanjing at a bar will usually cost ¥15–25. Many bars also sell Western draught beers such as Guinness and Boddingtons, which cost at least ¥40. The best – and cheapest – draught is available in those places that make their own, such as *Get Lucky* (see p.131) and the *Paulaner Brauhaus* (see p.118). The *Hidden Tree* (see below) deserves a mention for its impressive collection of Belgian brews.

Beijing's bars have given a huge boost to the city's **music scene**, providing much-needed venues. You can now hear live classical zither or bamboo flute tunes, jazz, deep house, or head-banging grindcore on some night each week. A couple of bars with a strong emphasis on live music are reviewed on pp.130–131.

Eastern Beijing

Sanlitun and the northeast

Just inside the northeast section of the third ring road, this busy area (see the map on p.80) can be reached by taking the subway to Dongsi Shitiao, then bus #113 east; get off at the third stop. The main strip – **Sanlitun Lu** – is sometimes called **Jiuba Jie**, literally "bar street". A second concentration on a *hutong* south and just to the west is referred to as **Nan Jiuba Jie** (also known as **Sanlitun Nan Jie** and by its official, largely unused name, Dongdaqiaoxie Jie). Many foreigners prefer it to the main strip, as most venues here are a bit cheaper and hipper.

We've listed the most deserving bars below, but there are plenty more in this area from which to choose. In addition to drinks, a few offer Western food, and there are plenty of decent places to eat in the area too (see p.118). Venues with a cover charge are listed under discos.

Frank's Place
万龙酒吧
wànlóng jiǔbā
Gongrentiyuchang Dong Lu.
One of the original expat hangouts, with a cosy neighbourhood feel, and packed with Americana. Come here to eat – the giant burgers and steaks are tasty – and for quiet drinks in the company of the local golfing set.

Hidden Tree
隐蔽的树
yǐnbìde shù
12 Sanlitun Nan Jie.
Cosy, relaxed and fashionable in an understated way, with a pleasant garden and a twisted oak growing through the bar. Has a good selection of draught beers.

Jam House
芥茉房酒吧
jiànmòfáng jiǔbā
Sanlitun Nan Jie ☏010/65063845.
Head south past *Nashville* for about 100m and look for the sign that points you down an alley. This little place is Sanlitun's hippest, largely thanks to Mimi, the colourful manageress. It's popular with both trendy locals and young expats, with the conversation usually conducted in Chinese. There's a live band at weekends –

usually rock or jazz – followed by a jam session which patrons are welcome to join in. If the raucous downstairs bar gets too heavy on your ears, head up to the rooftop seating.

Jazz Ya
李波餐厅
líbō cāntīng
18 Sanlitun Lu ☏010/64151227.
This mellow place, with rough-hewn wooden tables and moody music, has a better drinks menu than most of its neighbours. It's set back from the road; look for the yellow sign down an alley next to *Bella Coffee*. Occasional live jazz.

Minders Bar
明大酒吧
míngdà jiǔbā
Sanlitun Nan Jie.
One of the early 1990s bars, with an in-house Filipino band covering 1970s and 1980s pop and rock. Unpretentious.

Nashville
乡谣酒吧
xiāngyáo jiǔbā
Sanlitun Nan Jie.
Among the longest-established places, where you can hear country music, with an in-house band Wednesday to Saturday. A wide variety of draught beers available, including Hoegaarden and Boddingtons.

Poachers Inn
猎人俱乐部
lièrén jùlèbù
43 Bei Sanlitun Lu.
Head north up Sanlitun Lu, turn left after 200m at the sign for the *Cross Bar* and follow the road round, and the bar is on the right. This is Beijing's most popular expat bar – and plenty of locals like it too, in part at least thanks to the refreshingly low prices (draught beer is ¥5 a pint, cocktails ¥10). The dancefloor gets busy most nights and is crammed every weekend, and there's live jazz on Thursday night and bands occasional Saturdays.

Public Space
50 Sanlitun Lu.
Though the exterior looks like every other watering hole on the strip, this is actually Sanlitun's first bar, still very popular and one of the most pleasant in the area. Draught beer is ¥20, a gin and tonic ¥30.

Success
4 Gongrentiyuchang Dong Lu.
More of a nightclub than a bar, but

without a cover charge. Come to gawp at this irony-free monument to spiritual pollution and kitsch excess. An awful band plays Mando-pop nightly to a smug crowd of conspicuous consumers. Get one of the slick hostesses to light your cigarette for you and you'll feel like you've really arrived.

Tree Lounge
Dongsanhuan Lu (third ring road), just south of the Agriculture Exhibition Centre.
Tucked just around the corner from the *CD Café*, in the same building. New and modish, with music you can talk over, comfy dark nooks and a patio. Tsingtao ¥15.

Around Chaoyang Park

Bus #113 comes here from Dongsi Shitiao subway – get off at the fourth stop.

Goose and Duck
鹅和鸭酒吧
éhéyā jiǔbā
Outside the park's west gate.
A faux British pub run by an American, this is the place to play pool and darts and pick up anti-fashion and hick-hair tips. The clientele keep their shirts tucked into their jeans and never notice how great (and incongruous) the Saturday night house band are. Buy the band drinks and commiserate. Two drinks for the price of one 4–8pm.

World of Suzie Wong
苏西黄酒吧
sūxīhuáng jiǔbā
Outside the park's west gate, above the *Mirch Masala* restaurant – look for the discreet yellow neon sign outside.
Striking neo-Oriental decor – think lacquer and rose petals – but inexpensive prices (Tsingtao ¥12). Named after a fictional Hong Kong prostitute, this den is popular with Cantonese guys, beautiful bored women and fashionable expats thrilled by how decadent it all looks.

Northern Beijing

As well as the obvious strip that runs along the south side of **Houhai**, there's a chain of bars along **Yandaixie Jie**, the *hutong* leading towards the Drum Tower from

Yinding Bridge. All of these places are new, and charge between ¥15 and ¥20 for a bottle of Tsingtao; we've listed the only two well-established ones.

To reach the area, take bus #107 from Dongzhimen subway stop, get off at the north entrance to Beihai Park and walk north around the lake. The places listed here are marked on the map on pp.000–000.

Buddha Bar
不大酒吧
búdà jiǔbā
Yinding Bridge, opposite the *Kaorouji* restaurant.
The great location by the lake and the pleasant patio make this fashionably ramshackle, bric-a-brac-stuffed place popular for discreet people-watching. Especially good in summer; not cheap though (¥25 for a bottle of Tsingtao).

No Name Bar
3 Qianhai Dongyuan, just east of the *Kaorouji* Restaurant.
A hippy-ish café bar that thinks it's special because it doesn't have a sign. This was the first lakeside bar, and its trendy anonymity and bric-a-braccy interior design has informed every other one in the area.

Pass By Bar
过客酒吧
guòkè jiǔbā
108 Nan Luo Guo Xiang, off Di'anmen Dong Dajie ☏010/84038004,
A renovated courtyard house turned cosy bar/restaurant that's popular with foreign and Chinese backpackers and students. There are lots of books and pictures of China's far-flung places to peruse, and well-travelled staff to chat to – if you can get their attention. Pretty good pizzas too.

What?
什么酒吧
shénme jiǔbā
North of the third ring road on Tai Yang Gong Lu, the northern continuation of Hepingli Dongjie.
This has nightly jam sessions, open to all and very variable in quality. Popular with the rock-loving set.

Discos

Beijing's giant discos are very popular now that hedonism is politically acceptable. They may not be the hippest venues on the planet but they're certainly spirited, and cheaper than a night out in a Western capital. Another, much cooler, club scene exists, which mostly plays trance and funk music to punters wearing sunglasses in the dark. These smaller venues get closed down often, partly as the authorities take a dim view of use of the "shake-head drug" (ecstasy).

All places listed here have a cover charge, given in our reviews, which generally increases at weekends. Note that if you just want to dance, and aren't too prissy about the latest music, see the bar reviews above for venues with their own dancefloor.

Eastern Beijing

Sanlitun and the northeast

The Club
Opposite and just west of *Poachers Inn* (see opposite).
Small, dark venue for the in-crowd to check each other out while pretending to know the DJ. Decent music on the whole though, mostly house and funk. Women get in free on Thursdays. Daily 8pm–4am. ¥50

Orange
Off Xingfuyicun Lu.
Follow the sign north up the alley opposite the Workers' Stadium's north gate. Dark and minimalist with a big dancefloor, this is very chic and popular with those who think of themselves as trendsetters. Hip-hop on Thursdays and DJs at weekends, when there's a ¥30–50 cover charge.

Vics

威克斯

wēikèsī jiǔbā

Inside the Workers' Stadium's north gate, next to the *Outback* steakhouse.

Eighties LA decor, a sweaty dancefloor and a *Less Than Zero*-ambience of numb dissipation. The low cover charge and cheapish drinks (bottled beer ¥15) make it popular with students and embassy brats. Women get in free on Wednesdays and get free drinks till midnight. Thursday is ragga/reggae night. Hip-hop, R&B and techno all weekend. Daily 7pm–6am. ¥30 except Thurs, when it's free to get in.

Jianguomen

Club Banana

赛特饭店

sàitè fàndiàn (SCITECH Hotel)

Scitech Hotel, 22 Jianguomenwai Dajie.

Big, brash and in-your-face, this mega club has three sections – techno, funk and chill-out – and features go-go girls, karaoke rooms and an enthusiastic, young clientele. It's not subtle but it does the job. Mon–Thurs & Sun 8.30pm–4am, Fri & Sat 8.30pm–5am. ¥20, except weekends ¥40.

Northern Beijing

JJs

JJ迪斯科

JJ dísīkē

74–76 Xinjiekou Bei Dajie, just west of the Shicha lakes; see map, pp.82–83.

Another laser-lashed cavern hosting a young crowd dancing by numbers to a mild cocktail of techno, pop and house. Go-go girls demonstrate how it should be done. Bus #22 comes here from Qianmen. Daily 8pm–4am. ¥20–50.

Gay Beijing

Official attitudes towards homosexuality have softened of late – it's been removed from the official list of psychiatric disorders and is no longer a national crime, though gay men have occasionally been arrested under public disturbance statutes. That's unlikely to happen in cosmopolitan Beijing however, where pink power is a big influence on fashion and the media.

The **gay scene** is vibrant but discreet, with gay bars no longer required to hand out pamphlets urging clients to go home to their wives. One longstanding venue is the *On/Off* bar, at 5 Xingfuyicun Xili, Lian Bao Apartments, Chaoyang (☎010/64158083), mostly catering for men. It's all rather sedate and square, though, and the only pretty boys are those for rent (nicknamed "ducks" in Chinese). *Drag-On*, at the end of the alley behind Xingfucun Zhong Lu, near the Workers' Stadium, is livelier, with weekend amateur pole dancing and other activities for the *tongzhi* (literally, comrades, here given a new bent). Two venues popular with the young gay crowd, though not specifically gay clubs, are the *Rock and Roll* disco at Yard 4, Gongrentiyuchang Bei Lu, behind the *Loft* pub; and *Club Banana* (see above).

Entertainment and art

Most visitors to Beijing take in at least a taste of **Beijing opera** and the superb Chinese **acrobatics displays** – both of which are pretty timeless. Fewer investigate the equally worthwhile contemporary side of the city's entertainment scene – the new music, theatre and art happenings. There are also a number of **cinemas** where you can check out the weighty, often provocative movies emerging from a new wave of film-makers.

For officially approved cultural forms of expression – visiting ballet troupes, large-scale concerts and so forth, check the listings in the *China Daily*, available at most hotels, but for the real lowdown, including gigs, track down the expat-oriented magazine *That's Beijing* (see p19).

Traditional opera

Beijing opera (*jingxi*) is the most celebrated of the country's 350 or so regional operatic styles – a unique combination of song, dance, acrobatics and mime, with some similarity to Western pantomime. Highly stylized, to the outsider the performances can often seem obscure to the point of absurdity, rapidly growing tedious and ultimately painful, since shows

---

Shows at tea houses

A few tea-house theatres, where you can sit and snack and watch performances of Beijing opera, sedate zither music and martial arts, have appeared in the capital, though all are aimed at tourists rather than locals. You can watch a ninety-minute variety show – comprising all three genres – at the **Lao She Tea House**, Third Floor, Dawancha Building, 3 Qianmen Xi Dajie (daily 2.30pm & 7.40pm; ¥40–130; the afternoon performances are cheaper). Popular with tour groups, the show gives a gaudy taste of traditional Chinese culture. The **Tianqiao Theatre**, set in a mock-traditional building at 113 Tianqiao Nan Dajie (☏010/63040617), aims for an authentic atmosphere, right down to the Qing costumes of the staff. Performances, beginning at 7pm and lasting two hours, are mostly segments of traditional opera with a little acrobatics in between. The ticket price of ¥180 includes tea and snacks; for ¥330 you get a duck dinner too. Buying tickets a day in advance is advised as the place is sometimes booked out with tour groups.

The **Tianhai Tea House**, tucked away in an alley east off Sanlitun Lu, offers an elegant respite from the hedonism outside, and has free recitals of traditional music (Fri & Sat from 9pm). More the haunt of expats and arty Chinese is the tea house at the **Sanwei Bookstore**, at 60 Fuxingmennei Dajie (opposite the *Minzu Hotel*; ☏010/66013204). This is where to come for performances of light jazz on Fridays and Chinese folk music on Saturdays (8.30–10pm).

(which can last up to four hours) are punctuated by a succession of crashing gongs and piercing, discordant songs. But it's worth seeing once, especially if you can acquaint yourself with the plot beforehand. Most of the plots are based on historical or mythological themes – two of the most famous sagas, which any Chinese will explain to you, are *The White Snake* and *The Water Margin* – and full of moral lessons. An interesting, if controversial, variation on the traditions are operas dealing with contemporary themes – such as Mao's first wife, or the struggle of women to marry as they choose. Apart from checking out the venues below, you can visit a tea house for your opera fix (see p.127). Tea-house performances are short and aimed at foreigners, and you can also slurp tea or munch on snacks – often Beijing duck as well – while being entertained.

The **colours** used on stage, from the costumes to the make-up on the players' faces, are highly symbolic – red signifies loyalty; yellow, fierceness; blue, cruelty; and white, evil.

Chang'an Theatre
长安大剧场
chángān dàjùchǎng
7 Jianguomennei Dajie ☎010/65101309.
A modern, central theatre putting on nightly performances at 7.15pm. ¥40–150.

Liyuan Theatre
First floor of the *Jianguo Qianmen Hotel* (see p.108), 175 Yong'an Lu ☎010/63016688 ext 8860.
There aren't many Chinese faces in the audience as the opera staged here is a tour-group-friendly bastardization, merely lasting a hour and jazzed up with some martial arts and slapstick. A display board at the side of the stage gives a nonsensical English translation of the few lines of dialogue. Tickets for the nightly 7.30pm performances can be bought from the office in the front courtyard of the hotel (daily 9–11am, noon–4.45pm & 5.30–8pm; ¥30–120); the more expensive seats are at tables at the front, where you can sip tea and nibble pastries during the performance. Bus #66 from Hepingmen subway stop comes here.

Huguang Guild Hall
湖广会馆
húguǎng huìguǎn

3 Hufang Lu, a 1500m walk south from Hepingmen subway stop ☎010/63518284.
This reconstructed theatre with a fine performance hall has a small opera museum on site too, with costumes and pictures of famous performers, though no English captions. Nightly performances at 7.15pm; ¥60–150.

Prince Gong's Palace
恭王府
gōngwáng fǔ
Liuyun Jie ☎010/66186628.
Opera is put on nightly for tour groups in the grand hall at the Prince Gong mansion (see p.86). You have to call to book a seat. Performances start at 7.30pm and cost ¥80–120.

Zhengyici Theatre
正义祠剧场
zhèngyìcí jùchǎng
220 Qianmen Xiheyan Jie ☎010/63189454.
For the genuine article, performed in the only surviving wooden Beijing opera theatre, worth a visit just to check out the architecture. Duck dinners, available here, cost an additional ¥110. Though not cheap, this is a highly recommended night out, with performances at 7.30pm (¥150; 2hr).

Drama and dance

Spoken **drama** was only introduced into Chinese theatres in the twentieth century. The People's Art Theatre in Beijing became the best-known company and, prior to the Cultural Revolution, staged Chinese-language translations of European plays which had a clear social message – Ibsen and Chekhov were among the favourite playwrights. But in 1968, Jiang Qing, Mao's third wife, declared that "drama is dead". The company, along with most of China's cinemas, was almost completely out of action for nearly a decade afterwards, with a corpus of just eight plays (deemed socially improving) continuing to be performed. Many of the principal actors, directors and writers were banished, generally to rural hard labour. The past couple of decades have seen a turnaround, with the People's Art Theatre, reconstituted in 1979, establishing its reputation once again with a performance of Arthur Miller's *Death of a Salesman*.

Though a little glitzy for many foreigners' tastes, Chinese **song and dance** extravaganzas are the way they don't make them any more in the West. Most evenings, you can catch one of these revues simply by turning the TV on, though there is plenty of opportunity to see them live. One not to miss is the regularly staged *Red Detachment of Women*, a classic piece of retro communist pomp which celebrates a revolutionary women's fighting outfit – the dancers wear guerilla uniform and carry hand grenades and rifles. Some venues, such as the Beijing Exhibition Theatre, occasionally stage performances, in the original language, of imported musicals like *The Sound of Music* which, with tickets at ¥50–100, are a lot cheaper to watch here than at home.

Dance is popular in Beijing, generally more so at the traditional end of the spectrum, though a few small venues purvey more contemporary forms. Besides the venues listed below, the Poly Theatre (see p.131) is another place where you can watch theatrical and dance performances.

Beijing Exhibition Theatre
北京展览馆剧场
běijīng zhǎnlǎnguǎn jùchǎng
135 Xizhimenwai Dajie ☎010/68354455.
This giant hall stages classical concerts and large-scale song-and-dance revues.

Beijing Modern Dance Company Theatre
北京现代舞团实验剧场
běijīng xiàndàiwǔtuán shíyàn jùchǎng
8 Majiabao Dongli, in the south of the city beyond the Third Ring Road ☎010/67573879.
A small but very dedicated dance troupe performing modern pieces. Tickets only cost around ¥40.

Capital Theatre
首都剧场
shǒudū jùchǎng
22 Wangfujing Dajie ☎010/65253677.
Look out for the People's Art Theatre here – displayed in the lobby is their photo archive, documenting their history – as well as other companies. Tickets generally start at ¥40 and can cost as much as ¥300.

Experimental Theatre For Dramatic Arts
中央实验话剧院小剧场
zhōngyāng shíyànhuà jùyuàn xiaojùchǎng
45 Mao'er Hutong ☎010/64031099.
Just north of the Bell Tower, off Jiugulou Dajie, this has a reputation for putting on modern, avant-garde performances, in Chinese.

Puppet Theatre
中国木偶剧院
zhōngguó mù'ǒu jùyuàn
A1, Section 1, Anhua Xi Li, Bei Sanhuan Lu (third ring road), opposite the Sogo Department Store ☎010/64254798.
Once as important for commoners as opera was for the elite, Chinese puppetry usually involves hand puppets and marionettes. Occasionally shadow puppets made of thin translucent leather and supported by rods are used. Beijing opera, short stories and fairy tales. Shows daily at 6.30pm; ¥20.

Acrobatics and martial arts

Certainly the most accessible and exciting of the traditional Chinese entertainments, **acrobatics** covers anything from gymnastics through to feats of magic and juggling. The tradition of professional acrobats has existed in China for two thousand years and continues today at the country's main training school, at Wu Qiao in Hebei Province, where students begin training at the age of 5.

The style may be vaudeville, but performances are spectacular, with truly awe-inspiring feats of dexterity – sixteen people stacked atop a bicycle and the like. Just as impressive are martial-arts displays, which usually involve a few mock fights and feats of strength, such as breaking concrete slabs with one blow.

Chaoyang Theatre
朝阳剧场
cháoyáng jùchǎng
36 Dongsanhuan Bei Lu ☎010/65072421.
The easiest way to see acrobatics is to come to one of the shows here. At the end, the Chinese tourists rush off as if it's a fire drill, leaving the foreign tour groups to do the applauding. There are plenty of souvenir stalls in the lobby – make your purchases after the show rather than during the interval, as prices come down at the end. Shows nightly 7.15–9pm; tickets cost ¥60–80, though they can work out cheaper if you arrange them through your hotel.

Wansheng Theatre
万胜剧场
wànshèng jùchǎng
95 Tianqiao Market, at the eastern end of Beiwei Lu and west of Tiantan Park ☎010/63037449.
Tourist-friendly and great fun, the performances here are lighter on glitz than elsewhere. Nightly performances at 7.15pm; ¥100–150.

Xinrong Theatre
鑫融剧院
xīnróng jùchǎng
16 Baizhifang Xi Jie, the street leading west off the southern end of Niu Jie ☎010/63543344.
A popular kung fu show with a story about two competing schools used as an excuse for a monumental choreographed rumble. Nightly performances at 7.30pm; ¥70–280.

Live music venues

Traditional Han Chinese music is usually played on the *erhu* (a kind of fiddle) and *qin* (a seven-stringed zither). Most recent pieces are compositions in a pseudo-romantic, Western-influenced style; easy on the ear, they can be heard live in upmarket hotels and restaurants. To hear traditional pieces, visit the concert halls, the Sanwei Bookstore on a Saturday (see p.127) or the *Tianhai Tea House*. Western classical music is popular – the best place to catch it is the Beijing Concert Hall – but what has really caught on is jazz, which you can hear at a few venues, notably *Jazz Ya* (see p.124) and the Sanwei Bookstore on Fridays.

Mainstream **Chinese pop** – mostly slushy ballads sung by Hong Kong or Taiwanese heartthrobs – is hard to avoid; it pumps out of shops on every street and can be heard live at the Workers' Stadium. Beijing also has a thriving underground scene of edgy rock (see box opposite), showcased at a couple of the venues below.

Beijing Concert Hall
北京音乐厅
běijīng yīnyuè tīng
1 Beixinhua Jie, just off Xichang'an Jie ☎010/66057006.
South of Zhongnanhai, this thousand-seater hosts regular concerts of Western classical and Chinese traditional music by Beijing's resident orchestra and visiting orchestras from the rest of China and overseas. Tickets, usually priced in the ¥30–150 range, can be bought here, at the CVIK Plaza (see p.79) and at the Parkson Department Store (see p.135).

CD Café
CD 咖啡屋
CD kāfēiwù
Dongsanhuan Lu (third ring road), just south of the Agriculture Exhibition Centre ☎010/65018877 ext 3032.
The best and most accessible place to sample the local music scene, with a good stage, a spacious seating area, and bands on most nights. Check the expat listings magazines for their schedule. A Tsingtao costs ¥15 and there's table service. Can feel a bit froufrou despite the raw rock explosions it hosts.

The Beijing rock scene

Controversial local legend **Cui Jian**, a sort of Chinese Bob Dylan, was China's first real rock star, giving up a job as a trumpeter in a Beijing orchestra to perform gravel-voiced guitar rock with lyrics as dangerous as he could get away with. He still performs in the city's bars occasionally. Look out for his recent albums "Power to The Powerless" and "Egg Under the Red Flag".

Cui Jian is now seen as the granddaddy of Beijing's **indie music** scene. There are plenty of smoky bars to act as venues; government permission is not required for gigs, unlike theatre; and unlike literature, no party officials scrutinize the lyrics – so if you're an angsty young Beijinger with something to say, you start a band. Nobody makes any money as venues and bands struggle to survive against all-pervasive pop pap, and when an act does take off, piracy eats up any profits the recordings might have made – but fierce dedication keeps the scene alive.

The punks are the most obviously outrageous, if not the most original, element of the indie music scene; try to catch **Brain Failure**, **Reflector** or **Hang on the Box** for the most frenzied moshing in Asia. The Nirvana-influenced **Cold Blooded Animals** are another great live act, with some form of visual affront to the audience pretty much guaranteed, and they'd certainly smash their equipment if they could afford to.

At the time of writing, the most-hyped band was the **Second Hand Roses**, whose lead singer Liang Long dresses in drag and sings in the vaudevillean style of northeastern opera. Part of the reason for their critical approval (ironically, mostly with foreigners) is their inclusion of Chinese elements, such as a *suona* (horn) section. Other bands argue that such "authenticity" is irrelevant as rock is an international language, not a Western one.

At present the biggest bands to have broken out of the Beijing scene are indie popsters **New Pants** and **Flower** (it helps that they're pretty teens), though these days you're more likely to see them on a billboard than performing in a bar. Other Beijing stalwarts to look out for are rockers **Tongue**, **Zi Yue** and **Hopscotch**, rap-metal crowd pleasers **CMCB**, and poppy girl band **Colour** (Yanse). Promising newcomers include **Beautiful Pharmacy**, who decorate the stage to resemble a clinic, jazz funksters **SunJam**, and the electronica afficionados **Supermarket**.

Most bands of note are on the Scream, Badhead or Modern Sky labels. For the latest new releases, check out ⊛www.niubi.com.

Century Theatre
中日青年交流中心
zhōngrì qīngniánjiāoliú zhōngxīn
At the Sino-Japanese Youth Centre, 40 Liangmaqiao Lu, 2km east of the *Kempinski Hotel* ☎010/64663311.
An intimate venue that plays host to soloists and small ensembles. Mostly Chinese modern and traditional classical compositions. Evening performances; ¥120–150.

Forbidden City Concert Hall
Inside Zhongshan Park, Xi Chang'an Jie ☎010/65598285.
A stylish new hall, with performances of Western and Chinese classical music.

Get Lucky Bar
豪运酒吧
háoyùn jiǔbā
Tai Yang Gong Lu, off Huixingdong Jie (the northern continuation of Hepinglidong Jie) ☎010/64299109.
Miles out of the way, just beyond the third ring road in the northeast of the city, but you have to get here if you want to know what's going on in the local indie music scene – there are live bands most weekends. The very good draught beer, brewed on the premises, is a bonus. There have been rumours of an imminent move, so ring to check. The address given above is 500m east of the south gate of the Business and Economics University (*jingmao daxue nan men*) – look for the huge neon sign.

Poly Theatre
保利大厦国际剧院
bǎolìdàshà guójì jùyuàn
Poly Plaza, 14 Dongzhimen Nan Dajie, near Dongsi Shitiao subway stop ☏010/65001188 ext 5127.
A gleaming hall that hosts diverse performances of jazz, ballet, classical music, opera and modern dance for the enjoyment of Beijing's cultural elite. Tickets are on the pricey side, usually starting at ¥100. Performances begin 7.15pm.

Workers' Stadium
工人体育场
gōngrén tǐyùchǎng
In the northeast of the city, off Gongren Tiyuchang Bei Lu ☏010/65016655.
This is where giant gigs are staged, mostly featuring Chinese pop stars, though the likes of Björk have also played here.

Cinemas

There are plenty of cinemas showing Chinese films and dubbed Western films, usually action movies. Just ten Western films are picked by the government for release every year. Despite such restrictions, these days most Beijingers have an impressive knowledge of world cinema, thanks to the prevalence of cheap pirated DVDs.

Some of the largest screens in Beijing, showing mainstream Chinese and foreign films, are the newly renovated Capital Cinema at 46 Chang'an Jie, near Xidan (☏010/66055510), the old Dahua Cinema at 82 Dongdan Bei Dajie (☏010/65274420) and the Shengli Movie Theatre at 55 Xisi Dong Dajie (☏010/66175091). Tickets cost ¥15–50. Chinese movies are sometimes subtitled in English (call to check) at the Xin Dong'an Cinema on the fifth floor of the Sun Dong'an Plaza in Wangfujing (☏010/65281988) and at the UME Huaxing Cinema at 44 Kexueyuan Nan Lu, Haidian, next to the Shuang Yu Shopping Centre, just off the Third Ring Road (☏010/62555566).

Beijing on film

Chinese film is enjoying something of a renaissance. Foreigners are likely to be familiar with acclaimed work from the so-called "fifth generation" of film-makers such as **Chen Kaige**'s *Farewell My Concubine*, the epic tragedy of a gay Beijing opera singer, and **Zhang Yimou**'s hauntingly beautiful *Raise the Red Lantern*.

However, these films were criticized at home as being overly glamourous and made for foreigners. The new "sixth generation" of directors subsequently set out to make edgier work. Their films, usually low-budget affairs, shot in black and white – and difficult to see in China, depict what their makers consider to be the true story of modern urban life: cold apartments, ugly streets, impoverished people. The most well-known of these films is *Beijing Bastards*, the story of apathetic, fast-living youths, which included a role for rebel rocker Cui Jian (see p.131). *Beijing Feng Da Ba* ("Is Beijing Windy?") is a great underground documentary, consisting mostly of the ballsy film maker **Ju Anqi** walking into places he shouldn't and conducting absurdist interviews. The satirical *In The Heat of The Sun* was scripted by **Wang Shuo**, the bad boy of Chinese contemporary literature (see p.183), and perfectly captures the post-revolutionary ennui of 1970s Beijing in its tale of a street gang looking for kicks.

Recently, even the more commercial films have been influenced by this social-realist aesthetic; look out for *Beijing Bicycle*, the story of a lad trying to get his stolen bike back, and **Liu Fendou**'s *Spring Subway*, which uses the capital's gleaming new underground stations as a backdrop to the main character's soul-searching.

The biggest box-office director at the time of writing is **Feng Xiaogang**. His *Be There or Be Square*, *Sorry Baby* and *Big Shot's Funeral* are light, clever comedies set in Beijing.

Space for Imagination at 5 Xi Wang Zhuang Xiao Qu, Haidian, opposite Qinghua University's east gate, (☎010/62791280) is a cineastes' bar that shows avant-garde films every Saturday at 7pm. The best serious film venue though, is **Cherry Lane Movies**, usually housed at the Peking Opera Photo Studio, Kent Centre 29 Liangmaqiao Lu, 2km east of the Kempinski Hotel. (☎010/64301398, Ⓦwww.cherrylanemovies.com.cn; check as the venue changes occasionally). Their screenings, which include obscure and controversial underground Chinese films, usually with English subtitles, take place every Friday at 8pm (¥50), followed by a discussion, often featuring the director or cast members.

Art galleries

Chinese painting has an ancient history. The earliest brush found in China, made out of animal hairs glued to a hollow bamboo tube, dates from about 400 BC. The Chinese used silk for painting on as early as the third century BC, with paper being used as early as 106 AD. Traditional Chinese paintings are light and airy, with empty spaces playing an important element in the design, and rich in symbolism; they're decorated with a few lines of poetry and several names in the form of seals – the marks of past owners.

The best place to see fine classical Chinese paintings is the gallery in the Forbidden City (see p.54); examples from the Sui, Song and Tang dynasties are regarded as the high point. Respectable examples of Chinese painting are for sale at the Traditional Painting Store, at 289 Wangfujing Dajie. However, be wary in general of private art galleries selling classical-looking paintings. They're aimed at tourists, and almost all the images are worthless prints or produced en masse in art sweatshops.

Contemporary art is flourishing in Beijing, and worth checking out. Chinese art schools emphasize traditional crafts, but many students have been quick to plug themselves into international trends. At its best, this leads to art that is technically proficient and conceptually strong. Artists and photographers, unlike writers, have few problems with censorship and illegal copying, and the scene has been nurtured by considerable foreign interest – the best galleries are owned by expats, and Chinese art is seen as an attractive investment by foreign buyers. The following galleries will get you started, but for the more avant-garde art happenings, check listings magazines.

China Art Gallery
中国美术馆
zhōngguó měishù guǎn
1 Wusi Dajie.
At the northern end of Wangfujing Dajie (you can get here on bus #2 from Qianmen or trolleybus #104 from Beijing Zhan), this huge, recently renovated building usually holds a couple of shows at once. There's no permanent display; past exhibitions have included specialist women's and minority people's exhibitions, even a show of Socialist-Realist propaganda put up not to inspire renewed zeal but as a way to reconsider past follies. Once regarded as a stuffy academy – at the 1999 Venice Biennale Beijing artist Lu Hao filled a Plexiglas model of the building with parrots

– it now reluctantly embraces modern trends such as installation and video art. In July, the colleges hold their degree shows here. Tues–Sun 9am–4pm; entrance fee varies from ¥2 up to ¥50.

Courtyard Gallery
四合院画廊
sìhéyuàn huàláng
95 Donghuamen Dajie ☎010/65268882,
Ⓦwww.courtyard-gallery.com.
In an old courtyard house by the east gate of the Forbidden City, this is the best venue for contemporary art in the city, with frequent shows, and something of a meeting point for the cultural elite. There's also a cigar lounge and restaurant (see p.116). Mon–Sat 11am–7pm, Sun noon–7pm.

Beijing Tokyo Art Projects

东京画廊

dōngjīng huàláng

4 Jiuxianqiao Lu, Chaoyang ☎010/84573245,
Ⓦ **www.tokyo-gallery.com.**

Hip new arts centre, also called Factory
798, in that most piquant of modern
venues, an abandoned factory. There's
studio space, a restaurant and bar, as well
as a gallery for the wackier end of contemporary art. The giant Russian-built factory
complex is well off the road; look for the
signpost. Tues–Sat 10am–6pm.

Red Gate Gallery

红门画廊

hóngmén huàláng

**Dongbianmen watchtower, Chongwenmen Dong
Dajie** ☎010/65251005,
Ⓦ **www.redgategallery.com.**

Commercial gallery, run by a Western
curator, inside one of the last remnants of
the old city wall. A little more adventurous

than other Beijing galleries, it's used a
resource by foreign museum directors.
Daily 10am–5pm.

Soka Art Centre

索卡艺术中心

suōkǎyìshù zhōngxīn

**North end of Xiushui Dong Jie, behind the
British embassy and east of Ritan Park**
☎010/65860344.

Small space for contemporary painting.
Tues–Sun 10am–9pm.

Wanfung

云峰画苑

yúnfēng huàyuàn

**136 Nanchizi Dajie, in the old archive building
of the Forbidden City** ☎010/65233320,
Ⓦ **www.wanfung.com.cn.**

Shows the work – generally at the traditional end of modern – of established contemporary artists, sometimes from abroad.
Two viewing spaces, one for group
Chinese work, one for solo shows.

Shopping

Beijing has a good reputation for its shopping, much of it concentrated in four main **shopping districts**: Wangfujing has mostly small, expensive shops; Xidan hosts giant department stores; Dongdan, which mainly sells brand-name clothes; and Qianmen, perhaps the area that most rewards idle browsing, with a few quirky outlets among the cheap shoes and clothes stores. In addition to these areas, **Liulichang** (see p.57), a street of imitation Qing buildings aimed especially at visitors, is a good spot to get a lot of souvenir buying done quickly, while **Jianguomenwai Dajie** is the place to head for clothes. The shopping experience is more exciting in the city's many **markets**, even though they offer no guarantee of quality. You can – and should – **bargain** (aim to knock at least two thirds off the starting price), so the markets work out cheaper than the shops.

Remember that China has a massive industry in **fakes** – nothing escapes the counterfeiters. You'll no doubt hear assurances to the contrary, but you should assume that all antiques and collectable stamps and coins are replicas, the paintings are prints, and that the Rolex watch you could snap up will stop working as soon as you turn the corner. If you don't mind robbing artists of their livelihood, pirated CDs and DVDs are very cheap. Even more of a bargain are the widely available fake designer-label clothes and accessories.

Department stores and malls

For general goods, check out the city's **department stores**, which sell a little of everything, and provide a good index of current Chinese taste. A prime example is the Beijing Department Store at 255 Wangfujing Dajie, a 1980s remnant from the first phase of China's opening up. The newer Landao Store on Chaoyangmenwai Dajie is more impressive, as are the megashopaliths on Xidan. All of these are aimed at the middle class; to see what the wealthy fill their homes with, visit the Parkson Building on Fuxingmenwai Dajie or the Lufthansa Centre on Liangmaqiao Lu in the northeast of the city.

Rising living standards for some are also reflected in the new giant **malls** where everything (clothes mostly) costs as much as it does in the West. They have supermarkets and food courts too. If you don't already get enough of this at home, try the Sun Dong'an and Oriental Plazas on Wangfujing Dajie, the China World Plaza in the World Trade Centre on Jianguomenwai Dajie), or the Japanese SOGO Store on Xuanwumenwai Dajie.

The **Friendship Store** on Jianguomenwai Dajie deserves a mention here. The first modern department store in China, it was once the only place in Beijing selling imported goods, and Chinese shoppers, barred from entering, would bribe foreigners to buy things for them. The store has since failed to reinvent itself, and is known for high prices and insouciant staff – who may well be out of a job soon, as there is talk of shutting down this remnant of the bad old pre-consumerism days.

Shops are generally open Monday to Saturday from 8.30am to 8pm (7pm in winter), with the large shopping centres staying open till 9pm and opening on Sundays too. We've given specific opening times in the listings below where these differ markedly from standard hours. **Markets** don't have official opening times, but tend to trade from about 6am to 7pm. Phone numbers are given for shops that are particularly out of the way – head there in a taxi and ask the driver to call them for directions.

Antiques, curios and souvenirs

There's no shortage of **antique stores** and **markets** in the capital, offering opium pipes, jade statues, porcelain Mao figurines, mahjong sets, Red Guard alarm clocks, Fu Manchu glasses, and all manner of bric-a-brac, pretty much all fake. The jade is actually soapstone, inset jewels are glass, and that venerable painting is a print stained with tea. **Liulichang**, south of Hepingmen subway stop, has the densest concentration of curio stores in town, with a huge selection of wares, particularly of art materials, porcelain and snuff boxes, though prices are steep. Chairman Mao's *Little Red Book* is ubiquitous (and only costs about ¥10). The most popular memento is a soapstone **seal** for imprinting names in either Chinese characters or Roman letters (starting at around ¥40); to see ancient traditions meeting modern technology, go round the back and watch them laser-cut it.

Good, widely available, inexpensive souvenirs include seals, kites, art materials, papercuts, tea sets, and ornamental chopsticks. For something a little unusual, you could get hold of a real jade bracelet (Weiwenshi Jewellery Store, 23 Qianmen Dajie); a mahjong set (any department store); a specialist tea blend (stores on Dazhalan); a stylish Serve the People T-shirt (*Serve the People* restaurant, p.119); a silver Tian'anmen tie clip (from the Police Museum, p.74); or a metal Chinese shop sign character (Nanxinhua Jie, near Liulichang). And if you're after something decidedly outré, you could buy a model ear marked with acupuncture points or some goat penis aphrodisiac (Tongrentang pharmacy, p.57).

Serious **antique hunters** should head for Tianjin (see p.158), where the choice is more eclectic, prices are a little cheaper and you just might actually find something authentic to buy.

Beijing Curio City
北京古玩城
běijīng gǔwánchéng
Dongsanhuan Nan Lu, west of Huawei Bridge in the southeast of the city.
A giant arcade of over 250 stalls, best visited on a Sunday, when other antique traders come and set up in the streets around. Bus #300 from Guomao subway stop. Daily 9.30am–6.30pm.

Friendship Store
友谊商店
yǒuyí shāngdiàn
Jianguomenwai Dajie, south of Ritan Park.
A wide range of touristy souvenirs, but at higher prices than in the markets. Daily 9am–8.30pm.

Gongyi Meishu Fuwubu
工艺美术服务部
gōngyì měishù fúwùbù
200 Wangfujing Dajie.
A huge and well-reputed store selling art supplies. Soft Chinese brushes (some with tips up to 15cm long) and decorated blocks of solid ink are good value. Bus #111 from Wangfujing subway stop. Daily 8am–6pm.

Hongqiao Department Store
红桥百货中心
hóngqiáo bǎihuò zhōngxīn
Northeast corner of Tiantan Park.
The top floor of this giant mall is packed with stalls selling antiques and curios. One shop is given over solely to Cultural Revolution kitsch, such as alarm clocks with images of Red Guards on the face. The Socialist Realist posters are great, though it's tough getting a sensible price

for anything. The stalls share space with a pearl and jewellery market. Clothes and fake bags are sold on the second floor; the first floor is the place to go for small electronic items, including such novelties as watches that speak the time in Russian when you whistle at them. Bus #41 from Qianmen. Daily 9am–8pm.

Huaxia Arts and Crafts Store
293 Wangfujing Dajie.
Stocks a decent, if predictable, selection of expensive *objets d'art*. The selection upstairs is better, with clocks, rugs and wood carvings. Mon–Sat 8.30am–8pm.

Panjiayuan Market
潘家园市场
pānjiāyuán shìchǎng

Panjiayuan Lu, one of the roads connecting the southeastern sections of the second and third ring roads, east of Longtan Park.
Also called the dirt market, this is Beijing's biggest antique market, with a huge range of souvenirs and secondhand goods on sale (sometimes in advanced states of decay). It's at its biggest and best at weekends between 6am and 3pm, when the surrounding streets are packed with stalls, worth a visit even if you're not buying. The initial asking prices for souvenirs are more sensible than anywhere else. It's best to arrive by taxi as it's quite a way from the centre, though you could get here on bus #300 from Guomao subway stop.

Carpets and furniture

Made mainly in Xinjiang, Tibet and Tianjin, the beautiful handmade **carpets** on sale in Beijing aren't cheap, though they are pretty good value. Tibetan carpets are yellow and orange and usually have figurative mythological or religious motifs; carpets from Xinjiang in the northwest are red and pink with abstract patterns, while carpets from Tianjin come in all colours.

Check the colour for consistency at both ends – sometimes large carpets are hung up near a hot lamp, which causes fading. As well as the places mentioned below, you can get carpets at the Friendship Store (see opposite; bargain hard here), Yuanlong Silk Corporation (see p.139), and on Liulichang.

There's a huge market for reproduction Oriental furniture, and it represents a good buy if you can get it home (see p.143 for details of shipping companies in Beijing).

Carpet Shop
Tiyuguan Lu.
A good range of carpets, with much of the stock from Xinjiang, negligently displayed in an obscure warehouse. To get there, head through the gates of the sports centre on Tiyuguan Lu, directly over the road from the *Tiantan Hotel*; turn right at the weird sculpture and continue for about 50m. On your right you'll see an elegant white building that looks deserted – the dusty carpet shop is in here, on the second floor. Bus #39 comes here from Beijing Zhan. Mon–Sat 9am–6pm.

Linxia Flying Horse Carpet Shop
临下飞马毛纺地毯专
línxià fēimǎ máofǎngdìtǎn shìchǎng
66 Zhushikou Xi Dajie.
Wool and silk hand-woven rugs from Gansu Province, mostly with colourful mandala-like abstract designs.

Qianmen Carpet Shop
44 Xingfu Dajie, just north of the *Tiantan Hotel*.
A converted air-raid shelter selling carpets mostly from Xinjiang and Tibet; the silk carpets from Henan in central China are very popular. A typical 2m by 3m carpet can cost around ¥50,000, though the cheapest rugs start at around ¥2000. Bus #8 from Dongdan subway stop. Mon–Fri 8.30am–5pm.

Zhaojia Chaowai Market
朝外市场
cháowai shìchǎng
43 Dongsanhuan Lu, 100m north of Panjiayuan Junction.
Some carpets and enormous quantities of reproduction traditional Chinese furniture in all sizes and styles, for those without enough lacquer in their life.

Books

Plenty of English-language books on Chinese culture, many hard to find in the West, are on sale in Beijing, ranging from giant coffee-table tomes celebrating new freeways in China to comic-book versions of Chinese classics. Even if you're not buying, Beijing's bookshops are pleasant environments in which to browse – Chinese customers spend hours reading the stock, sometimes bringing along their own stool and cushions to make themselves comfortable. Some bookshops have cafés and art galleries attached.

In addition to the outlets listed below, there's a bookshop within the Friendship Store (see p.136), selling foreign newspapers (¥50) – a few days out of date – as well as a wide variety of books on all aspects of Chinese culture, though rather overpriced.

Cathay Bookstore
中国书店
zhōngguó shūdiàn
115 Liulichang.
Has an enormous selection, including specialist texts, dusty tomes and lavish coffee-table and art books. A little way south of Hepingmen subway stop. Mon–Sat 9am–6pm.

Foreign Language Bookstore
外交书店
wàijiāo shūdiàn
Main store at 235 Wangfujing Dajie; branch at 219 Wangfujing Dajie, above *Dunkin' Donuts.*
Their main store has the biggest selection of foreign-language books in mainland China. An information desk on the right as you go in sells listings magazines; opposite is a counter selling maps, including an enormous wall map of the city (¥80), which would be even better if only you could manage to take it home. The English books on offer downstairs include fiction, textbooks on Chinese medicine, and translations of Chinese classics. It's worth checking the upper floors too, which have

more fiction in English, magazines, wall hangings, and Japanese *manga*. Sometimes the same book is priced cheaper upstairs than downstairs. The branch store has some novels in English. Mon–Sat 9am–7pm.

Haidian Book City
海淀图书城
hǎidiàn túshūchéng
31 Haidian Nan Lu.
A great resource extensively used by foreign residents of the city, this giant complex of scholarly stores is full of books to help you learn Chinese, and also has a wide selection of English-language novels. Bus #302 comes here from Dongsanhuan Bei Lu – you can pick it up opposite the Great Bell Temple.

Tushu Daxia
图书大厦
túshū dàxià
Xichang'an Jie.
Beijing's biggest bookshop, with the feel of a department store. English fiction is on the third floor. Bus #22 from Qianmen. Mon–Sat 9am–7pm.

Clothes and fabrics

Clothes are a bargain in Beijing, but be sure to check the quality carefully. The best place to go is Jianguomen Dajie, where the **silk** and **cotton markets**, the Friendship Store and the plazas offer something for every budget. If you're particularly tall or have especially large feet, you'll generally have difficulty finding clothes and shoes to fit you, though there's a reasonable chance of finding clothes in your size at the Silk Market.

Beijing Silk Shop
前门妇女服装店
qiánmén fùnǚ fúzhuāngdiàn
5 Zhuaoshi Jie, just west of Qianmen Dajie.
Located just inside the first *hutong* to the west as you head south down Qianmen

Dajie, this is the best place in Beijing to buy quality silk clothes in Chinese styles, with a wider selection and keener prices than any of the tourist stores. The ground floor sells silk fabrics, while clothes can be bought upstairs.

Fou Clothing Company
85 Wangfujing Dajie.
Designer *qipaos* – long, elegant dresses slit up the thigh – and bespoke tailoring.

Mingxing Clothing Store
133 Wangfujing Dajie.
Well-made Chinese-style garments, such as *cheongsams* and *qipaos*. Once traditional evening wear for high-class ladies, these items are now most likely to be seen on waitresses.

PLA Official Factory Outlet
Dongsanhuan Bei Lu, about 1km north of the World Trade Centre.
As well as military outfits, they stock such oddments as wrist compasses, canteens, and police hats. There's also a huge selection of military footwear and chunky fur-lined coats. Bus #300 from Guomao subway stop.

Ruifuxiang Store
瑞蚨祥丝绸店
ruìfúxiáng sīchóudiàn
5 Dazhalan, off Qianmen Dajie; also at 190 Wangfujing Dajie.
Silk and cotton fabrics and a good selection of shirts and dresses. Mon–Sat 8.30am–8pm.

Silk Market
绣水市场
xiùshuǐ shìchǎng
Xiushui Jie, off Jianguomenwai Dajie, very near Yong'anli subway stop.
Loads of clothes. Good buys are silk dressing gowns, ties and scarves. Most of the designer labels are fake, but some of the Nike, North Face and J.Crew gear

is the genuine article. You'll need to bargain hard; you shouldn't pay more than ¥80 for a pair of jeans, or ¥70 for trainers.

Yabao Lu Cotton Market
雅宝路
yǎbǎo lù
Yabao Lu, west of Ritan Park.
As well as the huge variety of clothes (mostly badly made fake designer labels), the wallets, Filofaxes, sunglasses and shoes are all pretty good value if you bargain. Traders address all big noses in Russian, which gives you a good idea where most of this stuff ends up.

Yuanlong Silk Corporation
元隆顾绣绸缎商行
yuánlóng gùxiù chóuduàn shānghÁng
15 Yongnei Dong Jie, 200m west of the south gate of the Temple of Heaven.
A good selection of silk clothes. Mon–Sat 9am–6.30pm.

Yansha Outlets Mall
9 Dongsihuannan Jie, the southern end of the eastern section of the Fourth Ring Road ☎010/67395678.
A huge outlet for genuine designer clothes and bags, all old lines, at discounts of between thirty and fifty percent.

Yaxiu Clothing Market
58 Gongrentiyuchang Bei Lu.
A two-storey mall of stalls selling designer fakes. Not yet overrun with tourists, so the shopping experience and the prices are better than at the Silk Market.

CDs and DVDs

Pirated CDs and DVDs are sold by chancers who approach foreigners around the Friendship Store, on Dazhalan and in bars in Houhai and Sanlitun. The discs generally work, though sometimes the last few minutes are garbled. You can get DVDs for as little as ¥7, CDs for ¥4, though the asking price starts out at ¥15. Note that with DVDs of newly released films, you're likely to get a version shot illicitly in a cinema, with heads bobbing at the bottom of the screen.

Otherwise, music shops selling CDs can be found throughout the city, with a particularly dense cluster around Xinjiekou Dajie in the northwest. Two of the best stores are listed below.

Blue Line
北影宏运音像中心
běiyìng hóngyùnyīnxiàng zhōngxīn

62 Xinjiekou Bei Dajie.
Legitimate CDs, both Western or Mandopop, at less than half the cost at home.

Jing Hua Tong
51 Xinei Dajie, 100m west of the Xinjiekou
McDonald's.

Head to the back of the shop for a great
selection of genuine imports.

Computer equipment

Computer **hardware** is a bargain in China, though there's little after-sales support. Still, you can pick up memory chips or a palmtop for a fraction of what they cost at home. Pirated **software**, though a steal in more ways than one, should be given a wide berth as it may well fail to work.

One of the main areas for electronic goodies is **Zhongguancun** in northwest Beijng, nicknamed "silicon alley" for its plethora of small computer shops and hi-tech businesses.

Hi-Tech Mall
百脑汇
bǎinǎohuì
**Opposite the Dongyue Temple on
Chaoyangmenwai Dajie.**
Convenient and orderly mall of stores,
some of which will build you a PC for
around ¥5000.

Zhonghai Electronics Market
**At the corner of Zhongguancun Lu and Haidian
Lu.**
A veritable bazaar of poky stalls piled high
with all manner of gadgetry.

Directory

Airlines The following foreign airlines have offices in Beijing: Aeroflot, *Hotel Beijing Toronto*, Jianguomenwai Dajie ☎010/65002980; Air France, Rm512, Full Link Plaza, 18 Jianguomenwai Dajie ☎010/65881388; Air Ukraine, *Poly Plaza Hotel*, Dongsi Shitiao ☎010/65010282; Alitalia, Rm 141, *Jianguo Hotel*, 5 Jianguomenwai Dajie ☎010/65918468; All Nippon Airways, Fazhan Dasha, Rm N200, 5 Dongsanhuan Bei Lu ☎010/65909174; Asiana Airlines, Rm 102, Lufthansa Centre ☎010/64684000; Austrian Airlines, RmC215, Lufthansa Centre, 50 Liangmaqiao Lu ☎010/64622161; British Airways, Rm 210, SCITECH Tower, 22 Jianguomenwai Dajie ☎010/65124070; Canadian Airlines, Rm C201, 50 Liangmaqiao Lu ☎010/64637901; Dragonair, L107, China World Trade Centre, 1 Jianguomenwai Dajie ☎010/65182533; Finnair, Rm 204, SCITECH Tower, 22 Jianguomenwai Dajie ☎010/65127180; Garuda Indonesia, Poly Plaza, 14 Dongzhimen Nan Dajie ☎010/64157658; El Al, Rm 2906, Jing Guang Centre, Hujia Lou, Chaoyang ☎010/65014512; Japan Airlines, 1/F Changfugong Office Building, 26A Jianguomenwai Dajie ☎010/65130888; KLM, W501, West Wing, China World Trade Centre, 1 Jianguomen Dajie ☎010/65053505; Korean Air, Rm C401 China World Trade Centre, 1 Jianguomenwai Dajie ☎010/65050088; Lufthansa, Rm S101, Lufthansa Centre, 50 Liangmaqiao Lu, ☎010/64654488; Malaysia Airlines, Lot 115A/B, Level 1, West Wing, China World Trade Centre, 1 Jianguomenwai Dajie ☎010/65052681; Mongolian Airlines, China Golden Bridge Plaza, 1A Jianguomenwai Dajie ☎010/65079297; Pakistan Airlines, Rm 106A, China World Trade Centre, 1 Jianguomenwai Dajie ☎010/65052256; Qantas, Lufthansa Centre, 50 Liangmaqiao Lu ☎010/64674794; SAS Scandinavian Airlines, 1403 Henderson Centre, 18 Jianguomennei Dajie ☎010/65183738; Singapore Airlines, L109, China World Trade Centre, 1 Jianguomenwai Dajie ☎010/65052233; Swissair, Rm 201, SCITECH Tower, 22 Jianguomenwai Dajie ☎010/65123555; Thai International, S102B Lufthansa Centre, 50 Liangmaqiao Lu ☎010/64608899; United Airlines, Lufthansa Centre, 50 Liangmaqiao Lu ☎010/64631111. You can buy tickets for all flights on Chinese airlines at the Aviation Office at 15 Xichang'an Jie in Xidan (☎010/66013336 for domestic flights, ☎66016667 international; open 24hr); from CAAC offices in the *Beijing Hotel* on Dongchang'an Jie and in the China World Trade Centre; or from CITS offices at 103 Fuxingmenwai Dajie (☎010/66039321), in the China World Trade Centre (☎010/65053775) and in the *International Hotel* (☎010/65126688), just north of Beijing Zhan.

Airport information Ticket information ☎010/66013336; arrival/departure enquiries ☎010/64599567; shuttle bus information ☎010/64335835.

American Express Room L115D, China World Trade Centre ☎010/65052888, ☏65054972.

Banks and exchange See p.22.

Bungee jumping Thrill seekers can get their kicks at the Chaoyang Park Amusement Ground (daily10am–4pm; ¥150).

Contraception Condoms are widely available in pharmacies; stick to foreign, familiar brand names.

Couriers DHL has a 24hr office at 2 Jiuxian Qiao in the Chaoyang district

(☏010/64662211). More convenient are the offices in the *New Otani Hotel* (daily 8am–6pm; ☏010/65211309) and at L115, China World Trade Centre (daily 8am–8pm).

Departure tax ¥50 for internal flights, ¥90 if you are leaving the country.

Electricity The electrical supply is 220V AC, 50 cycles per second. Plugs come in four types: three-pronged with angled pins, three-pronged with round pins, two flat pins and two narrow round pins. Adaptor plugs are available from hardware and electronic stores; try the Hi-Tech Mall (see p.140).

Embassies Most embassies are either around Sanlitun in the northeast or in the Jianguomenwai compound, north of and parallel to Jianguomenwai Dajie. You can get passport-size photos for visas from an annexe just inside the front entrance of the Friendship Store. Visa departments usually open for a few hours every weekday morning (phone for exact times and to see what you'll need to take). Remember that during the application process they might take your passport off you for as long as a week, and that you can't change money or your accommodation without it. Australia, 21 Dongzhimenwai Dajie, Sanlitun ☏010/65322331; Azerbaijan, 7-2-5-1 Tayuan Building ☏010/65324614; Canada, 19 Dongzhimenwai Dajie, Sanlitun ☏010/65324546; France, 3 Dong San Jie, Sanlitun ☏010/65321331; Germany, 5 Dongzhimenwai Dajie, Sanlitun ☏010/65322161; India, 1 Ritan Dong Lu, Sanlitun ☏010/65321856; Ireland, 3 Ritan Dong Lu, Sanlitun ☏010/65322691; Japan, 7 Ritan Lu, Jianguomenwai ☏010/65322361; Kazakhstan, 9 Dong Liu Jie, Sanlitun ☏010/65326183; Kyrgyzstan, 2-4-1 Tayuan Building ☏010/65326458; Laos, 11 Dong Si Jie, Sanlitun ☏010/65321224; Mongolia, 2 Xiushui Bei Jie, Jianguomenwai ☏010/65321203; Myanmar (Burma), 6 Dongzhimenwai Dajie, Sanlitun ☏010/65321425; New Zealand, 1 Ritan Dong'er Jie, Sanlitun ☏010/65322731; North Korea, Ritan Bei Lu, Jianguomenwai ☏010/65321186; Pakistan, 1 Dongzhimenwai Dajie, Sanlitun ☏010/65322660; Russian Federation, 4 Dongzhimen Bei Zhong Jie ☏010/65322051; South Korea, 3rd & 4th Floor, China World Trade Centre ☏010/65053171; Thailand, 40 Guanghua Lu, Jianguomenwai ☏010/65321903; UK, 11 Guanghua Lu, Jianguomenwai ☏010/65321961; Ukraine, 11 Dong Lu Jie, Sanlitun ☏010/65324014; USA, 3 Xiushui Bei Jie, Jianguomenwai ☏010/65323831; Uzbekistan, 7 Beixiao Jie, Sanlitun ☏010/65326305; Vietnam, 32 Guanghua Lu, Jianguomenwai ☏010/65321155.

Emergencies See p.35.

Golf There are a few courses around Beijing; for information, visit *Franks Place*, the bar where the golfing crowd hang out (see p.123).

Gyms Most large hotels have gyms; the *International Hotel* at 1 Jianguomen Dajie has a good one (☏010/65126688), as does the *China World Hotel* in the China World Trade Centre on Jianguomenwai Dajie (☏010/65052266), though it's pricey. The best private gym is the Evolution Fitness Centre, Dabeiyao Centre, Sanhuan Dong Lu, behind the Motorola building (☏010/65670266). The Capital Gymnasium, at 5 Xizhimenwai Dajie (☏010/68335552), west of the zoo, is a sports centre offering badminton, basketball and climbing, at reasonable prices.

Hiking Beijing Hikers organize frequent, imaginative hikes in the city's environs, to dilapidated sections of the Great Wall, caves and the like. Adults pay ¥150 and reservations are required; for more details see ⊛www.bjhikers.com.

Hospitals See p.19.

Ice skating In winter, try Beida (see p.95), the Summer Palace (see p.97) or the Shicha Lakes. Otherwise, there's Le Cool in basement 2 of the China World Trade Centre (daily 10am–10pm except Tues & Thurs until 5.50pm, Sun until 8pm; ¥30/hr).

Internet access See p.30.

Kids' Beijing Attractions popular with kids include the Beijing Aquarium (see p.91) and the Puppet Theatre (see p.129) and the Explorascience Exhibition (see p.74). At the Five Colours Earth Craft Centre at 10 Dongzhimen Nan Lu, just north of the Poly Plaza, children can try their hand at pottery and tie-dyeing. There's an amusement park inside Chaoyang Park (daily 8.30am–6pm) with lots of rides – though it's no Disneyland.

Left luggage The main left-luggage office at Beijing Zhan is on the east side of the station (daily 5am–midnight; ¥5/day). There's also a left-luggage office in the foreigners' waiting room, signposted at the back of the station, with lockers for ¥10 a day (5am–midnight). The left-luggage office at Xi Zhan is downstairs on the left as you enter (¥10 a day).

Libraries The Beijing National Library, at 39 Baishiqiao Lu (Mon–Fri 8am–5pm; ☎010/68415566), just north of Zizhuyuan Park, is one of the largest in the world, with more than ten million volumes, including ancient manuscripts and a Qing-dynasty encyclopedia; the very oldest of its texts are Shang-dynasty inscriptions on bone. To take books out, you need to be resident in the city, though you can just turn up and get a day pass that lets you browse (apply in the office on the south side; ¥5). The library of the British Embassy, on the fourth floor of the Landmark Building, 8 Dongsanhuan Bei Lu (Mon–Fri 9am–5pm; ⓦwww.britishcouncil.org.cn), has a wide selection of books and magazines and is open to all.

Martial arts You can study martial arts under an English-speaking instructor at the Beijing Language and Culture Institute, 15 Xueyuan Lu, Haidian (☎010/62327531). Classes are taught in Mandarin at the Ruyi School, 152 Yuanmingyuan Lu, Haidian (☎010/62571596). Evolution Fitness Centre has kick-boxing classes (see "Gyms" opposite). For instruction in *tai ji* and *qi gong* at Ditan Park, contact daoist_gongfu@hotmail.com (☎010/13910534743).

Massage There are plenty of dubious places – some that aren't include Aibosen, Building 11, Area 2, An Zhen Xi Lu ☎010/64452015 (where all the masseuses are blind); Tai Pan Foot Massage, on the seventh floor of the Gangmei Building, 1 Xiagongfu Jie, behind the *Beijing Hotel* and off Wangfujing Dajie ☎010/65120868; and the Heping Centre, 1 Xiushui Jie, Jianguomen ☎010/64367370. The well-reputed Hanfangzhou foot massage clinic at 11 Xiushui Nan Jie, Jianguomen, is handy for stressed-out shoppers.

Pharmacies See p.19.

Shipping agents Asian Tigers (☎010/84585629, www.asiantigersgroup .com) is one of the largest of the many shipping companies that advertise widely in English language media.

Skiing Beijing has a number of decent new ski resorts. Nanshan (☎010/64450991, ⓦwww.nanshanski.com), northeast of the city, is the closest, only an hour and a half from downtown. Entrance is ¥20, and skiing costs ¥220 per day Mon–Fri, ¥340 Sat & Sun; gear rental is ¥30. To get there, take a bus from Dongzhimen bus station to Miyun Xidaqiao (¥10), then a taxi the rest of the way (¥10).

Snooker and pool Chengfeng Pool Hall, Olympic Stadium East Gate, 1 Anding Lu ☎010/64929199 (snooker ¥36/hr, pool ¥20); Xuanlong Pool Hall, 179 Hepingli Xi Jie ☎010/84255566 (snooker ¥25/hr, pool ¥16/hr).

Swimming Try the Olympic-size pool in the Asian Games Village, Anding Lu (daily 8am–9pm; ¥50), which boasts some of the city's fiercest showers; it's on the route of trolleybus #108 from Chongwenmennei Dajie or Andingmen subway stop, or the Dongdan Swimming Pool A2 Dahualu, (☎010/65231241). The *Kunlun, Great Wall Sheraton* and *Friendship* hotels all have pools open to non-guests, though you have to pay to use them, typically around ¥50.

Time Beijing (indeed, all of China) is 8hr ahead of GMT, 16hr ahead of US Pacific Time, 13hr ahead of US Eastern Standard Time and 2hr behind Australian Eastern Standard Time.

Toilets The old-fashioned public toilets, common in back streets and *hutongs*, are pungent, and offer little privacy; Westerners can find it disconcerting when the other squatters start up a conversation. Much of the plumbing is antiquated and can't handle paper – if there's a wastepaper basket by the loo, that's where it should go. Here are the characters you need to recognize:

Men's toilet	男厕所	*nán cèsuǒ*
Women's toilet	女厕所	*nǔ cèsuǒ*

Travel agents There are plenty of travel agents in Beijing. The biggest is the state-run CITS. They offer tours of the city and surroundings, and advance ticket booking within China for trains, planes and ferries, with a commission of around ¥20 added to ticket prices. You'll find CITS next to the *Gloria Plaza Hotel* at 28 Jianguomenwai

Dajie (daily 8.30–11.30am & 1.30–4.30pm; ☎010/65050231); next to the Parkson Building at 103 Fuxingmen Dajie (daily 9am–5pm; ☎010/66011122); in the *Beijing Hotel*, 33 Dongchang'an Jie (☎010/65120507); and at the *New Century Hotel* (☎010/68491426), opposite the zoo. CYTS has an office centrally located at 23C Dongjiaomin Xiang (☎010/6524 3388), the street east of Tian'anmen containing the old legations. Good, privately run alternatives to CITS include Sunshine Travel at 2 Nansanhuan Dong Lu (on the southeastern part of the third ring road; ☎010/65868069) and the R&R Travel Company, inside Ritan Park at Room B04, 9 Ritan Dong Lu (☎010/65868069); both are geared to corporate groups. For adventure travel within China, contact Wildchina, 70 Dongsi Qi Tiao (☎010/64039737, ⊛www.wildchina .com).

Spectator sport

The Chinese say they're good at racket sports such as squash and badminton, and of course table tennis, at which they are world champions, but acknowledge the need for improvement at games such as **football** – witness the national team's failure to score a goal at the last World Cup, one subject that should not be brought up if you want to win friends. Nevertheless, Chinese men follow foreign soccer avidly, particularly foreign teams with Chinese players. English, Spanish and German league games are shown on CCTV5 and BTV. The domestic football league is getting better, and decent wages have attracted a fair few foreign players and coaches (at the time of writing, former England player Paul Gascoigne plays for Gansu Tianma in Lanzhou, 900km southwest of the capital). **Guo'an**, Beijing's team, play at the Workers' Stadium on Sunday afternoons at 3pm. Tickets cost ¥15 and can be bought on the day; for a fixture list check ⊛www.soccerage.com /en/02/01278.html. Another team you can see in the capital is Shenyang from Dongbei province in the northeast. This stylish young squad plays at the Olympic Stadium in the north of the city, at least until they get their own stadium. The atmosphere at games is carnivalesque, and there's no trouble; no one sees the need to segregate fans for example.

Basketball is almost as popular, and has thrown up the unlikely hero of Yao Ming, a 211-centimetre-tall (6' 11") Inner Mongolian who, at the time of writing, was cutting a dash for the Houston Rockets in the USA's NBA. Chinese league teams, including Beijing's Ao Shen, play at the Workers' Stadium.

Around the city

Around the city

⑬

Around Beijing Shi

Outside the capital proper, Beijing Municipality ("*shi*" in Chinese) holds some great destinations, most compelling of which is the **Great Wall**, whose remains, either crumbling or spruced up, can be seen in a number of places in the hills a few hours north and east of the city. The hilly, wooded landscape to the **west of Beijing** is the most attractive countryside in the city's vicinity, and easily accessible from the centre. The **Botanical Gardens**, **Xiangshan Park** and **Badachu** – the last of these a collection of eight temples – make for an excellent day retreat; further west, the attractive **Tanzhe and Jietai temples** stand in superb rural isolation. All are at their quietest and best on weekdays.

Though less attractive than the Western Hills, the area **north of the city** contains a couple of sights of particular natural beauty as well as the vast **Aviation Museum** and the much-visited **Ming Tombs**. Unfortunately though, these places are so spread out that it's impractical to visit more than one in a day.

The Great Wall

This is a Great Wall and only a great people with a great past could have a great wall and such a great people with such a great wall will surely have a great future.

Richard M. Nixon

A practice begun in the fifth century BC, the building of walls along China's northern frontier continued until the sixteenth century. Over time, the discontinuous array of fortifications and ramparts came to be known as **Wan Li Changcheng** (literally, Long Wall of Ten Thousand Li, *li* being a Chinese measure of distance roughly equal to 500m), or the Great Wall to English speakers. Stretching from Shanhaiguan, where the wall meets the sea, to Jiayuguan Pass in the Gobi Desert, it's an astonishing civil engineering project. Even the most-visited section at **Badaling**, constantly overrun by Chinese and foreign tourists, is still easily one of China's most spectacular sights. The section at **Mutianyu** is somewhat less crowded; distant **Simatai** and **Jinshanling** are much less so, and far more beautiful. To see the wall in all its crumbly glory, head out to **Huanghua**, as yet untouched by development, though note that the authorities may try to curtail visits here to prevent further damage to the wall. If you want to make a weekend of it, visit the pretty little town of **Shanhaiguan**, covered on pp.168–169. For other trips to unreconstructed sections, check out ⓦ www.wildwall.com or contact Beijing Hikers (see p.142).

Aviation Museum	航空博物馆	*hángkōng bówùguǎn*
Badachu	八大处	*bādà chù*
Biyun Si	碧云寺	*bìyún sì*
Botanical Gardens	植物园	*zhíwù yuán*
Jietai Si	戒台寺	*jiètái sì*
Longqing Gorge	龙庆峡	*lóngqìng xiá*
Ming Tombs	十三陵	*shísān líng*
Miyun (Reservoir)	密云水库	*mìyún (shuǐkù)*
Tanzhe Si	潭柘寺	*tánzhé sì*
Western Hills	西山	*xīshān*
Wofo Si	卧佛寺	*wòfó sì*
Xiang Shan Park	香山公园	*xiāngshān gōngyuán*
Yanqing	延庆	*yánqing*
Great Wall	长城	*cháng chéng*
Badaling	八达岭	*bādá lǐng*
Huairou	怀柔	*huáiróu*
Huanghua Great Wall	黄花长城	*huánghuā chángchéng*
Jinshanling Great Wall	金山岭长城	*jīnshānlíng chángchéng*
Juyong Pass Great Wall	居庸关长城	*jūyōngguān chángchéng*
Mutianyu	慕田峪	*mùtián yù*
Simatai	司马台	*sīmǎ tái*

Some history

The Chinese have walled their cities since the earliest times and, during the Warring States period (around the fifth century BC), simply extended the concept by using walls to separate rival territories. The Great Wall's origins lie in these fractured lines of fortifications and in the vision of the first Emperor Qin Shi Huang, who, having unified the empire in the third century BC, joined and extended the sections to form one fairly continuous defence against barbarians. Under subsequent dynasties, whenever insularity rather than engagement drove foreign policy, the wall continued to be maintained and, in response to shifting regional threats, grew and changed course. It lost importance under the Tang, when borders were extended north, well beyond it. The Tang was in any case an outward-looking dynasty which kept the barbarians in check far more cheaply, by fostering trade and internal divisions. With the emergence of the insular Ming, however, the wall's upkeep again became a priority, and from the fourteenth to the sixteenth century military technicians worked on its reconstruction.

The irony, of course, is that the seven-metre-high, seven-metre-thick wall, with its 25,000 battlements, didn't work. Against the highly mobile nomads, the wall was only ever as strong as its weakest link. Successive invasions breached its defences (Genghis Khan is supposed to have merely bribed the sentries to get past them), and it was in any case of little use against the ocean barbarians – the nautical powers of Japan and, subsequently, Europe. But the wall did have other significant functions: it allowed the swift passage of troops and goods through the empire – there is room for five horses abreast most of the way – and it restricted the movement of the nomadic peoples of the distant, non-Han minority regions. In addition, smoke signals – made by burning wolf dung at the wall's beacon towers – swiftly sent news of enemy movements to the capital.

During the Qing dynasty, the Manchus let the wall fall into disrepair as it had proved no obstacle to their invasion. Slowly the wall crumbled away, useful only as a source of building material – recent demolitions of old *hutongs* in Beijing have turned up huge bricks from the wall, marked with the imperial seal. Now, though, this great pointless product of state paranoia is great business – the restored sections are besieged daily by rampaging hordes of tourists – and is touted by the government as a source of national pride. Its image adorns all manner of products, from wine to cigarettes, and is even used – surely rather inappropriately – on visa stickers.

Badaling and Juyong Pass

The best-known section of the wall, and the one most people see, is at **Badaling**, 70km northwest of Beijing (daily 8am–4.30pm;¥25). It was the first section to be restored (in 1957) and opened up to tourists. Here the wall is 6m wide, with regularly spaced watchtowers dating from the Ming dynasty. It follows the highest contours of a steep range of hills, forming a formidable defence, such that this section was never attacked directly but instead taken by sweeping around from the side after a breach was made in the weaker, low-lying sections.

Badaling may be the easiest part of the wall to get to from Beijing, but it's also the most packaged. At the entrance, a giant tourist circus – a plethora of restaurants and souvenir stalls – greets you. As you ascend to the wall, you pass a train museum (¥5), a cable car (¥30) and the **Great Wall Museum** (included in the main ticket). The wall museum, with plenty of aerial photos, models and construction tools, is worth a browse, though it's more interesting visited on the way down.

Once you're up on the wall, flanked by guardrails, it's hard to feel that there's anything genuine about the experience. Indeed, the wall itself is hardly original here, as the "restorers" basically rebuilt it wholesale on the ancient foundations. To get the best out of this part of the wall you need to walk – you'll quickly lose the crowds and, generally, things get better the further you go. You come to unreconstructed sections after heading 1km north (left) or 2km south (right). It's sometimes possible to continue along these – they're relatively deserted, and much more atmospheric; however, the authorities have recently wised up to attempts by tourists to escape being herded, and there may well be guards here to turn you back.

Practicalities

As well as CITS, all the more expensive Beijing hotels (and a few of the cheaper ones) run **tours** to Badaling, at prices that are sometimes absurd. If you come with a tour you'll arrive in the early afternoon, when the place is at its busiest, spend an hour or two at the wall, then return, which really gives you little time for anything except the most cursory of jaunts and the purchase of an "I climbed the Great Wall" T-shirt. It's just as easy, and cheaper, to travel under your own steam, and with more time at your disposal you can make for the more deserted sections. By far the easiest way to get here is on bus #919 from Deshengmen (a 2min walk east from Jishuitan subway stop) – there's an ordinary service (¥3; 2hr) and a much quicker a/c luxury bus (¥10; 1hr). Or there are plenty of tourist buses (outward journeys daily 6–10am; every 20min; ¥36–50): routes #1, #3 and #5 leave from Qianmen, #2 from the #103 terminus at Beijing Zhan, and #4 from outside the zoo. The journey to Badaling on one of these takes about an hour and a half, and the buses visit the Ming Tombs (see p.155) on the way back. Returning to Beijing shouldn't be a problem, as tourist buses run until about 6pm.

Juyong Pass

The closest section to Beijing, the wall at **Juyong Pass** (daily 8am–5pm;¥25), only fifteen minutes' bus ride south of the Badaling section, has been rather over-restored by enthusiastic builders. That said, it's not very popular, so not crowded, and is easily reached on the ordinary bus #919 (not the luxury version) from Deshengmen bus station. Strategically, this was an important stretch, guarding the way to the capital, only 50km away. From the two-storey gate the wall climbs steeply in both directions, passing through modern copies of the mostly Ming fortifications. The most interesting structure, one of the few genuinely old ones, is the intricately carved stone base of a long-vanished stupa just beyond here. Access to unreconstructed sections is blocked, but you can walk for about an hour in either direction.

Mutianyu

A two-kilometre section, the **Mutianyu Great Wall**, 90km northeast of the city (daily 8am–5pm; ¥20), is more appealing to most foreign visitors than Badaling, as it has rather fewer tourist trappings. Passing along a ridge through some lush, undulating hills, this part of the wall is well endowed with guard towers, built in 1368 and renovated in 1983.

From the entrance, steep steps lead up to the wall; you can get a cable car up (¥30, students ¥15) though it's not far to walk. The stretch of wall you can walk here is about 3km long (barriers in both directions stop you continuing any further). The atmospheric *Mutianyu Great Wall Guesthouse* (☎010/69626867; ❸), situated in a reconstructed watchtower 500m before the eastern barrier, is a good place for a quiet overnight stay, though be aware it has no plumbing.

Minibuses for Mutianyu leave from Dongzhimen and Xizhimen stations every morning (¥10 one way), but they take in photo stops and dubious amusement parks along the way. Alternatively, you can get tourist bus #6 (mid-April to mid-Oct outward journeys daily 7–8.30am; ¥50) from the south cathedral, near Xuanwumen subway stop, or the #42 bus station, just south of Dongsi Shitiao subway stop; they'll wait around at the site for an hour or two before heading back to Beijing. Returning by other means shouldn't be a hassle provided you do so before 6pm, as plenty of minibuses wait in the car park to take people back to the city. If you can't find a minibus back to Beijing, get one to the town of **Huairou**, from where you can get regular bus #916 back to the capital – the last bus leaves at 6.30pm.

Simatai and Jinshanling

Peaceful and semi-ruined, **Simatai** (daily 8am–4pm;¥20), 110km northeast of the city, is the most unspoilt section of the Great Wall around Beijing, though it seems about to gear up for mass tourism, with a cable car and toboggan ride already built. But with the wall snaking across purple hills that resemble crumpled velvet from afar, and blue mountains in the distance, it fulfils the expectations of most visitors more than the other sections, though it gets a little crowded at weekends. Most of this section is unrenovated, dating back to the Ming dynasty, and sporting a few late innovations such as spaces for cannon, with the inner walls at right angles to the outer wall to thwart invaders who breached the first defence. From the car park, a winding path takes you up to the wall, where most visitors turn right. Regularly spaced watchtowers allow you to measure your progress uphill along the ridge. The less energetic can take the new cable car to the eighth tower (¥20). The walk over the ruins isn't an easy one, and gets increasingly precipitous after about the tenth watchtower. The views are sublime, though. After about the fourteenth tower (2hr on), the wall peters out and the climb becomes quite dangerous, and there's no point going any further.

Jinshanling (¥25), 10km west of Simatai, is one of the least visited and best preserved parts of the wall, with jutting obstacle walls and oval watchtowers, some with octagonal or sloping roofs. It's presently being reconstructed so expect tourist buses out here some time soon, but for the moment it's not easy to reach without your own transport.

Practicalities

The journey out from the capital to Simatai takes about three hours. **Tours** run from the backpacker hotels and hostels for around ¥80, generally once a week in the off season, daily in the summer, and sometimes offer overnight stays. Most other hotels can arrange transport too, though expect to pay more. To travel here independently, catch a direct bus from Dongzhimen bus station (¥20) or take a bus to **Miyun** (see p.156) and negotiate for a minibus or taxi to take you the rest of the way (don't pay more than ¥20). The last bus back to Beijing from Miyun is at 4pm. Between mid-April and mid-October tourist bus #12 leaves for Simatai from the #42 bus station south of Dongsi Shitiao subway stop between 6 and 8am (¥50), and from opposite Xuanwumen subway stop; buses return between 4 and 6pm. A rented **taxi** will cost about ¥300, there and back including a wait. There's a small, reasonably comfortable though pricey **guesthouse** just inside the ticket gate (☎010/69931095; ❺) and plentiful, cheap simple lodgings with local villagers – the small guesthouse behind the car park, for example, isn't bad (❶).

Most people who want to visit both Simatai and Jinshanling visit the latter first, as it's easier to get a lift back to Beijing from Simatai. For Jinshanling, take a bus to Miyun, from where a taxi to the wall will cost around ¥100. It's a three-hour walk from here to Simatai, where there's a suspension bridge (¥30 toll) and they'll try and charge you a second entrance fee. If you start at Simatai, turn left from the path when you reach the wall, and you'll eventually come to the bridge. A popular day-trip from the backpacker hostels takes you to Jinshanling and picks you up at Simatai (¥80 excluding the entrance fee and toll).

Huanghua

The section of the wall at **Huanghua**, 60km north of Beijing, is completely unreconstructed. It's a good example of Ming defences, with wide ramparts, intact parapets and beacon towers. There's no entrance fee (though local peasants will try and charge you a few yuan), and you can hike along the wall for as long as you like, though some sections are a bit of a scramble. The government has expressed its intention to ban hiking here on the grounds that this was damaging the wall, though all they had done about it at the time of writing was put up a sign asking you not to hike. It's not too hard to get here: backpacker hotels have started taking tours, otherwise take bus #916 from Dongzhimen bus station to Huairou (¥8), and catch a minibus taxi from there (around ¥10; agree the fare before setting off, as the driver may try to overcharge foreigners). You'll be dropped off on a road that actually cuts through the wall. The section to the left is too hard to climb, but the section on the right, past a little reservoir, shouldn't present too many difficulties for the agile; indeed the climb gets easier as you go, with the wall levelling off along a ridge.

The wall here is attractively ruined – so watch your step – and its course makes for a pleasant walk through some lovely countryside. Keep walking the wall for about 2km, to the seventh tower, and you'll come to steps that lead south down the wall and onto a stony path. Follow this path down past an ancient barracks to a pumping station, and you'll come to a track that takes you south back to the main road, through a graveyard and orchards. When you hit the road you're about 500m south of where you started. Head north and after 150m you'll come to a bridge where taxis (¥10) and buses to Huairou congregate. The last bus from Huairou to Beijing is at 6.30pm.

The Western Hills

Like the Summer Palace (see p.97), the **Western Hills** are somewhere to escape urban life for a while, though they're more of a rugged experience. Thanks to their coolness at the height of summer, the hills have long been favoured as a restful retreat by religious men and intellectuals, as well as politicians in the modern times – Mao lived here briefly, and the Politburo assembles here in times of crisis.

The hills are divided into three parks, the nearest to the centre being the Botanical Gardens, 3.5km due west of the Summer Palace. Two kilometres farther west, **Xiangshan** is the largest and most impressive of the parks, but just as pretty is **Badachu**, its eight temples strung out along a hillside 2.5km to the south of Xiangshan.

About 20km from the centre, the hills take roughly an hour to reach on public transport. You can explore two of the parks in one day, but each deserves a day to itself. For a weekend escape and some in-depth exploration of the area, the *Xiangshan Hotel*, close to the main entrance of Xiangshan Park, is a good base (☎010/62591166; ❻). A startling sight, the light, airy hotel is one of the city's more innovative buildings, something between a temple and an airport lounge. It was designed by Bei Yuming (more usually known as I.M. Pei in the West), who also designed the pyramid at the Louvre in Paris and the Bank of China building at Xidan (see p.66).

The Botanical Gardens

Beijing's **Botanical Gardens** (daily 8am–6pm; ¥10) boast two thousand varieties of trees and plants, arranged in formal gardens that are particularly attractive in spring, when most of the flowers are in bloom. Plant varieties are labelled in English; some have whole gardens dedicated to them – the peony and cherry-tree gardens are worth seeking out. There's also a huge new hothouse which boasts tropical and desert environments (¥30), and has a lot of fleshy flora from Yunnan province in southwest China.

The path from the main gate, where the buses drop visitors (you can get here on bus #333 from outside the Yuanmingyuan or #360 from the zoo), leads after 1km to the **Wofo Si** (daily 8am–4.30pm; ¥2), housing a huge reclining Buddha, over 5m in length and cast in copper. Calm in repose, with two giant feet protruding from the end of his painted robe, and a pudgy baby-face, he looks rather cute, although he actually isn't shown sleeping or dying – about to enter nirvana. Suitably huge shoes, presented as offerings, are on display around the hall. Behind the temple is a bamboo garden, from which paths, signposted in English, wind off into the hills. One heads northwest to a pretty cherry valley, just under 1km away, where Cao Xueqiao is supposed to have written *The Dream of Red Mansions* (see p.183).

Xiangshan Park

Two kilometres west of the gardens lies **Xiangshan** (Fragrant Hills) **Park** (daily 7am–6pm; ¥5; same buses as for the botanical gardens, stopping at the main entrance), a range of hills dominated by Incense Burner Peak in the western corner. It's at its best in the autumn (before the sharp November frosts), when the leaves turn red in a massive profusion of colour. Though busy at weekends, the park is too large to appear swamped, and is always a good place for a hike and a picnic.

Just northeast of the park's main entrance, on the eastern side of the park, is the **Zhao Miao** (Temple of Clarity), one of the few temples in the area to escape being vandalized by Western troops in 1860 and 1900. Built by Qing Emperor Qianlong in 1780 in Tibetan style, it was designed to make visiting lamas feel at home. From here, it's worth following the path west up to the peak (an easy 1hr walk) from where, on clear days, there are magnificent views down towards the Summer Palace and as far as distant Beijing. You can hire a horse to ride down (¥20), though you're not free to go where you please; the horse will be led by a lackey to the park's north entrance, which is also where the cable car (¥20) from the summit sets you down.

Just outside the park gate here is the superb **Biyun Si** (Azure Clouds Temple; daily 7.30am–4.30pm; ¥10). A striking building, it's dominated by a bulbous dagoba and topped by extraordinary conical stupas. The giant main hall is now a maze of corridors lined with statues of *arhats* – five hundred of these Buddhist saints in all. The benignly smiling golden figures are all different – some have two heads or sit on animals (one is even pulling his own face off); you might see monks moving among them and bowing to each. The temple also contains a tomb containing just the hat and clothes of Sun Yatsen (president of the short-lived republic founded in 1911); his body was stored here for a while before being moved to Nanjing in 1924. Unfortunately, the tomb isn't open to public view.

Badachu

A forested hill 10km south of Xiangshan Park, **Badachu** (literally, eight great sites; daily 8am–5pm; ¥10) derives its name from the presence of eight temples here. Fairly small affairs, lying along the path that snakes around the hill, the temples and their surroundings are nonetheless quite attractive, at least on weekdays; don't visit at weekends when the place is swamped. Bus #347 comes here from the zoo, or you can take the east–west subway line to the westernmost stop, Pingguoyuan, and get a taxi the rest of the way (¥10).

At the base of the path is a new pagoda holding what's said to be one of Buddha's teeth, which once sat in the fourth temple, about halfway up the hill. The third, a nunnery, is the most pleasant, with a relaxing tea house in the courtyard. There's a statue of the rarely depicted, boggle-eyed thunder deity inside the main hall. The other temples make good resting points as you climb up the hill.

Inevitably, there's a cable car which you can ride to the top of the hill (¥20); you'll see it as you enter the park's main (north) gate. To descend, there's also a metal sled which you can use to slide down the hill (¥40).

The Tanzhe and Jietai temples

Due west of Beijing, two splendid temples sit in the wooded country outside the industrial zone that rings the city. Though **Tanzhe Si** and **Jietai Si** are relatively little visited by tourists, foreign residents rate them as among the best places to escape the city smoke. Take a picnic and make a day of it, as getting there and back can be time-consuming.

Tourist bus #7 visits both temples (mid-April to mid-Oct outward journeys 7–8.30am; ¥20 return), giving you ninety minutes at each, before returning to Qianmen. Otherwise, you could ride the east–west subway line all the way to its western terminus at Pingguoyuan, then catch bus #931 (¥3; this bus has two routes so make sure the driver knows where you're going) to Tanzhe Si. From here you'll be able to find a taxi on to Jietai Si (¥20), from where you'll have to get a cab back to the city. Or you can save yourself some hassle by hiring a taxi to visit both temples, which should cost around ¥180 if you start from the city centre.

Tanzhe Si

Forty kilometres west of the city, **Tanzhe Si** (daily 8am–6pm; ¥20) has the most beautiful and serene location of any temple near the city. The site is the largest of Beijing's temples, too, and one of the oldest, first recorded in the third century as housing a thriving community of monks. Wandering through the complex, past terraces of stupas, you reach an enormous central courtyard, with an ancient, towering gingko tree that's over a thousand years old (christened the "King of Trees" by Emperor Qianlong) at its heart.

Across the courtyard, a second, smaller gingko, known as "The Emperor's Wife", was once supposed to produce a new branch every time a new emperor was born. From here you can take in the other temple buildings, arrayed on different levels up the hillside, or look around the lush gardens, whose bamboo is supposed to cure all manner of ailments. Back at the temple entrance, the spiky *zhe* trees nearby (*Cudrania tricuspidata*, sometimes called the Chinese mulberry), after which the temple is named, "reinforce the essence of the kidney and control spontaneous seminal emission", so a sign here says.

Jietai Si

In complete contrast to the Tanzhe Si, the **Jietai Si** (daily 8am–6pm; ¥20, students ¥10), sitting on a hillside 12km east, looks more like a fortress than a temple, surrounded by forbiddingly tall, red walls. It's an extremely atmospheric, peaceful place, made slightly spooky by its dramatically shaped pines, eccentric-looking, venerable trees growing in odd directions. Indeed, one, leaning out at an angle of about thirty degrees, is pushing over a pagoda on the terrace beneath it.

In the main hall is an enormous tenth-century platform of white marble at which novice monks were ordained. Three metres high, it's intricately carved with figures – monks, monsters (beaked and winged) and saints. The chairs on top are for the three masters and seven witnesses who oversaw ordinations. Another, smaller side hall holds a beautiful wooden altar that swarms with dragons in relief.

The Ming Tombs (Shisan Ling)

After their deaths, all but three of the sixteen Ming-dynasty emperors were entombed in giant underground vaults, the **Shisan Ling** (literally, thirteen tombs, usually called the Ming Tombs in English). Two of the tombs, Chang Ling and Ding Ling, were restored in the 1950s; the latter was also excavated.

The tombs are located in and around a valley 40km northwest of Beijing. The location, chosen by the third Ming emperor, Yongle, for its landscape of gentle hills and woods, is undeniably one of the loveliest around the capital, the site marked above ground by grand halls and platforms. That said, the fame of the tombs is overstated in relation to the actual interest of their site, and unless you've a strong archeological bent, a trip here isn't worth making for its own sake. The tombs are, however, very much on the tour circuit, being conveniently placed on the way to Badaling Great Wall (see p.149). The site also makes a nice place to picnic, especially if you just feel like taking a break from the city and its more tangible sights. To get the most out of the place, it's better not to stick to the tourist route between the car park and Ding Ling, but to spend a day here and hike around the smaller tombs further into the hills. You'll need a map to do this – you'll find one on the back of some Beijing city maps, or you can buy one at the site.

The easiest way to get to the Ming Tombs is to take any of the **tourist buses** that go to Badaling (see p.149), which visit the tombs on the way to and from Beijing. You can get off here, then rejoin another tourist bus later either to continue to Badaling or to return to the city. To get there on ordinary public transport, take bus #845 from Xizhimen to the terminus at Changping, then get bus #345 the rest of the way. All buses drop you at a car park in front of one of the tombs, Ding Ling, where you buy your ticket (¥20).

The Spirit Way and Chang Ling

The approach to the Ming Tombs, the seven-kilometre **Spirit Way**, is Shisan Ling's most exciting feature, well worth backtracking along from the ticket office. The road commences with the **Dahongmen** (Great Red Gate), a triple-entranced triumphal arch, through the central opening of which only the emperor's dead body was allowed to be carried. Beyond, the road is lined with colossal stone statues of animals and men. Startlingly larger than life, they all date from the fifteenth century and are among the best surviving examples of Ming sculpture. Their precise significance is unclear, although it is assumed they were intended to serve the emperors in their next life. The animals depicted include the mythological *qilin* – a reptilian beast with deer's horns and a cow's tail – and the horned, feline *xiechi*; the human figures are stern, military mandarins. Animal statuary reappears at the entrances to several of the tombs, though the structures themselves are something of an anticlimax.

At the end of the Spirit Way stands **Chang Ling** (daily 8.30am–5pm; ¥20), which was the tomb of Yongle himself, the earliest at the site. There are plans to excavate the underground chamber, an exciting prospect since the tomb is contemporary with some of the finest buildings of the Forbidden City in the capital. At present the enduring impression above ground is mainly one of scale – vast courtyards and halls, approached by terraced white marble. Its main feature is the Hall of Eminent Flowers, supported by huge columns consisting of individual tree trunks which, it is said, were imported all the way from Yunnan in the south of the country.

Ding Ling

The main focus of the area is **Ding Ling** (daily 8.30am–5pm; ¥20), the under-ground tomb-palace of the Emperor Wanli, who ascended the throne in 1573 at the age of 10. Reigning for almost half a century, he began building his tomb when he was 22, in line with common Ming practice, and hosted a grand party within on its completion. The mausoleum, a short distance east of Chang Ling, was opened up in 1956 and found to be substantially intact, revealing the emperor's coffin, flanked by those of two of his empresses, and floors covered with scores of trunks containing imperial robes, gold and silver, and even the imperial cookbooks. Some of the treasures are displayed in the tomb, a huge musty stone vault, undecorated but impressive for its scale; others have been replaced by replicas. It's a cautionary picture of useless wealth accumulation, as pointed out by the tour guides you're bound to overhear.

Other sights north of Beijing

Out in the sticks 60km north of the city, the **Aviation Museum** is a fascinat-ing place (daily 8.30am–5.30pm; ¥40, students ¥20; bus #912 from Andingmen subway stop). This enormous museum contains over three hundred aircraft, dis-played in a giant hangar inside a hollow mountain and on a concourse. These range from the copy of the Wright brothers' plane flown by Feng Ru, a pio-neering Chinese aviator, in 1909, to Gulf War helicopter gunships. As well as plenty of fighter planes, many of which saw action in the Korean War, the bomber that flew in China's first atom-bomb test is here, as is Mao's personal jet (with his teacup and frilly cushions still inside) and the plane that scattered the ashes of the deceased Zhou Enlai, which is covered with wreaths and trib-utes. But unless you have a special interest in aircraft, it's the sight of archaic downed machines en masse, like the setting for a J.G. Ballard story, that makes the place memorable.

Miyun

The town of **MIYUN** lies some 65km northeast of Beijing, at the foot of the long range of hills along which the Great Wall threads its way. The area's claim to fame is the **reservoir** (where unnumbered buses from Dongzhimen bus sta-tion drop you; conductors shout out their vehicle's destination), built into the flat, wide valleys outside the town. It's a huge lake, scattered with islets and bays and backed by mountains. Supplying over half the capital's water, the reservoir has become a favourite destination for Beijing families, who flock here at weekends to go fishing, boating and walking (swimming is banned), and to visit the rash of amusement parks. However, it's easy enough to wander off on your own, a useful feature if you're here for a little solitude. Behind the reservoir, in the hills, you'll find rock pools large enough to swim in, lush vegetation and a rushing river – and on the hilltops, 4km away, there are outposts of the Great Wall, still in ruins.

To make a weekend of it, and perhaps combine your trip with a visit to Simatai, 50km to the northeast (see p.150), consider a night's stay at the *Miyun Yunhu Holiday Resort* (☎010/69044587; ❻) on the shores of the reservoir.

Longqing Gorge

Longqing Gorge is a local recreation spot at the edge of a reservoir some 90km northwest of the capital. The main attraction here is the **Ice Festival** held on the shore of the reservoir (late Jan & Feb, sometimes into March), at which groups of sculptors compete to create the most impressive ice sculpture. The enormous results depict cartoon characters, dragons, storks and figures from Chinese popular culture; with coloured lights inside for a gloriously tacky psychedelic effect, they look great at night.

There are two ways to reach the gorge by public **transport**: either tourist bus #8 (mid-April to mid-Oct, and during Ice Festival) from the #328 bus terminus near Andingmen subway stop, or train #575 from Xizhimen Zhan (daily at 8.30am; 2hr 30min). Unfortunately, the **hotels** around the reservoir are expensive and a bit dirty, and their rooms are especially pricey during the festival – though you needn't feel compelled to stay as there are buses back to Beijing until 10pm at least. The nearest decent hotel in this area is the *Yanqing Guesthouse* in **Yanqing**, a few kilometres to the south (℡010/69142363; ❸).

14

Tianjin, Chengde and Shanhaiguan

Beyond Beijing municipality lie two towns and one city that make for worthy short trips from the capital. China's third largest city, **Tianjin**, on the coast some 80km east of Beijing and easily visited as a day-trip, is a dynamic place, but for visitors its most attractive feature is its legacy of colonial buildings reflecting an assortment of foreign styles. See them while you can, however, as wide swaths of the city are being redeveloped. Though **Chengde**, a small country town 250km northeast of Beijing, is today a bland and unimportant place, its outskirts contain a string of gorgeous temples and a palace-and-park complex, the remnants of its glory days as the summer retreat of the Manchu emperors. In recent years it has once more become a summer haven, filling up at weekends with Beijingers escaping the hassles of the capital, and there's enough here to hold your interest for two or three days.

Finally, there's **Shanhaiguan**, its name literally meaning "The Pass Between the Mountains and the Sea". A town at the northern tip of the Bohai Gulf, it was originally built as a fortress in the Ming dynasty, to defend the eastern end of the **Great Wall**. The wall crosses the Yanshan Mountains to the north, forms the east wall of the town and meets the sea a few kilometres to the south. Despite the Great Wall, stretches of beach, scenic grandeur and historical importance, Shanhaiguan inexplicably remains a sleepy, dusty little place of low buildings and quiet streets. The best thing to do here is to rent a bike and spend a few days exploring.

Tianjin

Though **TIANJIN** is given over to industry and commerce today, it was as a **port** that the city first gained importance during the Ming dynasty. In the nineteenth century the city caught the attention of the seafaring Western powers, who used a minor infringement – the boarding of an English ship by Chinese troops – as an excuse to declare war. With well-armed gunboats, they were assured of victory, and the Treaty of Tianjin, signed in 1856, gave the Europeans the right to establish nine concessionary bases on the mainland, from where they could conduct trade and sell opium.

Tianjin

Tianjin	天津	tiānjīn
Ancient Culture Street	古文化街	gǔwénhuà jiē
Antique Market	旧货市场	jiùhuò shìchǎng
Catholic Church	西开教堂	xīkāi jiàotáng
Dabei Yuan	大悲院	dàbēi yuàn
Erduoyan	耳朵眼炸糕店	ěrduōyǎn zhágāodiàn
Fine Art Museum	艺术博物馆	yìshù bówùguǎn
Goubuli	狗不理包子铺	gǒubulì baozipu
Notre Dame des Victoires	望海楼教堂	wànghǎilóu jiàotáng
Quanye Bazaar	劝业场	quànyè chǎng
Zhongxin Park	中心公园	zhōngxīn gōngyuán

These separate **concessions**, along the banks of the Hai River, were self-contained European fantasy worlds: the French built elegant chateaux and towers, while the Germans constructed red-tiled Bavarian villas. The Chinese were discouraged from intruding, except for servants, who were given pass cards. Tensions between the indigenous population and the foreigners exploded in the **Tianjin Incident** of 1870, when a Chinese mob attacked a French-run orphanage and killed the nuns and priests, in the belief that the Chinese orphans were being kidnapped for later consumption. Twenty Chinese were beheaded as a result, and the prefect of the city was banished. A centre for secretive anti-foreign movements, the city had its genteel peace interrupted again by the **Boxer Rebellion** in 1900 (see p.98), after which the foreigners levelled the walls around the old Chinese city to enable them to keep an eye on its residents.

The City

Tianjin is a massive place, but the part of the city of interest to visitors, the dense network of ex-concession streets south and west of the main train station, and south of the Hai River, is fairly compact. There are few specific sights, and it's the city's streetscapes, an assemblage of nineteenth- and early twentieth-century foreign architecture, mostly European, juxtaposed with the concrete and glass monoliths of wealthy contemporary China, which are Tianjin's most engrossing attraction.

The **old city** was strictly demarcated into national zones, and each section of the city centre has retained a hint of its old flavour. The area northwest of the main train station, on the west side of the Hai River, was the old Chinese city. Running from west to east along the north bank of the river were the Austrian, Italian, Russian and Belgian concessions, though most of the old buildings here have been destroyed. Unmistakeable are the chateaux of the French concession, which now make up the downtown district just south of the river, and the haughty mansions the British built east of here. Further east, also south of the river, the architecture of an otherwise unremarkable district has a sprinkling of stern German constructions.

The majority of the colonial buildings are clustered in the grid of streets on the southern side of the river. From the main train station, **Jiefang Qiao** (Liberation Bridge), built by the French in 1903, leads south to an area given an oddly Continental feel by the pastel colours and wrought-iron scrollwork balconies of the French concession, which is at its most appealing around the glorified roundabout known as **Zhongxin Park**. At 12 Chengde Dao, the pink **Fine Art Museum** (daily 8.30am–noon & 1.30–5pm; ¥5), a slightly pompous old building, has a broad collection of paintings, kites, Chinese New Year prints and *ni ren*, literally "mud men", clay figurines which became a popular local craft in the nineteenth century. Their greatest exponent was a skilled caricaturist called Zhang who made copies of opera stars and other notables, and some of his work is on display; unfortunately none of his depictions of Tianjin's foreigners, which got him into trouble with the authorities, is here.

Zhongxin Park marks the northern boundary of the main **shopping district**, an area bounded by Dagu Lu, Jinzhou Dao and Chifeng Dao; Heping Lu and Binjiang Dao are the two busiest streets. Though stuffed with intrepid shoppers, the tree-lined narrow streets have a pleasingly laid-back feel, as traffic is light, and Heping Lu and Binjiang Dao are pedestrianized and lined with sculptures and benches. The **Quanye Bazaar Department Store**, a nine-storey turquoise fortress on the corner of Binjiang Dao and Heping Lu, has an enormous selection of goods. A wider selection of cheaper clothes is available from a massive **street market** that stretches the length of Binjiang Dao, terminating at the cathedral. Trolleybuses run the length of the shopping area (¥2).

The antique market

Just west of here is a shopping district of a very different character, the **antique market** (daily 8am–5pm), centred on Shenyang Jie but spilling over into side alleys. A great attraction even if you have no intention of buying, the alleys are lined with dark, poky shops, pavement vendors with their wares spread out in front of them on yellowed newspapers, and stallholders waving jade and teapots in the faces of passers-by. The market is open daily and expands and contracts according to the time of year (small in winter, big in the summer) but it's always at its largest on Sundays, swelled by Beijingers here for the weekend – it's generally cheaper than any in the capital. That said, the shopkeepers know the value of everything they are selling and you'll have to look hard for a bargain.

The variety of goods on display is astonishing: among the standard jade jewellery, ceramic teapots, fans and perfume bottles are Russian army watches, opium pipes, snuff boxes, ornate playing cards, old photographs, pornographic paintings, and rimless sunglasses.

At the southern end of Binjiang Dao, cross Nanjing Lu and continue south a minute or two to reach the **Catholic Church** (Sun only), a useful landmark and one of the most distinctive buildings in the city, with its odd facade of horizontal brown and orange brick stripes topped with three green domes.

North of the centre

The main sight in the northern part of the city, best reached by taxi, is the **Dabei Yuan**, on a narrow alleyway off Zhongshan Lu (daily 9am–4.30pm; ¥4). Tianjin's major centre for Buddhist worship, it's easy to find as the alleys all around are crammed with stalls selling a colourful mix of religious knick-knacks: incense, tapes of devotional music, mirror-glass shrines, and ceramic Buddhas with flashing lights in their eyes. Outside the first hall, built in the 1940s, the devout wrap their arms around a large bronze incense burner before lighting incense sticks and kowtowing. In the smaller, rear buildings – seventeenth-century structures extensively restored after an earthquake in 1976 –

you'll see the temple's jovial resident monks, while small antique wood and bronze Buddhist figurines are displayed in a hall in the west of the complex. Before you leave the area, be sure to wander the rapidly diminishing district of alleyways behind the temple.

The stern cathedral, **Notre Dame des Victoires**, stands over Shizilin Dajie, just over 1km south of here, on the north bank of the river. Built in 1904, it's the third to stand on this site – the first was destroyed in the massacre of 1870, a year after it was built, and the second was burnt down in 1900 in the Boxer Rebellion. The dark stone and rigorous formality of its lines give the cathedral an austere presence, in contrast to the Catholic Church further south. It's open to the public only on Sunday, when a morning service is held.

Cross the river from the cathedral and head a little way west along Beima Lu here to reach **Ancient Culture Street**, which runs off the southern side of the road, the entrance marked by a colourful arch. Like Liulichang in Beijing, this is a re-creation of a nineteenth-century Chinese street, minus beggars and filth and plus neon "OK Karaoke" signs, designed as a tourist shopping mall. It's all false, but with carved balconies and columns decorating the facade of red and green wooden shops topped with curling, tiled roofs, it's undeniably pretty. The shops sell pricey antiques and souvenirs, and there's an especially large range of teapots. The first shop on the right after the arch sells fifteen-centimetre-high clay figurines, in the style of Tianjin's master Zhang (see opposite). Look out, too, for the stalls selling *chatang*, soup made with millet and sugar, the stallholders attracting customers by pouring boiling soup from a long dragon-shaped spout into four bowls all held in one hand. About halfway down the street is the entrance to the heavily restored **Sea Goddess Temple** (daily 8am–4.30pm; ¥3), built in 1326 and the oldest building in Tianjin. There's an exhibition of local crafts in the side halls.

Practicalities

Double-decker trains for Tianjin (T-class; 1hr 10min; ¥30 one way) leave Beijing every hour starting at 7am. The city's huge **main train station** is located just north of the Hai River; the town centre is a few kilometres to the south (take bus #24). **Buses** from Beijing also arrive at the main train station – though the bus trip is comparatively long at nearly two hours. Maps of the city can be bought at station kiosks (¥2). Tickets for the trip back to Beijing are on sale at a special English-labelled kiosk to the right of the escalators at the main station. You can also buy your return ticket on the train from Beijing itself. At time of writing, the last train back to Beijing is the 9.16pm #4412/3, a creeper that pulls into the capital around midnight. Alternatively, follow one of the many touts in front of the station to their VW Santanas; these leave when full and take ninety minutes to do the journey (¥40).

Downtown and the old concession areas are just small enough to explore on foot, fortunately, as the **bus network** is both complicated and overcrowded, though bus maps are widely available around the train station. Bus fares around the centre are ¥0.5. Yellow *miandi* **taxis** are plentiful (minimum ¥5, which is sufficient for most journeys around town).

Tianjin is well known for its **food** – make sure you don't leave without sampling some of its speciality cakes and pastries. The *Erduoyan Fried Cake Shop* on Beima Lu, about 1km west of Ancient Culture Street, is a century-old institution that specializes in rice-powder cakes fried in sesame oil. Don't be put off by the name, which means "ear hole". Another local institution is the *Goubuli Stuffed Dumpling Restaurant* at 77 Shandong Lu, just off Binjiang Dao. The name *goubuli*, which means "dogs wouldn't believe it", is thought to be a reference either to the ugliness of the original proprietor or to the low-class status of dumplings, but the restaurant has grown from a poky little store to become the flagship of a chain with branches in the US and across Asia. There's a proper dining room upstairs, though most locals prefer to eat in the canteen-like place on the ground floor, where you get a lot of dumplings plus assorted condiments in an airline-food-style tray for a very reasonable ¥13. They also have an outlet at the main train station.

Chengde

The Qing-dynasty emperor **Kangxi** chanced upon **CHENGDE** at the end of the seventeenth century, while marching his troops to a hunting range. Attracted by the cool summer climate and the rugged landscape, he built lodges here from which he could indulge in a fantasy Manchu lifestyle, hunting and hiking like his northern ancestors. The building programme expanded when it became diplomatically useful to spend time north of Beijing forging closer links with the troublesome Mongol tribes. By 1711 there were 36 palaces, temples, monasteries and pagodas set in a great walled park, its ornamental pools and islands dotted with beautiful pavilions and linked by bridges. Craftsmen from all over China were gathered to work on the project, with Kangxi's grandson, **Qianlong** (1736–96), adding another 36 imperial buildings during his reign, which was considered to be the heyday of the town.

Chengde came to be seen as unlucky after two emperors died here, and so gradually lost its imperial popularity. Left empty and neglected for most of the twentieth century, its old buildings largely escaped the ravages of the Cultural Revolution. Restoration, in the interests of tourism, began in the 1980s and is still ongoing.

Bishu Shanzhuang

Surrounded by a ten-kilometre wall, Chengde's palace-and-park complex (daily 5.30am–6.30pm; ¥30), larger than the Summer Palace in Beijing, makes up the northern third of the town. Called **Bishu Shanzhuang** (the name literally means "mountain villa for avoiding the heat"), this was where, in the summer months, the Qing emperors lived, feasted, hunted, and occasionally dealt with affairs of state. The palace buildings are unusual for imperial China, being low, wooden and unpainted. Though simple, they have an elegance that's in marked contrast to the opulence and grandeur of Beijing's palaces. It's said that Emperor Kangxi wanted the complex to mimic a Manchurian village to show his disdain for fame and wealth – though with 120 rooms and several thousand servants, he wasn't exactly roughing it. The same principle of idealized naturalness governed the design of the adjoining park, whose whole is an attempt to combine water, buildings and plants in graceful harmony. Lord Macartney, a British diplomat who visited in 1793, noted its similarity to the "soft beauties" of an English Romantic-style manor park.

The complex's main gate, **Lizhengmen**, is in the south wall, off Lizhengmen Dajie; it's also possible to enter about halfway along the eastern side of the perimeter wall. The park is simply too big to get overcrowded; if you head north beyond the lakes, you're likely to find yourself alone.

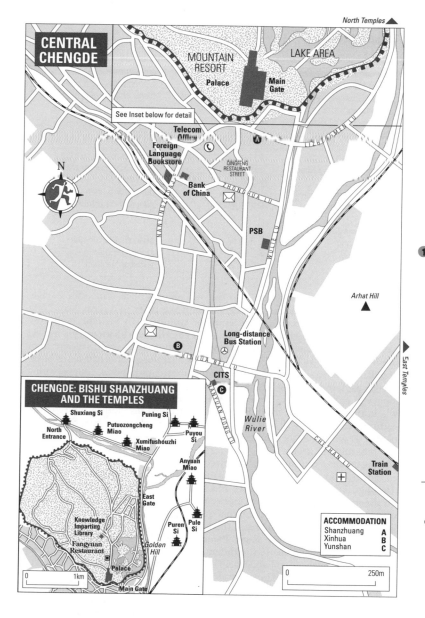

CENTRAL CHENGDE

MOUNTAIN RESORT

LAKE AREA

Palace

Main Gate

See Inset below for detail

Telecom Office

Foreign Language Bookstore

Ⓒ

QINGFENG RESTAURANT STREET

Ⓐ

ZHONGHUA LU

N

Bank of China

✉

PSB

NANYING

Arhat Hill ▲

✉

Ⓑ

Long-distance Bus Station

Ⓜ

NANYUAN DONG LU

CITS

Ⓒ

Wulie River

CHUAN LU

Train Station

✕

CHENGDE: BISHU SHANZHUANG AND THE TEMPLES

Shuxiang Si

Puning Si

North Entrance

Putuozongcheng Miao

Xumifushouzhi Miao

Puyou Si

Anyuan Miao

East Gate

Knowledge Imparting Library

Fangyuan Restaurant

Puren Si

Pule Si

Golden Hill

Palace

0   1km

Main Gate

0   250m

ACCOMMODATION

Shanzhuang	A
Xinhua	B
Yunshan	C

East Temples ▶

The palace quarter

The palace quarter, just inside and to the west of the main gate, consists of several groups of dark wooden buildings (the major ones are signposted in English), spread over an area of 100,000 square metres. The most interesting of the groups, the **Front Palace**, was where the emperors lived and worked; it's reached directly from the complex's main gate, which leads you to the **Outer**

Chengde

Chengde	承德	chéngdé
Anyuan Miao	安远庙	ānyuǎn miào
Arhat Hill	罗汉山	luóhàn shān
Bishu Shanzhuang	避暑山庄	bìshǔ shānzhuāng
Frog Crag	蛤蟆石	háma shí
Palace	正宫	zhèng gōng
Pule Si	普乐寺	pǔlè sì
Puning Si	普宁寺	pǔníng sì
Puren Si	溥仁寺	pǔrén sì
Putuozongcheng Miao	普陀宗乘之庙	pǔtuó zōngchéng zhīmiào
Shuxiang Si	殊像寺	shūxiàng sì
Sledgehammer Rock	棒锤山	bàngzhōng shān
Xumifushouzhi Miao	须弥福寿之庙	xūmífúshòu zhīmiào

Accommodation		
Shanzhuang	山庄宾馆	shānzhuāng bīnguǎn
Xinhua	新华饭店	xīnhuá fàndiàn
Yunshan	云山饭店	yúnshān fàndiàn

Wumen. This gate was where high-ranking officials once waited for a single peal of a large bell, indicating that the emperor was ready to receive them. Next is the **Inner Wumen**, where the emperor would watch his officers practise their archery. Directly behind, the **Hall of Frugality and Sincerity** is a dark, well-appointed room made of cedar wood imported at great expense from south of the Yangzi River, 1000km away, by Qianlong, who had none of his grandfather Kangxi's scruples about conspicuous consumption. Topped with a curved roof, the hall has nine bays; patterns on the walls include symbols of longevity and good luck. The **Four Knowledge Study Room**, behind, was where the emperor did his ordinary work, changed his clothes and rested. A vertical scroll on the wall here outlines the four knowledges required of a gentleman, as written in the Chinese classics: he had to be aware of what is small, obvious, soft and strong.

Many of the rooms in the Front Palace have been restored to their full Qing elegance, decked out with graceful furniture and ornaments. Even the everyday objects are impressive: brushes and ink stones on desks, ornate fly whisks on the arms of chairs, little jade trees on shelves. Other rooms house displays of ceramics, books, and exotic martial-art weaponry. The Qing emperors were fine calligraphers, and examples of their work appear throughout the palace.

The main building in the **Rear Palace** is the **Hall of Refreshing Mists and Waves**, the living quarters of the imperial family. This was where Emperor Xianfeng signed the humiliating Beijing Treaty in the 1850s, giving away more of China's sovereignty and territory after her defeat in the Second Opium War. A door leads from here to the **Western Apartments**, at the back of the complex, where the notorious Cixi (see p.98) lived when she was one of Emperor Xianfeng's concubines. It was through the partition here that she eavesdropped on the dying emperor's last words of advice to his ministers, intelligence which she used to help to force her way to power.

The park

With its twisting paths and streams, rockeries and hills, the park north of the palace buildings is a fantasy re-creation of the rough northern terrain and southern Chinese beauty spots that the emperors would have seen on their tours of inspection. The best way to get around the **lake area** – a network of pavilions, bridges, lakes and waterways, just to the northeast of the palace – is to rent a rowing boat from one of the many jetties (¥10/hr). Much of the architecture here is a direct copy of southern Chinese buildings. Just northwest of the lake area is the **Wenjinge**, or Knowledge Imparting Library, surrounded by rockeries and pools for fire protection.

A vast expanse of **grassland** extends from the north of the lakes to the foothills of the mountains, comprising Wanshu Wan (the Garden of Ten Thousand Trees) and Shima Di (the Horse Testing Ground). Genuine Qing-dynasty **yurts** sit here, the largest of which was once an audience hall where Qianlong received visiting dignitaries from ethnic minorities.

The hilly area in the northwest of the park has a number of rocky valleys, gorges and gullies with a few tastefully placed lodges and pagodas. The deer who used to graze here were wiped out by imperial hunting expeditions, though the animal has recently been reintroduced.

The temples

Originally there were twelve **temples** in the foothills of the mountains just east and north of Chengde, but two have been destroyed and another two are dilapidated. They're built in the architectural styles of China's different ethnic groups, so that wandering among them is rather like being in a religious theme park. This isn't far from the original intention, as they were constructed by Kangxi and Qianlong less to express religious sentiment than as a way of showing off imperial magnificence, and also to make envoys from anywhere in the empire feel more at home. Though varying in design, all the temples share Lamaist features – Qianlong found it politically expedient to promote Tibetan and Mongolian Lamaism as a way of keeping these troublesome minorities in line.

The northern temples

Just beyond the northern border of Bishu Shanzhuang stand five temples, once part of a string of nine. The **Puning Si** (Temple of Universal Peace; ¥20) here is a must, if only for its statue of Guanyin (the Goddess of Mercy), the largest wooden statue in the world. It's the only working temple in Chengde, with shaven-headed Mongolian monks manning the altars and trinket stalls. Built in 1755, the temple was based on the oldest of Tibet's temples, Samye. Like traditional Tibetan buildings, it lies on the south-facing slope of a mountain, though the layout of the front is typically Han Chinese, with a gate hall, stele pavilions, a bell and a drum tower. The statue of a fat, grinning monk holding a bag in the Hall of Heavenly Kings is Qi Ci, a tenth-century character with a jovial disposition who is believed to be a reincarnation of the Buddha. Four gaudy guardian demons here glare down at you with bulging eyeballs from niches in the walls.

The rear section of the temple, separated from the front by a wall, comprises 27 Tibetan-style buildings laid out symmetrically, with the Mahayana Hall in the centre. Some of the structures are solid throughout (their doors conceal walls), suggesting that the original architects were more concerned with appearances than function. The Mahayana hall itself is dominated by the awe-inspiring, 23-metre-high wooden **statue of Avalokiteshvara**, the Tibetan version of Guanyin. She has forty-two arms, with an eye in the centre of each palm, and three eyes on her face which symbolize her ability to see into the past, the present and the future. Once you've been suitably towered over at ground level, take a look at the statue from the balcony as this vantage point reveals new details, such as the eye sunk in her belly button, and the little Buddha on top of her head.

The **Xumifushouzhi Miao** (Temple of Sumeru Happiness and Longevity; ¥2), southwest of Puning Si, is being restored and much of it is closed to the public; the parts that are open are not in a good state of repair. The temple was built in 1780 for the sixth Panchen Lama when he came to Beijing to pay his respects to the emperor. Built in Mongolian style, it has as its finest feature eight sinuous gold dragons, each weighing over a thousand kilograms, sitting on the roof.

Based on the Potala Palace in Lhasa, the magnificent **Putuozongcheng Miao** (Temple of Potaraka Doctrine; ¥20) was built in 1771. It's the largest temple in Chengde, with sixty groups of halls, pagodas and terraces. The Tibetan-style facade, dominated by a grand red terrace, conceals a Chinese-style interior; many of the windows on the terrace are fake, and some of the whitewashed "buildings" around the base are merely filled-in shapes. The **Hall of All Laws Falling into One**, at the back, is worth a visit for the decorative religious furniture on display. Other halls hold displays of Chinese pottery and ceramics, and Tibetan religious artefacts, the last of these exhibitions slanted to portray the gorier side of Tibetan religion, including a drum made from children's skulls. The roof of the temple has a good view over the surrounding countryside.

The **Shuxiang Si** (Temple of Manjusri; ¥3), a short walk west, is Han in style, simple and unspectacular and, for that reason, relatively little visited. Built in 1744, it consists of towers and pavilions set in somewhat overgrown gardens and rockeries, and is a loose copy of a temple in the Wutai Mountains in central China. The statue of Manjusri, one of the Bodhisattvas in the main hall, looks suspiciously like Qianlong himself.

The eastern temples

The three temples east of Bishu Shanzhuang are easily accessible off a quiet road three or four kilometres from the town centre: from Lizhengmen Lu, cross over to the east bank of the river and head north.

The **Puren Si** (Temple of Universal Benevolence; ¥2), the first one out from the centre, is the oldest in the complex, dating from 1713. It was built by Kangxi as a sign of respect to the visiting Mongolian nobility, come to congratulate the emperor on the occasion of his sixtieth birthday. The best thing here is the collection of wooden *arhats* in a side hall, though most are fairly generic, rather stiff-looking figures. Still, the almost life-size image of an old man – whose lined face seems to radiate benevolence – being carried on a young disciple's back is attractively quirky.

The **Pule Si** (Temple of Universal Happiness; ¥20), 500m to the northeast, was built in 1766 by Qianlong as a place for Mongol envoys to worship, its style an odd mix of Han and Lamaist elements. The Lamaist back section, a triple-tiered terrace and hall, with a flamboyantly conical roof and lively, curved surfaces, steals the show from the more sober, squarer Han architecture at the front. The ceiling of the back hall is a wood-and-gold confection to rival the Temple of Heaven in Beijing.

The **Anyuan Miao** (Temple of Appeasing the Borders; ¥2), 500m north of Pule Si, was built in 1762 for a troop of Mongolian soldiers who were moved to Chengde by Qianlong. It's neither spectacular nor in great shape, but is a good place to stop especially if you're cycling, with sunflowers emerging from cracks in the flagstones and swaying against the background of crumbling red walls. The main building houses an ominous gilded figure of Ksitigarbha, the Buddha of the underworld; with nine heads and thirty-four arms, it looks quite sinister in the hall's murky, cobwebbed gloom.

Practicalities

The **train** journey from Beijing Zhan to Chengde takes four and a half hours (¥22 one-way). Chengde's **train station** is 2km from the centre, in the southeast corner of town; buses #2 and #3 head to the centre from here. Getting here by **bus** from Deshengmen station in the north of Beijing is slightly quicker (¥20 one-way), the buses terminating at Chengde's long-distance **bus station** just off Wulie Lu in the centre of town. On arrival, you can buy a bilingual **map** of the town (¥2) from kiosks around the stations.

Touts wait in ambush for new arrivals, and can be useful if you already have a hotel in mind, as you won't be charged for the ride there in their minibuses; however, they will hassle you throughout the journey to take a tour with them, and might unceremoniously dump you should you refuse. Onward train tickets can be bought in the station, or from **CITS**, 6 Nanyuan Lu (℡0314/2026827), near the *Yunshan Hotel*; or from any hotel, though you'll pay a surcharge of around ¥30.

If your time is limited, a **minibus tour** is worth considering as a way to cram in all the sights, though these tours tend to overlook the less spectacular, quieter temples. CITS's one-day organized tour, which takes you to Bishu Shanzhuang in the morning and the main temples in the afternoon, is something of a test of endurance (¥50 per person). For around the same price you can arrange your own English-language guided tour – you put together your own itinerary – through CITS or the larger hotels. Probably the best way to see everything in a short time is to rent a minibus or a bike to get around the temples one day, and explore Bishu Shanzhuang the next. Hotels can arrange for bike and vehicle rental; the latter, with a driver but without a guide, should cost around ¥150 a day (bargain hard).

Accommodation

Rooms in Chengde are slightly cheaper than in the capital, though standards are not as high and English may well not be spoken at reception. The best placed of the hotels is the *Shanzhuang* at 127 Lizhengmen Lu (℡0314/2023501; ❸), a grand (if slightly intimidating) complex with high ceilings and a cavernous, gleaming lobby. It's very good value if you get one of the large, comfortable rooms in the main building; rates in the ugly new building round the back are slightly lower. The main attraction at the simple, somewhat ageing *Xinhua*, 4 Xinhua Bei Lu (℡0314/2063181; ❸), west of the bus station (bus #7 comes here from the train station) is its restaurant, specializing in food from Shandong province. Among the most luxurious places to stay is the modern *Yunshan*, 6 Nanyuan Dong Lu (℡0314/2024551; ❼), popular with tour groups; bus #9 from the train station passes right by, or it's a ten-minute walk.

Eating

There are plenty of **restaurants** catering to tourists on Lizhengmen Lu, around the main entrance to Bishu Shanzhuang. The small places west of the *Shanzhuang* hotel are fine, if a little pricey, and lively on summer evenings, when rickety tables are put on the pavement outside. A meal for two here should cost about ¥60; plenty of diners stay on drinking well into the evening. Alternatively, head down Lizhengmen Lu to Qingfeng Restaurant Street, an alley signposted in English. Just about every building here is a restaurant, and there's enough variety to suit most price ranges and palettes.

Shanhaiguan and around

Far from being a solitary castle, **SHANHAIGUAN** originally formed the centre of a network of defences: smaller forts, now nothing but ruins, existed to the north, south and east, and beacon towers were dotted around the mountains. Today the town is still arranged along its original plan of straight boulevards following the compass points, intersected with a web of alleys. Dominating the town is a fortified gatehouse in the east wall, the **First Pass Under Heaven**, which for centuries was the entrance to the Middle Kingdom from the barbarian lands beyond. An arch topped by a two-storey tower, the gatehouse is the biggest structure in town, and makes the surrounding buildings look puny in comparison. It must have looked even more formidable when it was built in 1381, with a wooden drawbridge over a moat 18m wide, and three outer walls for added defensive strength. The arch remained China's northernmost entrance until 1644, when it was breached by the Manchus.

These days, the gate (daily 7.30am–5.30pm; ¥42) is overrun by hordes of marauding tourists, and is at its best in the early morning before most of them arrive. The gate's name is emblazoned in red above the archway, calligraphy attributed to Xiao Xian, a Ming-dynasty scholar who lived in the town. A steep set of steps leads up from Dong Dajie to the impressively thick wall, nearly 30m wide. The tower on top, a two-storey, ten-metre-high building with arrow slits regularly spaced along its walls, is now a **museum**, appropriately containing weapons, armour and costumes, as well as pictures of the nobility, who are so formally dressed they look like puppets. It's possible to stroll a little way along the wall in both directions; an enterprising man with a telescope stands at the far northern end, and through it you can watch tourists on the Great Wall at Jiaoshan several kilometres to the north, where the wall zigzags and dips along vertiginous peaks before disappearing over the horizon. There's plenty of tat for sale at the wall's base, including decorated chopsticks, hologram medallions and jade curios, while in a courtyard to the northern side, a statue of Xu Da, the first general to rule the fort, frowns sternly down on the scene.

Follow the city wall south from the gate, past CITS, and you come to the **Great Wall Museum** (daily 7.30am–6pm; ¥5). This modern imitation Qing building has eight halls, showing the history of the region in chronological order from Neolithic times. Though there are no English captions, the exhibits themselves are fascinating and well displayed. As well as the tools used to build the wall, the vicious weaponry used to defend and attack it is on display,

---

Shanhaiguan

Shanhaiguan		
Shanhaiguan	山海关	*shānhǎiguān*
First Pass Under Heaven	天下第一关	*tiānxià dìyīguān*
Great Wall Museum	长城博物馆	*chángchéng bówùguǎn*
Jiao Shan	角山	*jiǎo shān*
Lao Long Tou	老龙头	*lǎolóng tóu*
Longevity Mountain	长寿山	*chángshòu shān*
Mengjiangnü Miao	孟姜女庙	*mèngjiāngnǚ miào*
Yansai Hu	燕塞湖	*yànsài hú*

Accommodation

Jingshan	京山宾馆	*jīngshān bīnguǎn*
North Street Hotel	北街招待所	*běijiē zhāodàisuǒ*

including mock-ups of siege machines and broadswords that look too big to carry, let alone wield. The last three rooms contain dioramas, plans and photographs of local historic buildings – the final room's model of the area as it looked in Ming times gives an idea of the extent of the defences, with many small outposts and fortifications in the district around. It's much better than any CITS map or glossy brochure and should inspire a few bike rides. An annexe outside the museum holds temporary art exhibitions.

The Great Wall beyond Shanhaiguan

You'll see plenty of tourist **minibuses** grouped around the major crossroads in town and at the bus station (500m east of the southeastern gate in the city walls), all serving the sights outside Shanhaiguan. Public **buses** also travel these routes, but if you have the time you're best off travelling by **bike**, as the roads are quiet, the surrounding countryside is strikingly attractive and there are any number of pretty places off the beaten track where you can escape the crowds.

Intrepid hikers could try and make it to **Yangsai Hu**, a lake in the mountains directly north of Shanhaiguan, or to **Longevity Mountain**, a hill of rugged stones east of the lake, where many of the rocks have been carved with the character *shou* (longevity). There's also a pool here, a good place for a quiet swim.

Lao Long Tou

Follow the remains of the Great Wall south and after 4km you'll reach **Lao Long Tou** (Old Dragon Head, after a large stone dragon's head that used to look out to sea here), the point at which the wall hits the coast. **Bus #24** heads here from

△ The First Pass Under Heaven

Xinghua Jie, near Shanhaiguan's train station. The admission charge is ¥37 (daily 7.30am–5.30pm), though note you can simply climb up onto the wall from the beach, reached by taking the first fork to the left before the car park.

A miniature fortress with a two-storey temple in the centre stands right at the end of the wall. Unfortunately, everything here has been so reconstructed it all looks brand new, and the area is surrounded by a rash of tourist development, so it's not very atmospheric. The rather dirty beaches either side of the wall are popular bathing spots. Walk a few minutes past the restaurants west of Lao Long Tou and you'll come to the old British Army **barracks**, on the right; this was the beachhead for the Eight Allied Forces in 1900, when they came ashore to put down the Boxers. A plaque here reminds visitors to "never forget the national humiliation and invigorate the Chinese nation". Do your part by taking care not to trample the lawn.

Mengjiangnü Miao

Some 6.5km northeast of town is **Mengjiangnü Miao**, a temple dedicated to a legendary woman whose husband was press-ganged into one of the Great Wall construction squads. He died from exhaustion, and she set out to search for his body to give him a decent burial, weeping as she walked along the wall. So great was her grief, it is said, that the wall crumbled in sympathy, revealing the bones of her husband and many others who had died in its construction. The temple is small and elegant, with good views of the mountains and the sea. Statues of the lady herself and her attendants sit looking rather prim inside. To get here, take bus #23 from outside Shanhaiguan's south gate.

Jiaoshan

A couple of kilometres to the north of Shanhaiguan, it's possible to hike along the worn remains of the Great Wall all the way to the mountains. Head north along Bei Dajie and out of town, and after about 10km you'll come to a reconstructed section known as **Jiao Shan** (daily 8am–6pm; ¥17), passing the ruins of two forts – stone foundations and earthen humps – along the way. A steep path from the reconstructed section takes you through some dramatic scenery into the Yunshan Mountains, or you can cheat and take the cable car (¥10). The further along the wall you go the better it gets – the crowds peter out, the views become grander, and once the reconstructed section ends, you're left standing beside – or on top of – the real, crumbly thing. Head a few kilometres further east and you'll discover a trio of passes in the wall, and a beacon tower that's still in good condition. You can keep going into the mountains for as long as you like, so it's worth getting here early and making a day of it. A pedicab or taxi back into town from Jiao Shan's parking lot costs ¥5.

Practicalities

There are eight trains a day from Beijing, taking between three and seven hours. The cheapest tickets, costing ¥25–65, are for *yìngzuò* – literally, hard seats; it's well worth paying for *ruǎnzuò*, soft seats, at around twice the price. Shanhaiguan's **train station** is 500m south of town outside the city walls, where you'll be greeted by an eager mob of taxi drivers. The ¥5 flagfall covers a taxi or motor-rickshaw ride to any destination in town. **Bikes** can be rented from the affable man who runs an English-signed shop on the eastern side of Bei Dajie (daily 8am–7pm; ¥10 per day, plus ¥100 deposit), just north of the intersection of the walled city's four roads.

Shanhaiguan has two great **hotels**, ideally located next to the First Pass Under Heaven. The small, friendly *North Street Hotel*, at 2 Mujia Hutong (℡0335/5051680; ❷, dorm beds ¥20), feels like a temple: metal lions guard the gates, and inside, rooms lead off cloisters around a courtyard and garden. The rooms are large, though staff are perhaps a little too laid-back. Reception is the little shed inside the gate to the left. Note that the dorms do not have locks on the door, and you'll have to knock at the main gate to enter after 10pm. Nearby on Dong Dajie, the *Jingshan Hotel* is palatial (℡0335/5051130; ❹), built to imitate a Qing mansion, with high ceilings, decorative friezes, curling roofs and red-brick walls and balconies. Rooms with TV and fan are off a series of small courtyards.

Food in Shanhaiguan is very good if you find the right places – which invariably are those that don't have English menus. Avoid the *Jingshan's* fancy restaurant, which overcharges foreigners, and head for the small canteens on Dong and Nan Dajie. There's a great hotpot place at 33 Nan Dajie, though the owner's brand of home brew, with snakes and lizards marinating in it – is perhaps best avoided. Another friendly place is at 78 Nan Dajie – try their tasty beef stew (*niurou duen tudou*). Four doors east of the main crossroads on Nan Dajie is a tiny Muslim place that's good for breakfast – go for the crispy dumplings, *shaomai*. Across from the bike-rental shop on Bei Dajie is another Muslim canteen, serving excellent vegetable-stuffed fried dumplings (*shucai guotie*). For delicious, plump, steamed dumplings, there's *Jiaozi Wang*, next to the *Dongfang Hotel*.

Contexts

Contexts

A short history of Beijing

A centre of power for nearly a thousand years, Beijing is the creation of China's turbulent political history. Its pre-eminence dates back to the mid-thirteenth century, and the formation of **Mongol China** under **Genghis Khan**, and subsequently **Kublai Khan**. It was Kublai who took control of the city in 1264, and who properly established it as the capital, replacing the earlier power centres of Luoyang and Xi'an. Marco Polo visited him here and was clearly impressed with the city's sophistication: "So great a number of houses and of people, no man could tell the number . . .", he wrote. "I believe there is no place in the world to which so many merchants come, and dearer things, and of greater value and more strange, come into this town from all sides than to any city in the world . . ."

The wealth he described stemmed from Beijing's position at the start of the **Silk Road** (Marco Polo described "over a thousand carts loaded with silk" arriving in the city "almost each day", ready for the journey to central Asia). It allowed the Khans, who later proclaimed themselves emperors, to aspire to new heights of grandeur, with Kublai building himself a palace of astonishing proportions, walled on all sides and approached by great marble stairways; sadly, nothing remains of it now.

With the accession of the **Ming Dynasty**, who defeated the Mongols in 1368, the capital shifted temporarily to **Nanjing**. However, the second Ming emperor, Yongle, returned to Beijing, building around him prototypes of the city's two great monuments, the Forbidden City and the Temple of Heaven. It was during Yongle's reign, too, that the city's basic **layout** took shape, rigidly symmetrical, extending in squares and rectangles from the palace and inner-city grid to the suburbs, much as it is today. An inward-looking dynasty, the Ming also began constructing the **Great Wall** in earnest, in a grandiose but ultimately futile attempt to stem the incursions of northern Manchu tribes into China.

The Qing Dynasty

The city's subsequent history is dominated by the rise and eventual collapse of the **Manchus** who, as the **Qing dynasty**, ruled China from Beijing from 1644 to the beginning of the twentieth century. Three outstanding Qing emperors brought an infusion of new blood and vigour to government early on. **Kangxi**, who began his 61-year reign in 1654 at the age of 6, was a great patron of the arts – as is borne out by the numerous scrolls and paintings blotted with his seals, indicating that he had viewed them. His fourth son, the Emperor **Yongzheng** (1678–1735), ruled over what is considered one of the most efficient and least corrupt administrations ever enjoyed by China. This was inherited by **Qianlong** (1711–99), whose reign saw China's frontiers greatly extended and the economy stimulated by peace and prosperity. In 1750 the capital was perhaps at its zenith, the centre of one of the strongest, wealthiest and most powerful countries in the world. It was at this time that the extraordinary **Summer Palace** was constructed. With two hundred pavilions, temples and palaces, and immense artificial lakes and hills, it was the world's most extraordinary royal garden, a magnificent symbol of Chinese wealth and power, along with the Forbidden City.

China confronts European expansionism

At this time, expansionist European nations were in Asia, looking for financial opportunities. China's rulers, immensely rich and powerful, and convinced of their own superiority, had no wish for direct dealings with foreigners. When a British envoy, **Lord Macartney**, arrived in Chengde in 1793 to propose a political and commercial alliance between King George III and the emperor, his mission was unsuccessful. This was partly because he refused to kowtow to the emperor, but also because the emperor totally rejected any idea of allying with one whom he felt was a subordinate. Macartney was impressed by the vast wealth and power of the Chinese court, but later wrote perceptively that the empire was "like an old crazy first-rate man-of-war which its officers have contrived to keep afloat to terrify by its appearance and bulk".

Foiled in their attempts at official negotiations with the Qing court, the British decided to take matters into their own hands and create a clandestine market in China for Western goods. Instead of silver, they began to pay for tea and silk with **opium**, cheaply imported from India. As the number of addicts – and demand for the drug – escalated during the early nineteenth century, China's trade surplus became a deficit, as silver drained out of the country to pay for the drug. The emperor suspended the traffic in 1840 by ordering the destruction of over twenty thousand chests of opium, an act that led to the outbreak of the first **Opium War**. This brought British and French troops to the walls of the capital, and the Summer Palace was first looted, then burned, more or less to the ground, by the British.

The fall of the Qing dynasty

While the imperial court lived apart, within the **Forbidden City**, conditions for the civilian population, in the capital's suburbs, were starkly different. Kang Youwei, a Cantonese visiting in 1895, described this dual world. "No matter where you look, the place is covered with beggars. The homeless and the old, the crippled and the sick, with no one to care for them, fall dead on the roads. This happens every day. And the coaches of the great officials rumble past them continuously."

The indifference spread from the top down. China was now run by the autocratic, out-of-touch **Cixi**, who could hardly have been less concerned with the fate of her people. True to form, she squandered money meant for the modernization of the navy on building a new Summer Palace of her own. Her project was really the last grand gesture of imperial architecture and patronage – and like its predecessor was badly burned by foreign troops, in another outbreak of the Opium War. By this time, in the face of successive waves of occupation by foreign troops, the empire and the city were near collapse. The **Manchus abdicated** in 1911, leaving the northern capital to be ruled by warlords.

A short-lived republic, under the idealistic **Sun Yatsen**, failed to unify the country, and the post-imperial period was initially characterized by chaos and factionalism. In 1928 Beijing came under the military dictatorship of **Chiang Kaishek**'s nationalist Guomindang party, who held the city until the Japanese seized it in 1939. At the end of World War II, the city was controlled by an alliance of Guomindang troops and American marines.

21C–16C BC	Xia dynasty
16C–11C BC	Shang dynasty
11C–771 BC	Zhou dynasty
770 BC–476 BC	Spring and Autumn Period – China fragments into city states and small kingdoms
457 BC–221 BC	Warring States – China's fragmentation continues
221 BC–207 BC	Qin dynasty
206 BC–220 AD	Han dynasty

The Three Kingdoms: China is divided into three competing territories

220–265	Wei kingdom
221–263	Shu Han kingdom
222–280	Wu kingdom

265–420	Jin dynasty
420–581	Southern dynasties and Northern dynasties – rapid succession of short-lived dynasties
581–618	Sui dynasty – China united for the first time since Han dynasty
618–907	Tang dynasty
907–960	Five dynasties: a period of discord and instability
960–1271	Song dynasty
1271–1368	Yuan dynasty
1368–1644	Ming dynasty
1644–1911	Qing dynasty
1911–45	Short-lived republic founded, its fall followed by civil war and Japanese occupation
1945–49	Further period of civil conflict between Guomindang and People's Liberation Army
1949	Communists take power over all China; establishment of People's Republic

The Communist era

It wasn't until 1949, when **Mao Zedong**'s Communists defeated the Guomingdang, that the country was again united, and Beijing returned to its position as the centre of Chinese power. The rebuilding of the capital, and the erasing of symbols of the previous regimes, was an early priority for the Communists. The city that Mao inherited for the Chinese people was in most ways primitive. Imperial laws had banned the building of houses higher than the official buildings and palaces, so virtually nothing was more than one storey high. The roads, although straight and uniform, were narrow and congested, and there was scarcely any industry.

The Communists wanted to retain the city's sense of ordered planning, with **Tian'anmen Square**, laid out in the 1950s, as its new heart. Initially, their inspiration was Soviet, with an emphasis on heavy industry and a series of poor-quality high-rise housing programmes. Most of the traditional courtyard houses, which were seen to encourage individualism, were destroyed. In their place went anonymous concrete buildings, often with inadequate sanitation and little running water. Much of the new social planning was misguided; after the destruction of all the capital's dogs – for reasons of hygiene – in 1950, it was the turn of sparrows in 1956. This was a measure designed to preserve grain, but it only resulted in an increase in the insect population. To combat this, all the grass was pulled up, which in turn led to dust storms in the windy winter months.

In the zeal to be free of the past and create a modern, people's capital, much of Beijing was destroyed or co-opted: the Temple of Cultivated Wisdom became a wire factory and the Temple of the God of Fire produced electric lightbulbs. In the 1940s there were eight thousand temples and monuments in the city; by the 1960s there were only around a hundred and fifty. Even the city walls and gates, relics mostly of the Ming era, were pulled down, their place taken by ring roads and avenues.

More destruction was to follow during the Great Proletarian **Cultural Revolution** – to give it its full title – that began in 1966. Under Mao's guidance, Beijing's students organized themselves into a political militia – the **Red Guards**, who were sent out to destroy the Four Olds: old ideas, old culture, old customs and old habits. They attacked anything redolent of capitalism, the West or the Soviet Union; few of the capital's remaining ancient buildings escaped destruction.

The death of Mao

Mao's hold on power finally slipped in the 1970s, when his health began to decline. A new attitude of pragmatic reform prevailed, deriving from the moderate wing of the Communist Party, headed by Premier **Zhou Enlai** and his protégé **Deng Xiaoping**.

In July 1976, a catastrophic earthquake in the northeast of the country killed half a million people. The Chinese hold that natural disasters always foreshadow great events, and no one was too surprised when Mao himself died on September 9. Deprived of their figurehead, and with memories of the Cultural Revolution clear in everyone's mind, his supporters in the Party quickly lost ground to the right, and Deng was left running the country.

A degree of reform

The subsequent move away from Mao's policies was rapid: in 1978 anti-Maoist dissidents were allowed to display wall posters in Beijing, some of which actually criticized Mao by name. Though such public airing of political grievances was later forbidden, by 1980 Deng and the moderates were secure enough to sanction officially a cautious questioning of Mao's actions. In the capital, his once-ubiquitous portraits and statues began to come down. Criticism of Mao was one thing; criticism of the Party was viewed quite differently. When demonstrators assembled in **Tian'anmen Square** in 1989, protesting at corruption and demanding more freedom, the regime dealt with them brutally, sending tanks and soldiers to fire on them.

It was new social – rather than political – freedoms, and massive Westernization, that were brought about by Deng's "open door" policies of economic liberalization and opening up to foreign influences. In China, these changes are at their most evident in Beijing, where Western fast food, clothes and music, and Japanese motorbikes are all the rage. Many Chinese are much better off now than ever before. In the 1970s the "three big buys" – consumer goods that families could realistically aspire to – were a bicycle, a watch and a radio; in the 1980s they were a washing machine, a TV and a refrigerator. Today's educated Beijingers can aspire to the same standard of living as their counterparts in South Korea and Hong Kong.

The present day

Deng's successors, **Jiang Zemin** and now **Hu Jintao**, are neither as popular, as secure, nor as charismatic as Deng was, and, although China did not implode with Deng's death, as many had feared, the nation today is living up to Sun Yatsen's description of Chinese society as a "bowl of sand" – unstable, shifting and hard to predict. The new economy has brought with it new problems. Short-term gain has become the overriding factor in planning, with the result that the future is mortgaged for present wealth – Beijing's cultural heritage has vanished as *hutongs* are pulled down to clear space for badly made skyscrapers. As success is largely dependent on *guanxi* (personal connections), the potential for corruption is enormous; witness the men who stand outside Beijing subway stations, selling receipts so that cadres on junkets can pad their expense accounts. Many Chinese feel the price of modernization has become too high. Crime and unemployment, formerly seen as Western social diseases, have risen dramatically, and China's income disparities have become grotesque – eighty percent of the nation earns little more than a subsistence living, hard to imagine if you wander the new malls. It is only in the last decade that beggars have appeared in Beijing's underpasses. Peasants, attracted by the big city's prospects, now flood to Beijing en masse – you'll see plenty outside Beijing Zhan, many of them finding the capital as novel as any foreigner does. The lucky ones end up working on building sites, though even they, far from home and un-unionized, are often exploited. Though the majority are family men who send the little money that they earn home, they are treated with suspicion by most city-dwellers – indicative of China's new class divisions, or the resurfacing of old resentments.

As the showcase city of the face-conscious People's Republic, and soon host to the 2008 **Olympic games**, Beijing has become the recipient of a great deal of investment. Infrastructure has vastly improved, parks and verges have been prettified, fetid canals cleaned, and public facilities are better than anywhere else in China – the public toilets just west of Tian'anmen Square are the most expensive in the country, costing more than a million yuan. Historic sites have been opened, renovated, or, it sometimes appears, invented. There are plans to have fifty museums open in time for 2008. Pollution is less all-pervasive than it was, as factories have been relocated to the suburbs. A huge swath of new forest to the north of the city – nicknamed the Great Green Wall – has had some success in curbing the winter sandstorms that rage in from the Gobi desert. Though some complain that a ramshackle charm has been lost in the wholescale redevelopment, on the whole the city has improved. It will never perhaps be memorable for prettiness, but it's undeniably dynamic, new and exciting.

Books

D on't expect too much variety of English-language reading in Beijing, though you will be able to find a good many cheap editions of the Chinese classics, published in English translation by two Beijing-based firms, Foreign Languages Press (FLP) and Panda Books (some of these titles are published outside China, too). In the reviews below, books that are especially recommended are marked ★, while o/p signifies out of print; the publisher is listed only if it's based in China or elsewhere in Asia.

History

★ **Peter Fleming** *The Siege at Peking*. An account of the events which led up to June 20, 1900, when the foreign legations in Beijing were attacked by the Boxers and Chinese imperial troops.

Harrison Salisbury *The New Emperors* (o/p). Highly readable account of the lives of China's twentieth-century "emperors", Mao Zedong and Deng Xiaoping, which tries to demonstrate that communist rule is no more than an extension of the old imperial Mandate of Heaven.

Arthur Waldron *The Great Wall of China* (o/p). More for the academic than the casual reader, this book traces the origins and history of the wall.

Justin Wintle *The Rough Guide History of China* Pocket-sized but detailed chronicle of China's history, the key events and people put into context in a year-by-year format.

Jan Wong *Red China Blues*. Jan Wong, a Canadian of Chinese descent, went to China as an idealistic Maoist in 1972 at the height of the Cultural Revolution, and was one of only two Westerners permitted to enrol at Beijing University. She describes the six years she spent in China and her growing disillusionment, which led eventually to her repatriation. A touching, sometimes bizarre, inside account of the bad old days.

Culture and society

★ **Jasper Becker** *The Chinese*. Classic, weighty, erudite but very readable introduction to Chinese society and culture.

Gordon G. Chang *The Coming Collapse of China*. An antidote to the many titles predicting China's imminent world domination, this book theorizes that China's recent success is only skin deep, and that the country is about to fall apart

thanks largely to incompetent leadership. A lot of facts back up the scare mongering, and it's surprisingly persuasive.

Roger Garside *Coming Alive: China After Mao*. Garside was a diplomat at the British Embassy in Beijing in 1968–70 and 1976–79. Here he describes the aftermath of the Cultural Revolution.

Marco Polo *The Travels.* Said to have inspired Columbus, *The Travels* is a fantastic read, full of amazing insights picked up during Marco Polo's 26 years of wandering in Asia between Venice and the Peking court of Kublai Khan. It's not, however, a coherent history, having been ghost-written by a romantic novelist from Marco Polo's notes.

Joe Studwell *The China Dream.* Subtitled "The Elusive Quest for the Greatest Untapped Market On Earth", this is mandatory reading for foreign business people in China, this is a cautionary tale, written in layman's terms, debunking the myth that there's easy money to be made from China's vast markets. A great read for anyone interested in business, politics or human greed.

Tiziano Terzani *Behind the Forbidden Door* (o/p). In 1980, Terzani was one of the first Western journalists to be allowed to live in China; he was kicked out four years later for the unacceptable honesty of his writing. There is no better evocation of the bad old pre-reform years than this collection of essays, on such varied subjects as the rebirth of kung fu, mass executions and the training of crickets.

Zhang Xinxin and Sang Ye *Chinese Lives* (o/p). This Studs-Terkel-like series of first-person narratives, drawn from interviews with a broad range of Chinese people, is both readable and informative, full of fascinating details of day-to-day existence that you won't read anywhere else.

Guides and reference books

Giles Beguin and Dominique Morel *The Forbidden City.* A good introduction to the complex, and to the history of the emperors who lived there, though the best thing about this pocket book (as with most books about the Forbidden City) is the illustrations.

Lin Xiang Zhu and Lin Cuifeng *Chinese Gastronomy* (o/p). A classic work, relatively short on recipes but strong on cooking methods and the underlying philosophy. Wavers in and out of print, sometimes under different titles – look for Lin as the author name. Essential reading for anyone serious about learning the finer details of Chinese cooking.

Jessica Rawson *Ancient China: Art and Archaeology.* By the deputy keeper of Oriental antiquities at the British Museum, this scholarly introduction to Chinese art puts the subject in its historical context.

Beginning its account in Neolithic times, the book explores the technology and social organization which shaped the development of Chinese culture up to the Han dynasty.

Mary Tregear *Chinese Art.* Authoritative summary of the main strands in Chinese art from Neolithic times, through the Bronze Age and up to the twentieth century. Clearly written and well illustrated.

Wang Wenqiao and Gang Wenbin *Chinese Vegetarian Cuisine* (New World Press, Beijing). Compendium of Chinese vegetarian cooking, from simple boiled beans with ginger to complex, imitation meat dishes such as sweet-and-sour "spare ribs". The straightforward recipes are derived from the famous *Gongdelin* restaurant in Beijing.

Religion and philosophy

Asiapac Comics Series (Asiapac, Singapore). Available at Beijing's Foreign Language Bookstore, this entertaining series of books presents ancient Chinese philosophy in cartoon format, making the subject accessible without losing too much complexity. They're all well written and well drawn; particularly good is the *Book of Zen*, a collection of stories and parables, and the *Sayings of Confucius*. Unfortunately they're not cheap, costing at least ¥80 each.

Confucius *The Analects*. Good modern translation of this classic text, a collection of Confucius's teachings focusing on morality and the state. *I Ching*. Also known as *The Book of Changes*, this classic volume teaches a form of divination. It includes coverage of some of the fundamental concepts of Chinese thought, such as the duality of *yin* and *yang*.

Lao Zi *Tao Te Ching*. Said to have been translated into more languages than any other book except the Bible, the *Tao Te Ching* (*Daodejing* in pinyin) is a collection of mystical thoughts and philosophical speculation that form the basis of Taoist philosophy.

Arthur Waley (trans) *Three Ways of Thought in Ancient China*. Translated extracts from the writings of three of the early philosophers – Zhuang Zi, Mencius and Han Feizi. A useful introduction.

Biography and autobiography

E. Backhouse and J.O. Bland *China Under the Empress Dowager* (o/p). Classic work on imperial life in late nineteenth-century China. It's based around the diary of a court eunuch, which is now generally accepted to have been forged (Backhouse was a prime suspect; see the review of *Hermit of Peking* by Hugh Trevor-Roper).

Jung Chang *Wild Swans*. Enormously popular in the West, this family saga covering three generations was unsurprisingly banned in China for its honest account of the horrors of life in turbulent twentieth-century China. It serves as an excellent introduction to modern Chinese history, as well as being a good read.

Pu Yi *From Emperor to Citizen* (FLP, Beijing). The autobiography of the last Qing emperor, Puyi, who lost his throne as a boy and was later briefly installed as a puppet emperor during the Japanese occupation. He ended his life employed as a gardener.

Rius *Mao For Beginners*. Light-hearted, entertaining comic book about Mao Zedong and Maoism.

Jonathan Spence *Emperor of China: Self Portrait of Kang Xi*. A magnificent portrait of the longest-reigning and greatest emperor of modern China.

Hugh Trevor-Roper *Hermit of Peking: the Hidden Life of Sir Edmund Backhouse*. Sparked by its subject's thoroughly obscene memoirs, *Hermit of Peking* uses external sources in an attempt to uncover the facts behind the extraordinary and convoluted life of Edmund Backhouse – Chinese scholar, eccentric recluse and phenomenal liar – who lived in Beijing from the late nineteenth century until his death in 1944.

Marina Warner *The Dragon Empress*. Exploration of the life of Cixi, one of only two female rulers of China. Warner lays bare the complex personality of a ruthless woman whose reign, marked by vanity and greed, culminated in the collapse of the imperial ruling house and the founding of the republic.

Zhisui Li *The Private Life of Chairman Mao*. Written by Mao's personal doctor, this long memoir contains much useful material on the day-to-day workings of China's leadership, though most readers turn straight to the vivid descriptions of Mao's sexual proclivities, lack of personal hygiene and growing paranoia.

Chinese literature

Cyril Birch (ed) *Anthology of Chinese Literature from Earliest Times to the Fourteenth Century*. This survey spans three thousand years of Chinese literature, embracing poetry, philosophy, drama, biography and prose fiction. Interestingly, different translations of some extracts are included.

Cao Xueqing *Dream of Red Mansions* (available in a Penguin edition and from FLP, Beijing). Sometimes published under the English title *Dream of the Red Chamber*, this intricate eighteenth-century comedy of manners follows the fortunes of the Jia clan through the emotionally charged adolescent lives of Jia Baoyu and his two girl cousins, Lin Daiyu and Xue Baochai. The version published in the West by Penguin fills five paperbacks; the FLP edition, available in Beijing, is much simplified and abridged.

Lao She *Rickshaw Boy* (FLP, Beijing). One of China's great modern writers, Lao She was driven to suicide during the Cultural Revolution. This story is a haunting account of a young rickshaw puller in pre-1949 Beijing.

Lu Xun *The True Story of Ah Q* (FLP, Beijing). Widely read in China today, Lu Xun is regarded as the father of modern Chinese writing. Ah Q is one of his best tales, short, allegorical and cynical, about a simpleton who is swept up in the 1911 revolution. (You can pick a copy up at Beijing's Lu Xun Museum; see p.90.)

Luo Guanzhong *Romance of the Three Kingdoms* (various editions published in the West; also published by FLP, Beijing). One of the world's great historical novels. Though written 1200 years after the events it depicts, this vibrant tale vividly evokes the battles, political schemings and myths surrounding China's turbulent Three Kingdoms period.

Steven Owen *Anthology of Chinese Literature*. Unimaginably compendious, this colossal book contains delightfully translated excerpts and analyses from every era of Chinese literature up to 1911.

Wang Shuo *Playing For Thrills and Please Don't Call Me Human*. The enormously popular bad boy of contemporary Chinese literature, Wang Shuo writes in colourful Beijing dialect about the city's seamy underbelly. These are his only novels translated into English: the first is a mystery story whose boorish narrator spends most of his time drinking, gambling and chasing girls; the second, banned in China, is a bitter satire portraying modern China as a place where pride is nothing and greed is everything, as a dignified martial artist is emasculated in order to win an Olympic gold medal.

Wu Cheng'en *Journey to the West* (FLP, Beijing). Absurd, lively rendering of the Buddhist monk Xuanzang's pilgrimage to India to collect sacred scriptures, aided by – according to popular myth – Sandy, Pigsy, and the irrepressible Sun Wu Kong, the monkey king. Arthur Waley's version, published in the West under the title *Monkey*, retains the tale's spirit while shortening the hundred-chapter opus to paperback length.

Language

Language

Chinese

As the most widely spoken language on earth, Chinese is hard to overlook. **Mandarin Chinese**, derived from the language of Han officialdom in the Beijing area, has been systematically promoted over the past hundred years to be the official, unifying language of the Chinese people, much as modern French, for example, is based on the original Parisian dialect. It is known in mainland China as **putonghua**, "common language".

Chinese **grammar** is delightfully simple. There is no need to conjugate verbs, decline nouns or make adjectives agree – Chinese characters are immutable, so Chinese words simply cannot have different "endings". Instead, context and fairly rigid rules about word order are relied on to make those distinctions of time, number and gender that Indo-European languages are so concerned with. Instead of cumbersome tenses, the Chinese make use of words such as "yesterday" or "tomorrow" to indicate when things happen; instead of plural endings they simply state how many things there are. For English speakers, Chinese word order is very familiar, and you'll find that by simply stringing words together you'll be producing perfectly grammatical Chinese. Basic sentences follow the subject-verb-object format; adjectives, as well as all qualifying and describing phrases, precede nouns.

From the point of view of foreigners, the main thing which distinguishes Mandarin from familiar languages is that it is a **tonal language**. In order to pronounce a word correctly, it is necessary to know not only the sounds of its consonants and vowels but also its correct tone – though with the help of context, intelligent listeners should be able to work out what you are trying to say even if you don't get the tones quite right.

Pinyin

Back in the 1950s it was hoped eventually to replace Chinese characters with an alphabet of Roman letters, and to this end the **pinyin system**, a precise and exact means of representing all the sounds of Mandarin Chinese, was devised. It comprises all the Roman letters of the English alphabet (except "v"), with the four tones represented by diacritical marks, or accents, which appear above each syllable. The old aim of replacing Chinese characters with *pinyin* was abandoned long ago, but in the meantime *pinyin* has one very important function, that of helping foreigners pronounce Chinese words. However, there is the added complication that in *pinyin* the letters don't all have the sounds you would expect, and you'll need to spend an hour or two learning the correct sounds (see p.188).

You'll often see *pinyin* in Beijing, on street signs and shop displays, but only well-educated locals know the system very well. The Chinese names in this book have been given both in characters and in pinyin; the pronunciation guide below is your first step to making yourself comprehensible. For more information, see the *Rough Guide Mandarin Chinese Dictionary Phrasebook*, or *Pocket Interpreter* (FLP, Beijing; it's available at Beijing's Foreign Language Bookstore).

Pronunciation

There are four possible **tones** in Mandarin Chinese, and every syllable of every word is characterized by one of them, except for a few syllables which are considered toneless. In English, to change the tone is to change the mood or the emphasis; in Chinese, to change the tone is to change the word itself. The tones are:

First or "high" *ā ē ī ō ū*. In English this level tone is used when mimicking robotic or very boring, flat voices.

Second or "rising" *á é í ó ú*. Used in English when asking a question showing surprise, for example "*eh?*"

Third or "falling-rising" *ǎ ě ǐ ǒ ǔ*. Used in English when echoing someone's words with a measure of incredulity. For example, "John's dead." "*De-ad?!*"

Fourth or "falling" *à è ì ò ù*. Often used in English when counting in a brusque manner – "*One! Two! Three! Four!*".

Toneless A few syllables do not have a tone accent. These are pronounced without emphasis, such as in the English **u**pon.

Note that when two words with the third tone occur consecutively, the first word is pronounced as though it carries the second tone. Thus nǐ (meaning "you") and hǎo ("well, good"), when combined, are pronounced níhǎo, meaning "how are you"?

In Beijing, a croaky "r" sound is often added to words that end in a consonant, so "men" (door) becomes "menr".

Consonants

Most consonants, as written in *pinyin*, are pronounced in a similar way to their English equivalents, with the following exceptions:

c as in ha**ts**

g is hard as in **g**od (except when preceded by "n", when it sounds like sa**ng**)

q as in **ch**eese

x has no direct equivalent in English, but you can make the sound by sliding from an "s" to an "sh" sound and stopping midway between the two

z as in su**ds**

zh as in fu**dge**

Vowels and diphthongs

As in most languages, the vowel sounds are rather harder to quantify than the consonants. The examples below give a rough description of the sound of each vowel as written in *pinyin*.

a usually somewhere between f**a**r and m**a**n

ai as in **eye**

ao as in c**ow**

e usually as in f**u**r

ei as in g**ay**

en as in hyph**en**

eng as in s**ung**

er as in b**ar** with a stressed "r"

i usually as in b**ee**, except in *zi, ci, si, ri, zhi, chi* and *shi*, when *i* is a short, clipped sound, like the American military "sir".

ia as in **ya**k

ian as in **yen**

ie as in **yeah**

o as in s**aw**

ou as in sh**ow**

ü as in the German **ü** (make an "ee" sound and glide slowly into an "oo"; at the mid-point between the two sounds you should hit the *ü*-sound.

u usually as in f**oo**l, though whenever *u* follows j, q, x or y, it is always pronounced **ü**

uai as in **why**
ue as though contracting "you" and "air"
   together, **you'air**

ui as in **way**
uo as in **wo**re

Useful words and phrases

When writing or saying the name of a Chinese person, the surname is given first; thus Mao Zedong's family name is Mao.

Basics

I	我	wǒ
You (singular)	你	nǐ
He	他	tā
She	她	tā
We	我们	wǒmén
You (plural)	你们	nǐmén
They	他们	tāmén
I want...	我要	wǒ yào...
No, I don't want...	我不要	wǒ bú yào...
Is it possible...?	可不可以.....?	kěbùkěyǐ....?
It is (not) possible.	(不)可以	(bù) kěyǐ
Is there any/Have you got any...?	有没有.....?	yǒuméiyǒu...?
There is/I have.	有	yǒu
There isn't/I haven't.	没有	méiyǒu
Please help me	请帮我忙	qǐng bāng wǒ máng
Mr...	.....先生	xiānshēng
Mrs...	.....太太	tàitài
Miss...	.....小姐	xiǎojiě

Communicating

I don't speak Chinese.	我不会说中文	wǒ bú huì shuō zhōngwén
Can you speak English?	你会说英语吗?	nǐ huì shuō yīngyǔ ma?
Can you get someone who speaks English?	请给我找一个会说英语的人	qǐng gěi wǒ zhǎo yí ge huì shuō yīngyǔ de rén?
Please speak slowly.	请说地慢一点	qǐng shuōde màn yīdiǎn
Please say that again.	请再说一遍	qǐng zài shuō yí biàn
I understand.	我听得懂	wǒ tīngdedǒng
I don't understand.	我听不懂	wǒ tīngbudǒng
I can't read Chinese characters	我看不懂汉字	wǒ kànbudóng hànzi
What does this mean?	这是什么意思?	zhè shì shěnme yìsi?
How do you pronounce this character?	这个字怎么念?	zhè ge zì zénme niàn?

Greetings and basic courtesies

Hello/How do you do/ How are you?	你好	nǐ hǎo
I'm fine.	我很好	wǒ hěn hǎo
Thank you.	谢谢	xièxie

Don't mention it/ You're welcome	不客气	búkèqi
Sorry to bother you...	麻烦你	máfan nǐ
Sorry/I apologize.	对不起	duìbùqǐ
It's not important/ No problem.	没关系	méi guānxi
Goodbye.	再见	zài jiàn

Chitchat

What country are you from?	你是哪个国家的?	nǐ shì ná ge guójiā de?
Britain	英国	yīngguó
Ireland	爱尔兰	àiérlán
America	美国	měiguó
Canada	加拿大	jiānǎdà
Australia	澳大利亚	àodàlìyà
New Zealand	新西兰	xīnxīlán
China	中国	zhōngguó
Outside China	外国	wàiguó
What's your name?	你叫什么名字?	nǐ jiào shénme míngzi?
My name is...	我叫....	wǒ jiào...
Are you married?	你结婚了吗?	nǐ jiéhūn le ma?
I am (not) married.	我(没有)结婚(了)	wó (méiyǒu) jiéhūn
Have you got (children)?	你有没有孩子?	nǐ yǒu méiyǒu háizi?
Do you like...?	你喜不喜欢.....?	nǐ xǐ bù xǐhuan....?
I (don't) like...	我不喜欢....	wǒ (bù) xǐhuan...
What's your job?	你干什么工作?	nǐ gàn shénme gōngzuò?
I'm a foreign student.	我是留学生	wǒ shì liúxuéshēng
I'm a teacher.	我是老师	wǒ shì lǎoshī
I work in a company.	我在一个公司工作	wǒ zài yí ge gōngsī gōngzuò
I don't work.	我不工作	wǒ bù gōngzuò
Clean/dirty	干净/脏	gānjìng/zāng
Hot/cold	热/冷	rè/lěng
Fast/slow	快/慢	kuài/màn
Pretty	漂亮	piàoliang
Interesting	有意思	yǒuyìsi

Numbers

Zero	零	líng
One	一	yī
Two	二/两	èr/liǎng*
Three	三	sān
Four	四	sì
Five	五	wǔ
Six	六	liù
Seven	七	qī
Eight	八	bā
Nine	九	jiǔ
Ten	十	shí
Eleven	十一	shíyī
Twelve	十二	shíèr
Twenty	二十	èrshí
Twenty-one	二十一	èrshíyī

One hundred	一百	yìbǎi
Two hundred	二百	èrbǎi
One thousand	一千	yìqiān
Ten thousand	一万	yíwàn
One hundred thousand	十万	shíwàn
One million	一百万	yìbǎiwàn
One hundred million	一亿	yíyì
One billion	十亿	shíyì

* liáng is used when enumerating, for example "two people" liǎng ge rén. èr is used when counting.

Time

Now	现在	xiànzài
Today	今天	jīntiān
(In the) morning	早上	zǎoshàng
(In the) afternoon	下午	xiàwǔ
(In the) evening	晚上	wǎnshàng
Tomorrow	明天	míngtiān
The day after tomorrow	后天	hòutiān
Yesterday	昨天	zuótiān
Week/month/year	星期/月/年	xīngqī/yuè/nián
Monday	星期一	xīngqī yī
Tuesday	星期二	xīngqī èr
Wednesday	星期三	xīngqī sān
Thursday	星期四	xīngqī sì
Friday	星期五	xīngqī wǔ
Saturday	星期六	xīngqī liù
Sunday	星期天	xīngqī tian
What's the time?	几点了?	jǐdiǎn le?
10 o'clock	十点钟	shídiǎn zhōng
10.20	十点二十	shídiǎn èrshi
10.30	十点半	shídiǎn bàn

Travelling and getting about town

North	北	běi
South	南	nán
East	东	dōng
West	西	xī
Airport	机场	jīchǎng
Left luggage office	寄存处	jìcún chù
Ticket office	售票处	shòupiào chù
Ticket	票	piào
Can you buy me a ticket to…?	可不可以给我买到.....的票?	kěbùkěyǐ gěi wǒ mǎi dào… de piào?
I want to go to…	我想到.....去	wǒ xiǎng dào … qù
I want to leave at (8 o'clock)	我想(八点钟)离开	wǒ xiǎng (bā diǎn zhōng) líkāi
When does it leave?	什么时候出发?	shénme shíhòu chūfā?
When does it arrive?	什么时候到?	shénme shíhòu dào?
How long does it take?	路上得多长时间?	lùshàng děi duōcháng shíjiān?
CAAC	中国民航	zhōngguó mínháng
CITS	中国国际旅行社	zhōngguó guójì lǚxíngshè
Train	火车	huǒchē

Train station	火车站	huǒchēzhàn
Bus	公共汽车	gōnggòng qìchē
Bus station	汽车站	qìchēzhàn
Long-distance bus station	长途汽车站	chángtú qìchēzhàn
Hard seat	硬座	yìngzuò
Soft seat	软座	ruǎnzuò
Platform	站台	zhàntaí
Express train/bus	特快车	tèkuài chē
Fast train/bus	快车	kuài chē
Ordinary train/bus	普通车	pǔtōng chē
Minibus	小车	xiǎo chē

Getting about town

Map	地图	dìtú
Where is…?	……在哪里?	…zài nǎlǐ?
Go straight on	往前走	wàng qián zǒu
Turn right	往右拐	wàng yòu guǎi
Turn left	往左拐	wàng zuǒ guǎi
Taxi	出租车	chūzū chē
Underground/Subway station	地铁站	dìtiě zhàn
Rickshaw	三轮车	sānlún chē
Bicycle	自行车	zìxíngchē
I want to rent a bicycle	我想租自行车	wǒ xiǎng zū zìxíngchē
How much is it per hour?	一个小时得多少钱?	yí gè xiǎoshí děi duōshǎo qián?
Can I borrow your bicycle?	能不能借你的自行车?	néng bùnéng jiè nǐ de zìxíngchē?
Bus	公共汽车	gōnggòngqìchē
Which bus goes to…?	几路车到……去?	jǐ lù chē dào … qù?
Number (10) bus	(十)路车	(shí) lù chē
Does this bus go to…?	这车到……去吗?	zhè chē dào … qù ma?
When is the next bus?	下一班车几点开?	xià yì bān chē jǐ diǎn kāi?
The first bus	头班车	tóubān chē
The last bus	末班车	mòbān chē
Please tell me where to get off	请告诉我在哪里下车	qǐng gàosu wǒ zài nǎlǐ xià chē
Museum	博物馆	bówùguǎn
Temple	寺院	sìyuàn

Accommodation

Hotel (upmarket)	宾馆	bīnguǎn
Hotel (downmarket)	招待所，旅馆	zhāodàisuǒ, lǚguǎn
Hostel	旅社	lǚshè
Foreigners' guesthouse (at universities)	外国专家楼	wàiguó zhuānjiā lóu
Is it possible to stay here?	能不能住在这里?	néng bù néng zhù zài zhèlǐ?
Can I have a look at the room?	能不能看一下房间？	néng bù néng kàn yíxià fángjiān?
I want the cheapest bed you've got.	我要你最便宜的床位	wǒ yào nǐ zuì piányi de chuángwèi

Single room	单人间	dānrén jiān
Double room	双人间	shuāngrén jiān
Three-bed room	三人间	sānrén jiān
Dormitory	多人间	duōrén jiān
Suite	套房间	tàofángjiān
Bed	床位	chuángwèi
Passport	护照	hùzhào
Deposit	押金	yājīn
Key	钥匙	yàoshi
When is the hot water on?	什么时候有热水?	shénme shíhòu yǒu rèshuí?
I want to change my room	我想换一个房间	wǒ xiǎng huàn yí ge fángjiān

Shopping, money and banks, and visa extensions

How much is it?	这是多少钱?	zhè shì duōshǎo qián?
That's too expensive	太贵了	tài guì le
I haven't got any cash	我没有现金	wǒ méiyǒu xiànjīn
Have you got anything cheaper?	有没有便宜一点的?	yǒu méiyǒu pián yí yìdiǎn de?
Do you accept credit cards?	可不可以用信用卡?	kě bù kěyí yòng xìnyòngkǎ?
Department store	百货商店	bǎihuò shāngdián
Market	市场	shìchǎng
¥1 (RMB)	一块(人民币)	yí kuài (rénmínbì)
US$1	一块美金	yí kuài měijīn
£1	一个英磅	yí gè yīngbàng
HK$1	一块港币	yí kuài gǎngbì
Change money	换钱	huàn qián
Bank of China	中国银行	zhōngguó yínháng
Travellers' cheques	旅行支票	lǚxíngzhīpiào
PSB	公安局	gōng'ān jú

Mail and telephones

Post Office	邮电局	yóudiànjú
Envelope	信封	xìnfēng
Stamp	邮票	yóupiào
Airmail	航空信	hángkōngxìn
Surface mail	平信	píngxìn
Poste restante	邮件侯领处	yóujiàn hòulǐngchù
Telephone	电话	diànhuà
International telephone call	国际电话	guójì diànhuà
Reverse charges/ collect call	对方付钱电话	duìfāngfùqián diànhuà
Fax	传真	chuánzhēn
Telephone card	电话卡	diànhuàkǎ
I want to make a telephone call to (Britain)	我想给(英国)打电话	wǒ xiǎng gěi (yīngguó) dǎ diànhuà
I want to send a fax to (USA)	我想给(美国)发一个传真	wǒ xiǎng gěi (měiguó) fā yí ge chuánzhēn
Can I receive a fax here?	能不能在这里收传真?	néng bù néng zài zhèlǐ shōu chuánzhēn

Health

Hospital	医院	yīyuàn
Pharmacy	药店	yàodiàn
Medicine	药	yào
Chinese medicine	中药	zhōngyào
Diarrhoea	腑泻	fǔxiè
Vomit	呕吐	outù
Fever	发烧	fāshāo
I'm ill	我生病了	wǒ shēngbìng le
I've got flu	我感冒了	wǒgǎnmào le
I'm (not) allergic to...	我对.....(不)过敏	wǒ duì ... (bù) guòmǐn
Antibiotics	抗生素	kàngshēngsù
Quinine	奎宁	kuíníng
Condom	避孕套	bìyùntào
Mosquito coil	蚊香	wénxing
Mosquito netting	蚊帐纱	wénzhàngshā

A menu reader

The following lists should help out in deciphering the characters on a Chinese menu – if they're written clearly. If you know what you're after, try sifting through the staples and cooking methods to create your order, or sample one of the everyday or regional suggestions, many of which are available all over the country. Don't forget to tailor your demands to the capabilities of where you're ordering, though – a street cook with a wok isn't going to be able to whip up anything more complicated than a basic stir-fry. Note that some items, such as seafood and *jiaozi*, are ordered by weight.

General

Restaurant	餐厅	cāntīng
Chopsticks	筷子	kuàizi
House speciality	拿手好菜	náshǒuhǎocài
How much is that?	多少钱?	duōshǎo qián?
I don't eat (meat)	我不吃(肉)	wǒ bù chī (ròu)
I'm Buddhist/I'm vegetarian	我是佛教徒/我只吃素	wǒ shì fójiàotú/wǒ zhǐ chī sù
I would like...	我想要....	wǒ xiǎng yào...
Local dishes	地方菜	dìfāng cài
Menu/set menu/English menu	菜单/套菜/英文菜单	càidān/tàocài/yīngwén càidān
Small portion	少量	shǎoliàng
Spoon	勺	sháo
Waiter/waitress	服务员/小姐	fúwùyuán/xiǎojiě
Bill/cheque	买单	mǎidān
Cook together	一快儿	yíkuàir
50 grams	两	liǎng
250 grams	半斤	bànjīn
500 grams	斤	jīn
1 kilo	公斤	gōngjīn

Drinks

Beer	啤酒	píjiǔ
Sweet fizzy drink	汽水	qìshuǐ
Coffee	咖啡	kāfēi
Tea	茶	chá
(Mineral) water	(矿泉)水	(kuàngquán) shuǐ
Wine	葡萄酒	pútáojiǔ
Spirits	白酒	báijiǔ
Soya milk	豆浆	dòujiāng

Staple foods

Aubergine	茄子	qiézi
Bamboo shoots	笋尖	sǔnjiān
Beans	豆	dòu
Bean sprouts	豆芽	dòuyá
Beef	牛肉	niúròu
Bitter gourd	葫芦	húlu
Black bean sauce	黑豆豉	hēidòuchǐ
Buns (plain)	馒头	mántou
Buns (filled)	包子	bāozi
Carrot	胡萝卜	húluóbo
Cashew nuts	坚果	jiānguǒ
Cauliflower	菜花	càihuā
Chicken	鸡	jī
Chilli	辣椒	làjiāo
Coriander (leaves)	香菜	xiāngcài
Crab	蟹	xiè
Cucumber	黄瓜	huángguā
Duck	鸭	yā
Eel	鳝鱼	shànyú
Fish	鱼	yú
Garlic	大蒜	dàsuàn
Ginger	姜	jiāng
Green pepper (capsicum)	青椒	qīngjiāo
Green vegetables	绿叶素菜	lǜyè sùcài
Jiaozi (ravioli, steamed or boiled)	饺子	jiǎozi
Lamb	羊肉	yángròu
Lotus root	莲心	liánxīn
MSG	味精	wèijīng
Mushrooms	磨菇	mógū
Noodles	面条	miàntiáo
Omelette	炒鸡蛋	chǎojīdàn
Onions	洋葱	yángcōng
Oyster sauce	蚝油	háoyóu
Pancake	摊饼	tānbǐng
Peanut	花生	huāshēng
Pork	猪肉	zhūròu
Potato	土豆	tǔdòu
Prawns	虾	xiā
Preserved egg	皮蛋	pídàn
Rice, boiled	白饭	báifàn

Rice noodles	禾粉	héfěn
Rice, fried	炒饭	chǎofàn
Rice porridge (aka "congee")	粥	zhōu
Salt	盐	yán
Sesame oil	芝麻油	zhīma yóu
Shuijiao (ravioli in soup)	水饺	shuǐjiǎo
Sichuan pepper	四川辣椒	sìchuān làjiāo
Soup	汤	tāng
Soy sauce	酱油	jiàngyóu
Star anise	茴香	huíxiāng
Straw mushrooms	草菇	cǎogū
Sugar	糖	táng
Squid	鱿鱼	yóuyú
Tofu	豆腐	dòufu
Tomato	蕃茄	fānqié
Vinegar	醋	cù
Water chestnuts	马蹄	mǎtí
White radish	白萝卜	báiluóbo
Wood ear fungus	木耳	mùěr
Yam	芋头	yùtóu

Cooking methods

Casseroled	焙	bèi
Boiled	煮	zhǔ
Deep fried	油煎	yóujiān
Fried	炒	chǎo
Poached	白煮	báizhǔ
Red-cooked (stewed in soy sauce)	红烧	hóngshāo
Roast	烤	kǎo
Steamed	蒸	zhēng
Stir-fried	清炒	qīngchǎo

Everyday dishes

Chicken and sweetcorn soup	玉米鸡丝汤	yùmǐ jīsī tāng
Chicken with bamboo shoots and babycorn	笋尖嫩玉米炒鸡片	sǔnjiān nènyùmǐ chǎojīpiàn
Chicken with cashew nuts	坚果鸡片	jiānguǒ jīpiàn
Crispy aromatic duck	香酥鸭	xiāngsūyā
Egg flower soup with tomato	蕃茄蛋汤	fānqié dàn tāng
Egg fried rice	蛋炒饭	dànchǎofàn
Fish ball soup with white radish	萝卜鱼蛋汤	luóbo yúdàn tāng
Fish casserole	焙鱼	bèiyú
Fried shredded pork with garlic and chilli	大蒜辣椒炒肉片	dàsuàn làjiāo chǎoròupiàn
Hotpot	火锅	huǒguō
Kebab	串肉	chuànròu
Noodle soup	汤面	tāngmiàn
Pork and mustard greens	芥末肉片	jièmò ròupiàn
Pork and water chestnut	马蹄猪肉	mǎtí zhūròu

Pork and white radish pie	白萝卜肉馅饼	báiluóbo ròuxiànbǐng
Prawn with garlic sauce	大蒜炒虾	dàsuàn chǎoxiā
Roast duck	烤鸭	kǎoyā
Sandpot	沙锅	shāguō
Scrambled egg with pork on rice	滑蛋猪肉饭	huádàn zhūròufàn
Sliced pork with yellow bean sauce	黄豆肉片	huángdòu ròupiàn
Steamed rice packets wrapped in lotus leaves	荷叶蒸饭	héyè zhēngfàn
Stewed pork belly with vegetables	回锅肉	huíguōròu
Stir-fried chicken and bamboo shoots	笋尖炒鸡片	sǔnjiān chǎojīpiàn
Stuffed beancurd soup	豆腐汤	dòufutāng
Sweet and sour spare ribs	糖醋排骨	tángcù páigǔ
Sweet bean paste pancakes	赤豆摊饼	chìdòu tānbǐng
Wonton soup	馄饨汤	húntun tāng

Vegetables and eggs

Aubergine with chilli and garlic sauce	大蒜辣椒炒茄子	dàsuàn làjiāo chǎoqiézi
Egg fried with tomatoes	蕃茄炒蛋	fānqié chǎodàn
Fried beancurd with vegetables	豆腐素菜	dòufu sùcài
Fried bean sprouts	炒豆芽	chǎodòuyá
Monks' vegetarian dish (stir-fry of mixed vegetables and fungi)	罗汉斋	luóhànzhāi
Pressed beancurd with cabbage	卷心菜豆腐	juǎnxīncài dòufu
Stir-fried bamboo shoots	炒冬笋	chǎodōngsǔn
Stir-fried mushrooms	炒鲜菇	chǎoxiāngū
Vegetable soup	素菜汤	sùcài tāng

Regional dishes

Northern

Aromatic fried lamb	炒羊肉	chǎoyángròu
Fried prawn balls	炒虾球	chǎoxiāqiú
Mongolian hotpot	蒙古火锅	ménggǔ huǒguō
Beijing (Peking) duck	北京烤鸭	běijīng kǎoyā
Red-cooked lamb	红烧羊肉	hóngshāo yángròu
Lion's head (pork rissoles casseroled with greens)	狮子头	shīzitóu

Eastern

Beggars' chicken (baked)	叫花鸡	jiàohuājī
Dongpo pork casserole (steamed in wine)	东坡焙肉	dōngpō bèiròu
Drunken prawns	醉虾	zuìxiā
Five flower pork (steamed in lotus leaves)	五花肉	wǔhuāròu

| Steamed sea bass | 清蒸鲈鱼 | qīngzhēnglúyú |
| Yangzhou fried rice | 杨州炒饭 | yángzhōu chǎofàn |

Sichuan and western China

Crackling-rice with pork	爆米肉片	bàomǐ ròupiàn
Carry-pole noodles (with a chilli-vinegar-sesame sauce)	棒棒面	bàngbàngmiàn
Dong'an chicken (poached in spicy sauce)	东安鸡子	dōng'ān jīzi
Double-cooked pork	回锅肉	huíguōròu
Gongbao chicken (with chillies and peanuts)	宫爆鸡丁	gōngbào jīdīng
Green pepper with spring onion and black bean sauce	豆豉青椒	dòuchǐ qīngjiāo
Hot and sour soup (flavoured with vinegar and white pepper)	酸辣汤	suānlà tāng
Hot-spiced beancurd	妈婆豆腐	māpódòufu
Smoked duck	熏鸭	xūnyā
Strange flavoured chicken (with sesame-garlic-chilli)	怪味鸡	guàiwèijī

Southern Chinese/Cantonese

Claypot rice with sweet sausage	香肠饭	xiāngchángfàn
Crisp-skinned pork on rice	脆皮肉饭	cuìpíròufàn
Fish-head casserole	焙鱼头	bèiyútóu
Fish steamed with ginger and spring onion	清蒸鱼	qīngzhēngyú
Fried chicken with yam	芋头炒鸡片	yùtóu chǎojīpiàn
Honey-roast pork	叉烧	chāshāo
Kale in oyster sauce	蚝油白菜	háoyóu báicài
Lemon chicken	柠檬鸡	níngméngjī
Salt-baked chicken	盐鸡	yánjī
Scallops in taro patties	带子	dàizi

Dim sum

Dim sum	点心	diǎnxīn
Barbecue pork bun	叉烧包	chāshāo bāo
Custard tart	蛋挞	dàntà
Pork and prawn dumpling	烧麦	shāomài
Fried taro and mince dumpling	蕃薯糊饺	fānshǔ hújiāo
Lotus paste bun	莲蓉糕	liánrónggāo
Moon cake (sweet bean paste in flaky pastry)	月饼	yuèbǐng
Paper-wrapped prawns	纸包虾	zhǐbāoxiā
Prawn crackers	虾片	xiāpiàn
Shanghai fried meat and vegetable dumpling ("potstickers")	锅帖	guōtiē
Spring roll	春卷	chūnjuǎn
Steamed spare ribs and chilli	排骨	páigǔ

LANGUAGE | A menu reader

Stuffed rice-flour roll	肠粉	chángfěn
Stuffed green peppers with black bean sauce	豆豉馅青椒	dòuchǐ xiànqīngjiāo
Sweet sesame balls	芝麻球	zhīma qiú
Turnip-paste patty	萝卜糕	luóbo gāo

Glossary

Arhat Buddhist saint.

Avalokitshvara See Guanyin.

Bei North.

Binguan Hotel – generally a large one, for tourists.

Bodhisattva A follower of Buddhism who has attained enlightenment, but has chosen to stay on earth to teach rather than enter nirvana; Buddhist god or goddess.

Boxers The name given to a xenophobic organization which originated in Shandong in 1898. Encouraged by the Qing Empress Dowager Cixi, they roamed China attacking Westernized Chinese and foreigners in what became known as the Boxer Rebellion (see p.98).

Canting Restaurant.

Cheongsam Long, narrow dress slit up the thigh.

CITS China International Travel Service. A state-owned tourist organization whose primary interest is in selling tours, though they can help with obtaining train tickets.

CTS China Travel Service. Tourist organization similar to CITS.

Cultural Revolution Ten-year period, beginning in 1966, characterized by a drive for ideological purity and fanatical devotion to Mao, resulting in destruction of old buildings and the persecution of intellectuals.

Dagoba Dome-shaped shrine containing Buddhist relics.

Dong East.

Fandian Restaurant (sometimes also used for a hotel).

Fen Smallest denomination of Chinese currency – there are one hundred fen to the yuan.

Feng Peak.

Feng shui Literally meaning wind and water; a system of geomancy used to determine the auspicious positioning of buildings.

Gong Palace.

Guanyin The ubiquitous Buddhist goddess of mercy, who postponed her entry into paradise in order to help ease human misery. Derived from the Indian deity Avalokiteshvara, she is often depicted with up to a thousand arms.

Gulou Drum tower, traditionally marking the centre of a town, from which a drum was beaten at nightfall and in times of need.

Guomindang The Nationalist Peoples' Party, who, under Chiang Kaishek, fought communist forces for 25 years before being defeated. It moved to Taiwan in 1949, where it remains a major political party.

Han Chinese The main body of the Chinese people, as distinct from other ethnic groups such as Uigur, Miao, Hui, and Tibetans.

Hui Muslims; officially a minority, China's Hui are, in fact, ethnically indistinguishable from Han Chinese.

Hutong A narrow alleyway.

Immortal Taoist saint.

Jiao (or mao) Ten fen.

Jie Street.

Jiuba Bar or pub.

Lamaism The esoteric Tibetan and Mongolian branch of Buddhism, influenced by local shamanist and animist beliefs.

Ling Tomb.

Little Red Book A selection from *The Quotations from Chairman Mao Zedong*, produced in 1966 as a philosophical treatise for Red Guards during the Cultural Revolution.

Lu Street.

Luohan Any of Buddha's original disciples.

Maitreya Buddha The Buddha of the future, at present awaiting rebirth.

Mandala Mystic diagram which forms an important part of Buddhist iconography, especially in Tibet; mandalas usually depict deities and are stared at as an aid to meditation.

Men Gate/door.

Miao Temple.

Middle Kingdom A literal translation of the Chinese term for China.

Nan South.

Palanquin A covered sedan chair, used by the emperor.

Peking The old English term for Beijing.

PLA The People's Liberation Army, the official name of the Communist military forces since 1949.

PSB Public Security Bureau.

Pagoda Tower with distinctively tapering structure.

Pinyin The official system of transliterating Chinese script into Roman letters.

Putonghua Mandarin Chinese; literally "common language".

Qiao Bridge.

Qipao Another word for a cheongsam (see opposite).

RMB Renminbi, another name for Chinese currency, literally meaning "the people's money".

Red Guards The unruly factional forces, unleashed by Mao during the Cultural Revolution, to find and brutally destroy any "reactionaries" among the populace.

Renmin The people.

Si Temple.

Shan Mountain or hill.

Shui Water.

Siheyuan Traditional Beijing courtyard house.

Spirit wall Wall behind the main gateway to a house, designed to thwart evil spirits, which, it was believed, could move only in straight lines.

Spirit Way The straight road leading to a tomb, lined with guardian figures.

Stele Freestanding stone tablet carved with text

Stupa A multi-tiered tower containing Buddhist relics.

Ta Tower or pagoda.

Tai ji A discipline of physical exercise, characterized by slow, deliberate, balletic movements.

Tian Heaven or the sky.

Uigur Substantial minority of Turkic people, living mainly in Xinjiang.

Waiguoren Foreigner.

Xi West.

Yuan China's unit of currency, also called renminbi. Also a courtyard or garden (and the name of the Mongol dynasty).

Zhan Station.

Zhong Middle; China is referred to as *zhong guo*, the Middle Kingdom.

Zhonglou Bell tower, usually twinned with a *gulou*. The bell it contained was rung at dawn and in emergencies.

Zhuang Villa or manor.

LANGUAGE | Glossary

Index

and small print

Index

Map entries are in colour

INDEX

INDEX

INDEX

A rough guide to Rough Guides

In the summer of 1981, Mark Ellingham, a recent graduate from Bristol University, was travelling round Greece and couldn't find a guidebook that really met his needs. On the one hand there were the student guides, insistent on saving every last cent, and on the other the heavyweight cultural tomes whose authors seemed to have spent more time in a research library than lounging away the afternoon at a taverna or on the beach.

In a bid to avoid getting a job, Mark and a small group of writers set about creating their own guidebook. It was a guide to Greece that aimed to combine a journalistic approach to description with a thoroughly practical approach to travellers' needs – a guide that would incorporate culture, history and contemporary insights with a critical edge, together with up-to-date, value-for-money listings. Back in London, Mark and the team finished their Rough Guide, as they called it, and talked Routledge into publishing the book.

That first *Rough Guide to Greece*, published in 1982, was a student scheme that became a publishing phenomenon. The immediate success of the book – with numerous reprints and a Thomas Cook prize shortlisting – spawned a series that rapidly covered dozens of destinations. Rough Guides had a ready market among low-budget backpackers, but soon also acquired a much broader and older readership that relished Rough Guides' wit and inquisitiveness as much as their enthusiastic, critical approach. Everyone wants value for money, but not at any price.

Rough Guides soon began supplementing the "rougher" information about hostels and low-budget listings with the kind of detail on restaurants and quality hotels that independent-minded visitors on any budget might expect, whether on business in New York or trekking in Thailand.

These days the guides – distributed worldwide by the Penguin group – offer recommendations from shoestring to luxury and cover more than 200 destinations around the globe, including almost every country in the Americas and Europe, more than half of Africa and most of Asia and Australasia. Our ever-growing team of authors and photographers is spread all over the world, particularly in Europe, the USA and Australia.

In 1994, we published the *Rough Guide to World Music* and *Rough Guide to Classical Music*, and a year later the *Rough Guide to the Internet*. All three books have become benchmark titles in their fields – which encouraged us to expand into other areas of publishing, mainly around popular culture. Rough Guides now publish:

- Travel guides to more than 200 worldwide destinations
- Dictionary phrasebooks to 22 major languages
- History guides ranging from Ireland to Islam
- Maps printed on rip-proof and waterproof Polyart™ paper
- Music guides running the gamut from Opera to Elvis
- Restaurant guides to London, New York and San Francisco
- Reference books on topics as diverse as the Weather and Shakespeare
- Sports guides from Formula 1 to Man Utd
- Pop culture books from Lord of the Rings to Cult TV
- World Music CDs in association with World Music Network

Visit **www.roughguides.com** to see our latest publications.

Rough Guide credits

Text editor: Richard Lim
Layout: Andy Hilliard and Dan May
Picture research: Veneta Bullen
Proofreader: David Price

....

Editorial: London Martin Dunford, Kate Berens, Helena Smith, Claire Saunders, Geoff Howard, Ruth Blackmore, Ann-Marie Shaw, Gavin Thomas, Polly Thomas, Richard Lim, Lucy Ratcliffe, Clifton Wilkinson, Alison Murchie, Fran Sandham, Sally Schafer, Alexander Mark Rogers, Karoline Densley, Andy Turner, Ella O'Donnell, Andrew Lockett, Joe Staines, Duncan Clark, Peter Buckley, Matthew Milton; **New York** Andrew Rosenberg, Richard Koss, Yuki Takagaki, Hunter Slaton, Chris Barsanti, Thomas Kohnstamm, Steven Horak
Design & Layout: London Helen Prior, Dan May, Diana Jarvis; **Delhi** Madhulita Mohapatra, Umesh Aggarwal, Ajay Verma

Production: Julia Bovis, John McKay, Sophie Hewat
Cartography: London Maxine Repath, Ed Wright, Katie Lloyd-Jones; **Delhi** Manish Chandra, Rajesh Chhibber, Jai Prakash Mishra, Ashutosh Bharti, Rajesh Mishra, Animesh Pathak
Cover art direction: Louise Boulton
Picture research: Sharon Martins, Mark Thomas, Jj Luck
Online: New York Jennifer Gold, Cree Lawson, Suzanne Welles; **Delhi** Manik Chauhan, Amarjyoti Dutta, Narender Kumar
Marketing & Publicity: London Richard Trillo, Niki Smith, David Wearn, Chloë Roberts, Demelza Dallow; **New York** Geoff Colquitt, David Wechsler, Megan Kennedy
Finance: Gary Singh
Manager India: Punita Singh
Series editor: Mark Ellingham
PA to Managing Director: Julie Sanderson
Managing Director: Kevin Fitzgerald

Publishing information

This 2nd edition published January 2004 by
Rough Guides Ltd,
80 Strand, London WC2R 0RL.
345 Hudson St, 4th Floor,
New York, NY 10014, USA.
Distributed by the Penguin Group
Penguin Books Ltd,
80 Strand, London WC2R 0RL
Penguin Putnam, Inc.
375 Hudson Street, NY 10014, USA
Penguin Books Australia Ltd,
487 Maroondah Highway, PO Box 257,
Ringwood, Victoria 3134, Australia
Penguin Books Canada Ltd,
10 Alcorn Avenue, Toronto, Ontario,
Canada M4V 1E4
Penguin Books (NZ) Ltd,
182–190 Wairau Road, Auckland 10,
New Zealand
Typeset in Bembo and Helvetica to an original design by Henry Iles.

Printed in China

244pp includes index
A catalogue record for this book is available from the British Library

ISBN 1-854353-242-5

The publishers and authors have done their best to ensure the accuracy and currency of all the information in **The Rough Guide to Beijing**, however, they can accept no responsibility for any loss, injury, or inconvenience sustained by any traveller as a result of information or advice contained in the guide.

3   5   7   9   8   6   4   2

Help us update

We've gone to a lot of effort to ensure that the 2nd edition of **The Rough Guide to Beijing** is accurate and up to date. However, things change – places get "discovered", opening hours are notoriously fickle, restaurants and rooms raise prices or lower standards. If you feel we've got it wrong or left something out, we'd like to know, and if you can remember the address, the price, the time, the phone number, so much the better.

We'll credit all contributions, and send a copy of the next edition (or any other Rough Guide if you prefer), for the best letters. Everyone who writes to us and isn't already a subscriber will receive a copy of our full-colour thrice-yearly newsletter. Please mark letters: **"Rough Guide Beijing Update"** and send to: Rough Guides, 80 Strand, London WC2R 0RL, or Rough Guides, 4th Floor, 345 Hudson St, New York, NY 10014. Or send an email to **mail@roughguides.com**

Have your questions answered and tell others about your trip at **www.roughguides.atinfopop.com**

SMALL PRINT

Acknowledgements

Thanks from the **author** to Rick, Joyce, Qian Fan, Simon Fireman, Deniz, Penny, and Du. The **editor** thanks Jo Mead for the index, Veneta Bullen for picture research, Daniel May for typesetting, all the Delhi cartographers for the maps, and David Price for proofreading.

SMALL PRINT

Readers' letters

Thanks to all the following for their letters and emails, and apologies to anyone we've inadvertently omitted:

Ruth Brown, Andrew Canter, Sara Elinson, Elizabeth Godfrey, Fredrik S. Heffermehl, Judy Heiser, Arjen van Loenen and Edith Beerdsen, Anna McDonald, Joke Meindersma, Michael Rak, Stan Sweeney, Toby Sykes, David Thomas, Lucy Tickell.

Photo credits

Visit us online
roughguides.com

Information on over 25,000 destinations around the world

- **Read** Rough Guides' trusted travel info
- **Share** journals, photos and travel advice with other readers
- Get exclusive Rough Guide **discounts** and travel **deals**
- Earn membership points every time you contribute to the Rough Guide **community** and get **free** books, flights and trips
- Browse thousands of CD reviews and artists in our **music** area

Rough Guides travel...

UK & Ireland
Britain
Devon & Cornwall
Dublin
Edinburgh
England
Ireland
Lake District
London
London mini guide
London Restaurants
London & SE England,
  Walks in
Scotland
Scottish Highlands &
  Islands
Wales

Europe
Algarve
Amsterdam
Andalucía
Austria
Baltic States
Barcelona
Belgium & Luxembourg
Berlin
Brittany & Normandy
Bruges & Ghent
Brussels
Budapest
Bulgaria
Copenhagen
Corfu
Corsica
Costa Brava
Crete
Croatia
Cyprus
Czech & Slovak
  Republics
Dodecanese & East
  Aegean
Dordogne & The Lot
Europe
First-Time Europe
Florence
France

Germany
Greece
Greek Islands
Hungary
Ibiza & Formentera
Iceland
Ionian Islands
Italy
Languedoc & Roussillon
Lisbon
The Loire
Madeira
Madrid
Mallorca
Malta & Gozo
Menorca
Moscow
Netherlands
Norway
Paris
Paris Mini Guide
Poland
Portugal
Prague
Provence & the Côte
  d'Azur
Pyrenees
Romania
Rome
Sardinia
Scandinavia
Sicily
Slovenia
Spain
St Petersburg
Sweden
Switzerland
Tenerife & La Gomera
Turkey
Tuscany & Umbria
Venice & The Veneto
Vienna

Asia
Bali & Lombok
Bangkok
Beijing

Cambodia
China
First-Time Asia
Goa
Hong Kong & Macau
India
Indonesia
Japan
Laos
Malaysia, Singapore &
  Brunei
Nepal
Philippines
Singapore
South India
Southeast Asia
Thailand
Thailand Beaches &
  Islands
Tokyo
Vietnam

Australasia
Australia
Gay & Lesbian
  Australia
Melbourne
New Zealand
Sydney

North America
Alaska
Baltic States
Big Island of Hawaii
Boston
California
Canada
Chicago
Florida
Grand Canyon
Hawaii
Honolulu
Las Vegas
Los Angeles
Maui
Miami & the Florida
  Keys

Montréal
New England
New Orleans
New York City
New York City Mini
  Guide
New York Restaurants
Pacific Northwest
Rocky Mountains
San Francisco
San Francisco
  Restaurants
Seattle
Skiing & Snowboarding
  in North America
Southwest USA
Toronto
USA
Vancouver
Washington DC
Yosemite

**Caribbean
& Latin America**
Antigua & Barbuda
Argentina
Bahamas
Barbados
Belize
Bolivia
Brazil
Caribbean
Central America
Chile
Costa Rica
Cuba
Dominican Republic
Ecuador
First-Time Latin
  America
Guatemala
Jamaica
Maya World
Mexico
Peru
St Lucia
South America
Trinidad & Tobago

Rough Guides are available from good bookstores worldwide. New titles are
published every month. Check www.roughguides.com for the latest news.

...music & reference

Africa & Middle East
Cape Town
Egypt
The Gambia
Jerusalem
Jordan
Kenya
Morocco
South Africa, Lesotho
& Swaziland
Syria
Tanzania
Tunisia
West Africa
Zanzibar
Zimbabwe

Travel Theme guides
First-Time Around the
World
First-Time Asia
First-Time Europe
First-Time Latin
America
Gay & Lesbian
Australia
Skiing & Snowboarding
in North America
Travel Online
Travel Health
Walks in London & SE
England
Women Travel

Restaurant guides
French Hotels &
Restaurants
London
New York
San Francisco

Maps
Algarve
Amsterdam
Andalucia & Costa del Sol
Argentina
Athens

Australia
Baja California
Barcelona
Boston
Brittany
Brussels
Chicago
Crete
Croatia
Cuba
Cyprus
Czech Republic
Dominican Republic
Dublin
Egypt
Florence & Siena
Frankfurt
Greece
Guatemala & Belize
Iceland
Ireland
Lisbon
London
Los Angeles
Mexico
Miami & Key West
Morocco
New York City
New Zealand
Northern Spain
Paris
Portugal
Prague
Rome
San Francisco
Sicily
South Africa
Sri Lanka
Tenerife
Thailand
Toronto
Trinidad & Tobago
Tuscany
Venice
Washington DC
Yucatán Peninsula

Dictionary
Phrasebooks
Czech
Dutch
Egyptian Arabic
European
French
German
Greek
Hindi & Urdu
Hungarian
Indonesian
Italian
Japanese
Mandarin Chinese
Mexican Spanish
Polish
Portuguese
Russian
Spanish
Swahili
Thai
Turkish
Vietnamese

Music Guides
The Beatles
Cult Pop
Classical Music
Country Music
Cuban Music
Drum'n'bass
Elvis
House
Irish Music
Jazz
Music USA
Opera
Reggae
Rock
Techno
World Music (2 vols)

100 Essential CDs series
Country
Latin

Opera
Rock
Soul
World Music

History Guides
China
Egypt
England
France
Greece
India
Ireland
Islam
Italy
Spain
USA

Reference Guides
Books for Teenagers
Children's Books, 0–5
Children's Books, 5–11
Cult Football
Cult Movies
Cult TV
Digital Stuff
Formula 1
The Internet
Internet Radio
James Bond
Lord of the Rings
Man Utd
Personal Computers
Pregnancy & Birth
Shopping Online
Travel Health
Travel Online
Unexplained
Phenomena
The Universe
Videogaming
Weather
Website Directory

Also! More than 120 Rough Guide music CDs are available from all good book and record stores. Listen in at www.worldmusic.net

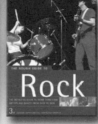

NOTES

NOTES

NOTES

NOTES

NOTES

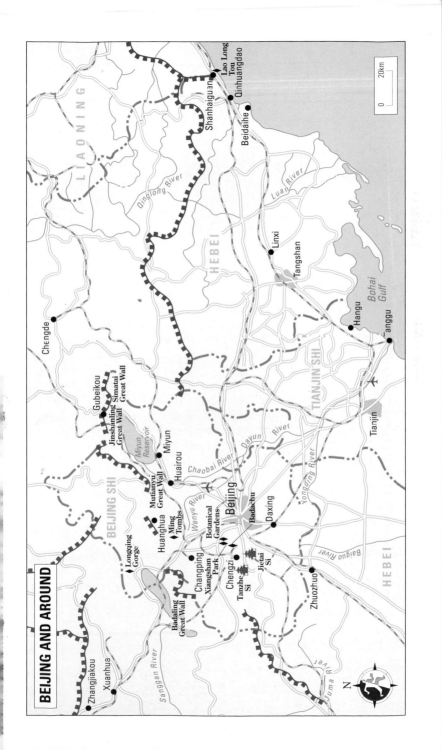

BEIJING AND AROUND

0   20km

N

Yuanmingyuan

Summer
Palace

Tsinghua
University

Wudaokou

Beijing
University

BEISIHUAN XI LU

Zhichunlu

ZHONGGUANCUN DAJIE

Dazhong Si

BEISANHUAN XI LU

BAISHIQIAO LU

Dazhong Si

XIZHIMEN BEI DAJIE

XISANHUAN BEI LU

Beijing
Library

Zizhuyuan
Park

Zoo

Xizhimen
Zhan

Xizhimen

ZIZHUYUAN LU

Exhibition
Hall

Chegongzhuang

CHEGONGZHUANG XI LU

SANLIHE LU

Fuchengmen

FUCHENG LU

Fuxingmen

CCTV
Tower

Yuetan
Park

Yuyuantan
Park

Military
Museum

Nanlishi
Lu

FUXINGMEN BEI DAJIE

Yuquan Lu

Gongzhufen

FUXING LU

Wukesong

Wanshou Lu

Junshi Bowuguan

Muxidi

Fuxingmen

Baiyun Guan

LIANHUACHI DONG LU

Xi Zhan

GUANG'ANMEN DAJIE

XISANHUAN ZHONG LU

Second Ring Road

Third Ring Road

Fourth Ring Road

0   4 km

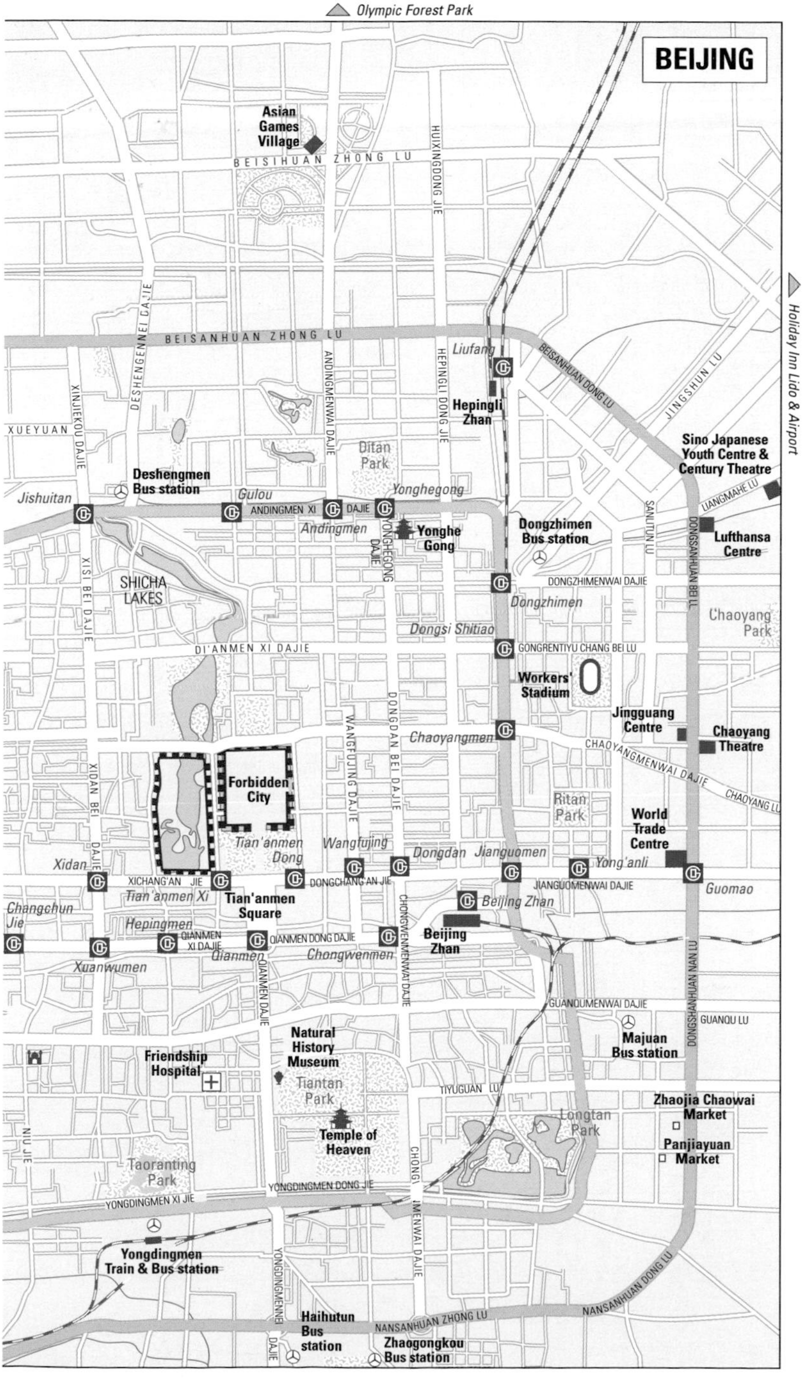

Olympic Forest Park
BEIJING
Holiday Inn Lido & Airport
Asian Games Village
BEISIHUAN ZHONG LU
HUIXINGDONG JIE
BEISANHUAN ZHONG LU
DESHENGMENNEI DAJIE
ANDINGMENWAI DAJIE
HEPINGLI DONG JIE
Liufang
Hepingli Zhan
BEISANHUAN DONG LU
JINGSHUN LU
XINJIEKOU DAJIE
XUEYUAN
Ditan Park
Sino Japanese Youth Centre & Century Theatre
Deshengmen Bus station
Jishuitan
Gulou
Yonghegong
ANDINGMEN XI DAJIE
LIANGMAHE LU
Andingmen
YONGHEGONG DAJIE
Yonghe Gong
Dongzhimen Bus station
SANLITUN LU
DONGSANHUAN BEI LU
Lufthansa Centre
SHICHA LAKES
XISI BEI DAJIE
DONGZHIMENWAI DAJIE
Dongzhimen
Chaoyang Park
Dongsi Shitiao
DI'ANMEN XI DAJIE
GONGRENTIYU CHANG BEI LU
Workers' Stadium
DONGDAN BEI DAJIE
WANGFUJING DAJIE
Jingguang Centre
Chaoyangmen
Chaoyang Theatre
CHAOYANGMENWAI DAJIE
CHAOYANG LU
XIDAN BEI DAJIE
Forbidden City
Ritan Park
World Trade Centre
Tian'anmen Dong
Wangfujing
Dongdan
Jianguomen
Yong'anli
Xidan
XICHANG'AN JIE
DONGCHANG'AN JIE
JIANGUOMENWAI DAJIE
Guomao
Tian'anmen Xi
Tian'anmen Square
Beijing Zhan
Changchun Jie
Hepingmen
QIANMEN XI DAJIE
QIANMEN DONG DAJIE
CHONGWENMENWAI DAJIE
Beijing Zhan
Qianmen
Chongwenmen
Xuanwumen
QIANMEN DAJIE
DONGSANHUAN NAN LU
GUANGQUMENWAI DAJIE
GUANQU LU
Natural History Museum
Majuan Bus station
Friendship Hospital
Tiantan Park
TIYUGUAN LU
Longtan Park
Zhaojia Chaowai Market
Temple of Heaven
NIU JIE
Panjiayuan Market
Taoranting Park
YONGDINGMEN DONG JIE
YONGDINGMEN XI JIE
CHONGWENMENWAI DAJIE
Yongdingmen Train & Bus station
YONGDINGMENNEI DAJIE
NANSANHUAN DONG LU
NANSANHUAN ZHONG LU
Haihutun Bus station
Zhaogongkou Bus station

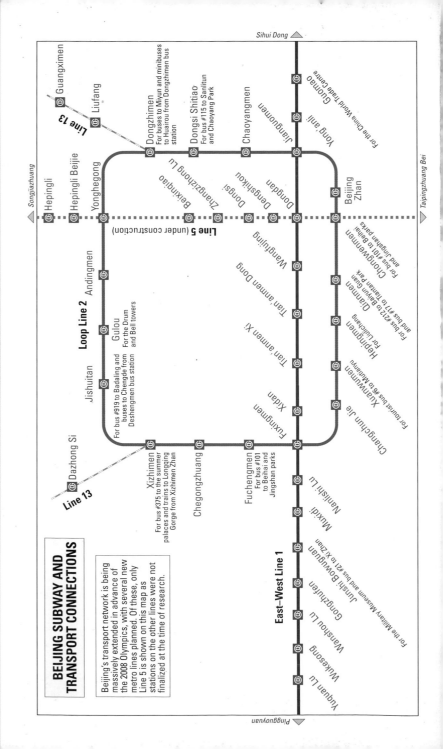

BEIJING SUBWAY AND TRANSPORT CONNECTIONS

Beijing's transport network is being massively extended in advance of the 2008 Olympics, with several new metro lines planned. Of these, only Line 5 is shown on this map as stations on the other lines were not finalized at the time of research.